HEROIC RESCUES AT SEA

True Stories of the Canadian Coast Guard

Carolyn Matthews

NIMBUS PUBLISHING LTD

Nimbus Publishing Limited
PO Box 9166
Halifax, NS   B3K 5M8
(902) 455-4286

Printed and bound in Canada

Design: Kathy Kaulbach, Paragon Design Group

National Library of Canada Cataloguing in Publication

Matthews, Carolyn
      Heroic rescues at sea :
      true stories of the Canadian Coast Guard

ISBN 1-55109-394-4

      1. Canadian Coast Guard--Search and rescue operations. I. Title.

VG55.C3M37 2002   363.12'381'0971   C2002-901302-X

Canada

The Canada Council | Le Conseil des Arts
for the Arts | du Canada

We acknowledge the financial support of the Government of Canada through the Book Publishing Industry Development Program (BPIDP) and the Canada Council for our publishing activities.

This book is dedicated

to my late father, William Haddock

of Te Pahu, New Zealand,

and to my mother,

Lilian Haddock,

now of Hamilton, New Zealand.

Table of Contents

Acknowledgements

A PLEASURABLE PART OF FINISHING A BOOK is giving thanks to those who contributed to its creation, and to the people who provided me with assistance and support.

Glenn French introduced me to the impact of trauma counselling by recounting his experiences at the site of the Swissair disaster and by describing how it changed his life. The researching of material for an article on this subject led me to Manone Dulude in Georgetown, Ontario, and to interviews with other trauma counsellors, many of whom work as lifeboat station search and rescue workers for the Canadian Coast Guard. Thus began my appreciation of these people and the work they do.

Heartfelt thanks to Marjorie Ludlow Green for editing my work and for her mentoring; without her ongoing encouragement and her belief in me and my project, writing this book would have been a lonely endeavour indeed.

Thanks to my husband, Tony Matthews, for his patient support and enthusiasm, and for making sure I had all the equipment necessary for my work. Thanks to my friend Norah Taylor for helping me to begin.

I feel much gratitude for Ron Miller, Director of Search and Rescue in Ottawa, for his interest and support. This included making available to me Coast Guard records, personnel and other contacts, and providing some financial assistance—and refusing to exercise any editorial control over the material. My gratitude extends also to other Coast Guard personnel in operations: Mike Voigt, Chief, Rescue Coordination, Ottawa; Danny Coultis, Supervisor, Central and Arctic Regions; Peter Stow, Supervisor, Marine Search and Rescue, Maritimes Region; and Michel Brisebois, Officer in Charge, Rescue Coordination Centre, Halifax. There are many others...

I have much appreciation for the search and rescue workers who spent much time and effort on my behalf. I value them, and what they do, more than they will ever know. In particular I'll mention Tim MacFarlane of Abbotsford, British Columbia who gave his time, stories and insights, even though revisiting some of his experiences rekindled old pain and trauma. Thanks to Dave Griffiths in St. John's, who drove me about Newfoundland in his time off and took care of the myriad details involved in setting up interviews, Wade Buell in Kingston, for searching out historical information, and Dave Hegstrom in Bamfield on Vancouver Island.

Special thanks to East Coast fishermen Bob Berringer, who took me into his home, and Randy Feener. Thanks also to Jim Mosher of the Scotia Trawler Fishing Fleet for his time, and for his frankness about his commercial enterprises and the fishing industry in Nova Scotia.

I feel a debt of gratitude to my publisher, Dorothy Blythe in Halifax, who took a chance on me and believed in my project.

I appreciate all those who assisted me, and I feel I have made friends across the country.

Not least, I thank my mother in New Zealand, who tiptoed about her own house while I was there so that I would not be interrupted in the writing of my book.

Foreword

MY INSPIRATION TO WRITE about the Canadian Coast Guard's search and rescue workers (SAR) was born in the summer of 1999 when I interviewed several people who toiled at the site of the Swissair disaster. I felt inspired by their courage and compassion and by their willingness to do what most of us would not even contemplate: brave the fury of the elements and our inland seas and oceans to rescue people in trouble, and act as paramedics, midwives, grief counsellors, and firefighters on the water, often at short notice. They are sailors, navigators, engineers, and mechanics, on call twenty-four hours a day for periods of seven or fourteen days at a stretch, and they do all this for relatively small pay and scant recognition.

Of course, marine search and rescue work is also carried out by other organizations: the RCMP, provincial and municipal police forces, firefighters, and the military, some of whom are mentioned in this book. But these groups have their feet planted on terra firma with some degree of control over, and refuge from, the elements. They also have a public profile: what they do is acknowledged in the public consciousness.

Search and rescue workers have to deal with seas that cannot be tamed, organized, or conquered. There is nothing firm beneath their feet, and no refuge from the raging tempests. As a professional group, the Coast Guard and their search and rescue workers have little public profile; their story has yet to be told.

Many people profiled here expressed discomfort at receiving recognition for what they have contributed when their co-workers may have given much more. There are many, many other stories of heroic work and self-sacrifice; the people acknowledged here are those I happened to meet.

The people in these stories represent all those who love ships and the sea, and who have the desire to help people in need, to make a difference in the lives of others; in so doing, they find meaning in their own. Here you will meet rescue workers who have an unstoppable flow of empathy and compassion, who test themselves physically and emotionally against the violence of sea and sky. For some, search and rescue work is a means of probing into the heart of life. For others, it is an escape from the humdrum and the routine, from the sometimes frightening thought of having to face life in all its ordinariness and predictability. Or sometimes this work is simply what they know how to do. *Heroic Rescues* is not so much a historical record as a human interest story. While some of the Coast Guard's history and present-day activities and responsibilities are portrayed, the emphasis is on the search and rescue workers and their stories.

The evolution of the organization we know as the Canadian Coast Guard is fascinating. In the early years of Canada's shipping, there was a near-total lack of safety measures and a lack of concern for the welfare of sea travellers; navigation was by means of "by guess, and by God." Crews were inexperienced and untrained. Yesterday's mariners suffered great hardship, prompting the great English sage, Samuel Johnson, to remark that "no one would put themselves onto a ship who had means enough to get himself into a jail." If fire and storm did not immobilize a ship, then pirates, marauders, and buccaneers would lure them to certain disaster. Frequent shipwrecks meant repeated heroic rescue attempts by captain, crew, the crews of nearby ships, and folk who lived along the shores where ships foundered.

Establishing life-saving support along Canada's extensive, sparsely populated coastlines bordering the Atlantic, Pacific, and Arctic oceans presented a challenge to the new country. It wasn't until the late 1700s, after a series of terrible wrecks, that the government was pressured to provide lifeboat stations and provisions to shipwrecked mariners in Eastern Canada. The government established Canada's first light station on Sable Island, Nova Scotia in 1733, followed by others on Sambro Island, Nova Scotia in 1758, Cape Breton in 1777, and St. John's, Newfoundland in 1791.

The origins of our modern life-saving system began with volunteer efforts in the form of people helping people, of coastal folk and fishermen paddling out in giant seas in small wooden boats, often putting their own ships, cargo, and passengers at risk for the relief of others.

More formal assistance to shipwrecked sailors began with specific crews of volunteers called "soldiers of the surf," or "storm warriors," engaged to protect ships of commerce. As shipbuilding gained significance in the economic life of the colonies, there was an urgent need to keep ships and seamen safe, to protect fishermen and the industry, to patrol their vessels, and to enforce regulations along the eastern seaboard. This need extended to the Great Lakes region (larger in size than the British Isles), once its extensive system of canals and waterways was built and once Lake Ontario became connected to Lake Erie by the first Welland Canal in 1829.

At Confederation in 1867, the Federal Government acquired a large collection of aid systems, lifesaving stations, canals and waterways, regulatory bodies, and associated vessels, along with the shore infrastructure that supported them. The Department of Marine and Fisheries was established to oversee these marine responsibilities. In 1936 the government passed the Department of Transportation Act, bringing all these components under a single federal authority. In 1962, the fleet of vessels used in marine service was named the Canadian Coast Guard. In 1995 the Coast Guard amalgamated with the Department of Fisheries and Oceans.

If it is true that the mark of a mature, civilized nation is the extent to which a government cares for its people, then Canada is truly a mature and civilized nation. Our government, through the Coast Guard, demonstrates the value it places on human life by the resources it devotes to the protection of the lives of its people, as well as of our maritime interests.

Internationally, the country's reputation is excellent: Canada today is considered one of the world's great maritime nations and its Coast Guard one of the finest. It is signatory to the International Civil Aviation and Maritime conventions; Canada's area of SAR responsibility extends from the Canada-United States border to the North Pole, and from eight hundred nautical miles offshore in the Pacific Ocean to about one thousand miles offshore in the Atlantic. It has an historic effectiveness ratio averaging ninety to ninety-four percent. And volunteer organizations such as the Canadian Coast Guard Auxiliary play a vital and indispensable role.

The Coast Guard is respected because of the amount of money it dedicates to search and rescue work, its generosity in providing training to emerging Coast Guard organizations around the world that seek its help, and the ratio of lives saved to lives at risk in marine distress. Canada is known near and far for its efficient search and rescue coordination and communication systems, its advanced computer technology (such as the computer search planning program) and for other sophisticated technology employed by its mariners. Its SAR workers are recognized for their extraordinary ability to accomplish seemingly impossible rescues. Not the least is the devotion that they and their auxiliary counterparts bring to their work.

"People say to us, 'geez, there are guys down in the middle of the Atlantic, down in Norfolk, talking to you, and asking you what would you do in a particular situation,'" says one marine controller. "Many Coast Guard organizations around the world tell us that they don't have anyone with experience there at the moment, and say, 'if you guys see us doing something wrong, would you tell us?' We're not a military organization like the United States Coast Guard. With us, you're not going to see a whole lot of saluting. We're a bunch of hands-on guys; we get the work done without formality." Of course, the crew aren't always "guys"; today, women go to sea alongside men.

What the Canadian Coast Guard particularly values is experience. It knows that the majority of its workers will stay in the service because it is a way of life they are passionately dedicated to. The Coast Guard also recognizes the importance of having people in lifeboat stations who have grown up in the communities where they work—who have lived on, and in, boats all their lives. When these workers go out to help fishermen, commercial craft, and pleasure boaters, they understand exactly what they are getting into. They also know many of the people they assist, and this knowledge is key to the excellent work they do. As one observer commented, "It's really about loyalty, inspiration, and dedication."

Recent years, however, have seen unsettling changes. The system of recruitment and training for positions at the lifeboat stations has altered, creating a degree of upheaval.

"There is always difficulty when you change a system, introduce new requirements such as a more formalized training," says Peter Stow, regional supervisor of Marine Search and Rescue, Maritimes Region. "We established a Coast Guard college at Sydney, from which someone would graduate, for example, with certification for the position of a commanding officer. Up until that time, the system saw seamen/deckhands work their way up into these positions after achieving the required certificates. They may well have felt displaced by the new college system. But we would never parachute a newly certified officer straight into such a position. He or she would first be required to get experience on the boats. Eventually the graduate would assume an officer's position, but only if they won it through competitions."

In the 1990s, downsizing and re-structuring have changed the face of the Canadian Coast Guard. Our rescuers now work much harder with less. Many are kept on contract, with all its insecurity, for sometimes ten years or more, in spite of exemplary dedication and a superior level of skills and qualifications. Resources have been rationed, and people and equipment deployed to other functions.

Lifelong careers at the Coast Guard are disappearing, and some find the job is not as glamorous as they thought it would be. There are great surges of adrenaline when sudden, desperate rescue missions are underway, but these are interspersed with periods of mundane maintenance work, like washing solar panels. The challenge is to stay on the edge, like a coiled spring, when it might have been a month since the last dangerous rescue.

The tasks required have become more varied: the original Coast Guard mandate to save the lives of those in jeopardy in Canada has been expanded to include maintenance work at the base; buoy tending and lighthouse supply missions; and crewing for Coast Guard ships on multi-tasking expeditions that include water quality monitoring, scientific sampling for pollution, and other missions like hydrographic work and ice breaking. Coast Guard responsibilities now also include approving safety equipment, developing construction standards for vessels, conducting marine radio communications, and teaching boating safety. Interspersed are search and rescue missions that include retrieving body parts and transporting ill and injured people to waiting ambulances when airplanes and helicopters are grounded because of fog or freezing rain. The only multi-tasking duty not considered acceptable is fisheries enforcement; Coast Guard workers believe that if you police people suspected of doing something wrong, they are not likely to call you when they need help, which could result in loss of life.

Boats are not the only means of transport; the airforce has a large role in the national search and rescue work. Because of Canada's international obligations, in 1947 the Canadian government gave a mandate to the Royal Canadian Airforce (RCAF) to provide search and rescue services across the country. In 1951, maritime services were also delegated to the RCAF under the umbrella of the Department of National Defence.

Ice-breaking expeditions like this one in the Gulf of St. Lawrence now complement the original Coast Guard mandate to save the lives of those in peril.

"But we, the airforce, didn't have the expertise for the marine part—guys who fly airplanes don't drive boats," says Major Michel Brisebois, officer in charge of the Rescue Coordination Centre in Halifax. "So the maritime interests were delegated to the Coast Guard. It's an organization that encompasses both marine and air services, all part of the federal search and rescue system."

The Coast Guard is a public service with its own mandate, goals and objectives, standards, and mandatory training programmes, but many exercises are conducted jointly with the military. "The benefits of cooperation are many," says Brisebois. "Coast Guard personnel at a lifeboat station have only a Coast Guard view, out of necessity, but those in the control room and at the joint rescue coordination centres have backgrounds in commercial shipping, the airforce, Coast Guard College, and the sea. This provides a strong collective in one room, as opposed to the limitation of having one view of the world." The on-scene coordinator is generally the first SAR asset to arrive. He or she assumes command under Brisebois's responsibility, who, in turn, answers to the rear admiral, who reports to the Cabinet.

"The mandate is ours, the RCAF," says Brisebois, "but we are very much a team player; rendering the service is a team effort. We're very attuned to each other on the things we do together.

"This is a national program involving various branches of the federal government, provinces and territories, municipalities and volunteer organizations. Whatever has been its evolution over the years, at its heart it remains a marine search and rescue system demanding a significant amount of effort in our marine search and rescue environment."

For many of us, the Canadian Coast Guard is associated with light-keepers and their lighthouses, braving the seas in their wooden rowing boats to go to the aid of the besieged helmsman. While much has changed, including the closing of most of the manned lighthouses, the image of the dedicated rescuer deserves to remain. The knowledge that the Coast Guard will always come often sustains those in desperate situations. The sight of the red and white Coast Guard cutter and its crew in their light blue and navy uniforms continues to inspire hope and courage.

Even today, when fear of liability and its ensuing costs often inhibit humanitarian action, the Coast Guard does not restrain their search and rescue workers by keeping them on shore while tempests rage and people perish on the seas. Those behind desks in the marine control rooms know that, in spite of all the sophisticated technology that allows them virtual presence at the scene of a shipwreck, they can never really understand the conditions, and therefore the risks to the rescue workers. They have deep respect for the experience and judgement of their frontline rescue crews, and allow them freedom to make their own decisions about the risks they take. This respect is deserved.

While search and rescue workers may have various motives in choosing this work, they all share a dedication to saving the lives of others. Deep human emotions are engendered by the sharing of difficult and dangerous experiences, and the need for trust in others for one's very life. This is a heady experience, bonding those who participate.

In these pages, you will travel from coast to coast, live at a lifeboat station, and enter the joint rescue coordination centres and marine control rooms to see how search and rescue works. I hope you will enjoy going on dramatic rescue missions and entering the lives of our rescue workers for a little while. I hope too that when you turn the last page, you will have a keener appreciation of who they are and what they do.

Carolyn Matthews

ATLANTIC

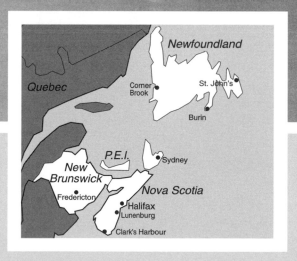

Newfoundland

Quebec

Corner
Brook

St. John's

Burin

P.E.I.

Sydney

New
Brunswick

Nova Scotia

Fredericton

Halifax
Lunenburg

Clark's Harbour

The Hard Face
of the Sea

Newfoundland has nearly six thousand miles of deeply indented and rugged shorelines, its convoluted harbours hiding 'sunkers,' reefs that lurk beneath the water's surface. These harbours offer hope to ships seeking shelter, only to repulse them with treacherous reefs, their very names tragic: Cape aux Morts, Rocks of Massacre, Malignant Cove, Bay of Despair, Dead Sailor's Rock, Wreck Cove.

This far-flung province forms the seventh largest island in the world, encompassing almost the same land mass as Great Britain. Unlike Great Britain, however, it is a place of rock and shallow soil with no gulf stream to warm its shores. During the summer and autumn, Newfoundland, is a world of water, of granite and shale rock that lies bare to sun and wind, of spruce and pine, and green in the hollows. Always, there is the hard, turbulent face of the sea.

For much of the year, the island can be gaunt and grey, a universe of ice and snow. Beginning in late November, a great tongue of polar pack ice begins thrusting southward from Baffin Bay in huge continental masses. By Christmas, the ice has reached the coast of Labrador and Belle Isle Strait. Late January sometimes sees ice engulfing the northern reaches of Newfoundland, perhaps creeping up to the Grand Banks. Then this all-encompassing watery world is hidden beneath ice fields, under floes that ride over each other to form icy mountainous ridges below which stretches a vast, unbroken plain extending to the horizon. There is no season of the year when the coastal waters and shipping lanes are free of ice and icebergs.

The people once lived among rocks, between wind and water in houses that crowded on the land lash—that indeterminate area where land meets water. Early morning dawned to the chugging of fishing boats, a familiar, comforting sound that signalled

One of the deadliest risks in the North Atlantic is ice, which begins to build almost the moment water touches railings and decks.

the vibrant heart of the community. Beyond the point, a dory dawdled; below, on the docks, someone hauled in herring nets while another shovelled snow from a roof. Shouts and whistles came from along the wharves that lay at the foot of the village.

This is winter in a small Newfoundland fishing community where snow lies heavy in the hollows and is scattered on the exposed rock. The bay is not crowded, but neither is it empty: old wharves brood over water, tidal wrack, upturned boats, fish stores. Smells suffuse the air: tar, salt, fish and pickled herring, old net twine, spruce logs crackling in the fire. It is a world of discarded brass and copper, of old shoes and boots and tangled wire. In corners of the sheds are piles of old conch shells that once were used as foghorns. Brilliant colours of turquoise, blue, yellow and red are flung on the walls of houses that cling haphazardly to the rocks above the shore, a startling contrast to the sombre backdrop of winter cliffs. People tread, heads bent into the wind, on pathways that meander about slopes and valleys, and among wooden fence enclosures. For nearly four hundred years, Newfoundlanders have lived here, wresting their living from the sea, sometimes facing winters of starvation. Those who survived are like no others, and it is believed that there are no finer seamen in the world.

Sealers historically have faced the greatest danger of all those who risk life and ship on the seas about Newfoundland. Most families depended on a successful seal hunt in order to eat and

Coast Guard ice-breakers like the *Henry Larsen* patrol ice-heavy seas year round.

so to survive. It was especially so in 1931, "that year of black adversity," described so chillingly in the story of the explosion of the sealing vessel *Viking*, told by Farley Mowat in his book *Grey Seas Under*. The disaster that struck the *Viking* is one among many tales that chill the heart of the reader.

In that year, all able-bodied men and many boys—all those who wished to go—crowded old, rotten vessels to pursue the herds of seals. The captain drove his ship deep into the pack ice, he and his men fully aware that none of them might return. The decision to go was a measure of their desperation as the survival of the communities was at stake.

The owners used dynamite in an attempt to free the ship from thick pack ice off Horse Island in the Straits of Belle Isle, and the steamer went up in flames. The rescuers—other sealers who had

Crest of the Marine subcentre of St. John's, Newfoundland.

Canadian Coast Guard
Newfoundland Region

begun their harvest farther north—turned about in heavy seas and drove themselves into the bitter ice in an attempt at rescue.

The bitter ice remains, still claiming a life here and there. But it is no longer the hazard it once was. In the seventy years that have passed since the tragic sinking of the *Viking* and the loss of many of her crew near Horse Island, the Canadian government has established an extensive system of search and rescue, provided under the Department of National Defence, and focused on the Coast Guard and its auxiliary. The use of sophisticated navigational and communications technology allows identification of vessel and location, and fast rescue of those in jeopardy, wherever they might be. The *Henry Larsen* patrols the northwest coasts of Newfoundland during the winter months and the Arctic waters during the summer. Other Coast Guard ships, including the *Ann Harvey*, are also involved in ice-breaking activities as need dictates; Hercules aircraft and Labrador helicopters are on standby to fly to the rescue of the stranded.

In the marine subcentre in St. John's, there is a desk known as Ice Operations, dedicated to monitoring ice conditions and formation, responding to the needs of vessels, large and small. Ruby Strang alternates with Ray Bartlett in taking responsibility for monitoring conditions around the clock at this desk. But, however sophisticated the means of patrol and the efficiency of search and rescue methods, the hazards of the seas, especially of the North Atlantic, continue to haunt the people who live along its shores.

To the Ends of the Earth

St. John's, Newfoundland

"Daddy might be up in a big airplane when Santa Claus comes," Greg Smit says to his children as he puts the finishing touches to the Christmas tree in the living room. "Some people have to work at Christmas on big ships that sail the ocean. When the weather's bad, they might get in trouble and need someone to fly out to rescue them. So if the phone rings and I'm needed, I'll have to race out the door in a flash...but hey, don't worry, I'll be back."

Canadian Armed Forces personnel like Greg Smit—pictured here at 103 Search and Rescue Squadron in Gander—work closely with the Canadian Coast Guard.

Greg Smit, search and rescue technician for the Canadian Armed Forces, speaks nonchalantly to his children on Christmas Eve—December 25, and the days that follow, are quiet. His wife hears him say much the same thing as New Year's Eve approaches: Daddy might have to be away up in that big plane when other people are having parties to celebrate the beginning of a new year.

The call that sees Greg Smit hurry out the door comes on New Year's Day. His words "Hey, I'll be back," echo in the room that, to wife and children, seems suddenly empty. This is one call from which Greg Smit might not return.

"I walked up the gangway of the ship that day, and that was it for me: I never looked back." This is how Dave Griffiths, a young university graduate, describes his entry into search and rescue work for the Canadian Coast Guard. Like Greg Smit and all his mates in the business, he might one day never look back simply because he might never come back.

Queen's Battery, looking seaward.

Dave also gets a call on that New Year's Day, a call that he feels is sending him to the ends of the earth.

Unlike Greg, Dave does not spend Christmas in 1993 at home with family, but at St. John's harbour on board the Coast Guard ship the *Sir Wilfred Grenfell*. Snow lies heavy on the slopes above the harbour, and glittering icicles hang precariously from rocky outcrops. Temperatures are very cold.

The crew's Coast Guard patrol ship has been in refit: deck heads replaced, protective deck covering in alleyways and cabins removed, electronic systems brought back on line, engine room cleaned up. On December 27, the crew assumed regular activities on board ship. New Year's Eve sees them patrolling the harbour waters as thousands of people crowd the shores to watch fireworks at the height of the city's big party. The Coast Guard's fast rescue craft patrols throughout the evening; for its crew, it is an effective means of retrieving members of a once-happy crowd who accidentally find themselves in the water, drunk and wet.

Little does the on-duty Coast Guard search and rescue crew know that before many hours of the new year have passed, they, as well as their counterparts in the Armed Forces, will find themselves thrown into a SAR mission that will test the limits of their endurance.

Dave Griffiths is at home this evening in St. John's, celebrating the evening quietly with family and friends. He is on call, and must be available for departure on a search and rescue mission within half an hour of receiving summons. No drinking or partying for him this night.

There are no celebrations either this New Year's Eve for Greg Smit. A call to duty for him will not be on a Coast Guard ship, but in a Canadian Armed Forces Hercules aircraft. He, too, is at

Dave Griffiths, whose first-ever search and rescue mission took place almost eight hundred nautical miles from his home in Newfoundland.

home with his family and not drinking because he must be ready within thirty minutes to respond to a rescue mission. The pager is in his pocket, and, later, at his bedside. For both young men, this is to be their first ever SAR mission, one that will live long in lore and legend of both the Coast Guard and the Armed Forces.

New Year's Day dawns cold and grey, the temperature registering minus twenty degrees. Winds are fierce. Snow still lies deep in the hollows and about rocks that dot the slopes above the harbour; like sentries, the few trees stand guard over water and ships below. The streets bordering the waterfront are pot-holed, layered with old snow and slush. The Coast Guard crew is at the harbour going about the usual tasks of general ship maintenance. Because it is New Year's Day, Captain Bergeron orders in special food so the cook can prepare a lavish lunch for crew separated from family and friends. The captain tells them he will release them an hour or two early from their twelve-hour shifts so they can be free to participate in some of the day's celebrations.

Toward three in the afternoon, the call comes—a source of light 786 nautical miles from St. John's has been spotted. The summons is received from the Halifax Joint Rescue Coordination Centre, where the signal of an electronic positioning-indicating radio beacon (EPIRB)[1] has been relayed.

"The call comes into the bridge," says Dave. "Being a deckhand, I don't know all the details, just that we are heading out

[1] Emergency position-indicating radio beacons are battery-operated transmitters which, when activated, transmit a coded signal. Any signal received from an EPIRB is considered to indicate distress, and search and rescue forces in Canada will respond. Each coded signal identifies the country in which the ship is registered and provides a unique identification of the beacon, allowing the SAR forces to identify the vessel and its owner.

Class 1 EPIRB is designed to float free from the vessel and its signal is activated automatically. A class 11 type is portable, and is also able to float, but can only be activated manually.

The *Sir Wilfred Grenfell*, stationed at St. John's, Newfoundland.

to sea. We begin to prepare, taking in the mooring lines and stowing them, but there's a problem. We carry two fast rescue boats on board; one is on shore, about to be replaced by another, but it hasn't arrived yet." Dave explains that it is critical that the ship leave within thirty minutes of a tasking; failure to do so is a serious event. SAR marine controllers plan their response to an emergency based on the knowledge that any resource they task will respond within the allotted time.

"I know it's a cliché," says Dave, "but in life-and-death emergencies, every second counts. Any crew who cannot respond within the given time frame has some explaining to do."

The captain, concerned about meeting the thirty-minute deadline, makes the decision with one of his officers that Dave will remain behind to wait for the second fast rescue craft. Dave will have it deployed by crane into the harbour waters, then race after the departing ship; once alongside, it will be lifted on board.

The *Sir Wilfred Grenfell* is lining up in the ranges to head out to sea when the second fast rescue craft arrives on the docks.

"What timing!" says Dave. "The service technician and I work fast to launch her, hook her on [to the *Grenfell*], recover her…it's a kind of tricky maneuver, but it goes pretty well. Then, as we pass through the narrows into the open sea beyond, we look up to see what we're in for. I have to confess I'm stunned. I see, then that we are going to be in for quite a punch."

What Dave sees beyond the shelter of the harbour is a heaving ocean swept up into monstrous green swells by winds

A Labrador helicopter helps a Coast Guard vessel, the *Sir Wilfrid Laurier,* respond to a distress call. Hercules and Aurora aircraft are also called upon regularly for assistance by air.

gusting to seventy knots, as well as freezing rain and snow—a threatening wintry atmosphere where sea and sky create an indistinguishable horizon. The crew goes about quickly fastening down all the hatches—"battening down the hatches really does come into play here," says Dave. "We double-check every single one on deck, every door, because, as we pass Fort Amherst, the ship starts to punch right away into the swells; within hours she's taking on heavy seas and we're making very slow progress." It is an indication of what the crew is about to face and the beating the ship will take: high winds and heavy seas in swells reaching heights of forty to sixty feet.

The crew has finished the ship inspections. As they go below decks to scrub off crustings of salt and get dry, they hear the captain over the PA system.

"This will be no ordinary rescue," he announces. "It's not an incident fifty to one hundred miles off shore." He explains that the ship will be sailing outside Canadian territorial waters, far beyond the two hundred-mile limit, and that it will take some time to get there. What he does not say is that the *Sir Wilfred Grenfell* is heading almost eight hundred nautical miles from Newfoundland's shores toward the western coasts of North Africa and Portugal. It will take three to four days to arrive at the spot in the ocean where a ship has been torn apart by storm, its crew of thirty-six men in the water. The crew learn more details as the ship bucks its way across the hostile Atlantic: the *Marika* is a commercial bulk carrier flying a Liberian flag and carrying heavy shipments of iron ore. It and its crew have disappeared, in an area near the mid-Atlantic Ridge and West European Basin.

The Coast Guard crew rig a wire about the ship, slip on their safety harnesses and attach these to the wire while going about their duties. But this is a universe of treacherous decks where seas wash over. One minute a ship is perpendicular to the water, the next it is horizontal in a landscape of high winds and water that, to Dave's imagination, has the appearance of some evil creature reaching up and over the ship, its giant fist raised to crush it. Survival is what the voyage is about, and it means hanging on.

"The captain orders Tony Ryan, our cook, not to try to make hot meals," says Dave. "The ship is pitched at such severe angles that he's afraid he might scald himself. Poor fellow, he's down in the galley, surrounded by food, and the everyday objects of his business have become a very real hazard to him. Day after day, he prepares us drinks and sandwiches under tremendous difficulty without a word of complaint."

Life is not a picnic for the men in the engine room either. They might not have to endure hardships of the kind their counterparts in old sailing schooners did, when the stoke hold and engine room were closed off tight and fresh air entered only through the draft for the fires, temperatures rose to 120 degrees, and the all-pervasive stink of ashes, bilge, and engine oil made the men sick. But the difficulties for today's crew are severe nevertheless, and they perform their tasks with humour and good cheer.

Sleep eludes the crew: one has first to negotiate getting into a bunk. If the violence of the ship's pitching and rolling doesn't throw them out, they are called to go up on deck and re-secure the life rafts. Before the first long night is over, one raft is lost overboard, torn loose by huge seas tearing at the ship.

"For almost four days," says Dave. "this is what we know: bucking wet decks, freezing cold, and bruises from the pounding and buffeting we're getting."

When he gets the call this New Year's morning from the Armed Forces and a summons to the base for an operation far out on the Atlantic, Greg Smit experiences a moment of pure exhilaration. "Quite a start to the year," he says laconically to his wife. "Perhaps this will be the real thing, not just a false alarm."

Greg has been with the forces for nine years, a paramedic at the army base, and, in more recent years, an SAR technician. Training has been long and arduous, his participation in training exercises, mock disasters, and rescue attempts seemingly never-ending. He has not yet been part of a real search and rescue operation, where he can put into practice all he has learned. Although he does not yet know it, this call is an extremely rare type of rescue mission: he is about to soar and dip above the earth's waters for prolonged periods, returning only to go out again to face severe buffeting in turbulent skies above hostile seas.

"Thirty-six people shipwrecked far out in the Atlantic in serious trouble—this was what I'd trained and waited for; I was just raring to go," says the young Greg. "We would be the first to get there, the first to do something. We've had many false alarms in the past, and, for a moment, I wondered if this was one: that the EPIRB had just fallen overboard and self-activated—it's happened before."

The Hercules C306 aircraft had not often been far off the coast, and it had never travelled anywhere close to this distance. Greg is the designated spotter, and it is the first time he has been the only spotter on the team. He is quiet, deep into his own thoughts about what he might have to do as the crew prepares the aircraft for takeoff.

The large doors at the back of the plane are removed, and a window is installed, with a chair facing out. Greg Smit, the spotter, becomes the eyes of the pilots up front. If he sees anything in the water, he and another SAR technician will prepare to jump. Greg hangs on tight as the aircraft attempts to race across the skies, its speed reduced as it is flung about, tossed like a paper bag in the wind; objects scatter throughout the cabin. Greg becomes violently sick, but he is not alone: all the crew but one of the pilots and the flight engineer are sick for the entire duration of the mission. Nothing has prepared him, or any of them, for this horrendous ordeal.

After four to five hours, the crew reaches their destination far out in international waters: latitude near the fortieth parallel, longitude, thirty degrees. Here, SAR shares jurisdiction with Great Britain and the United States, but for twenty-four hours, the Canadian Hercules is the only aircraft searching the ocean. It sweeps down from the skies to fly as low as possible for this type of craft: one hundred to three hundred feet above angry seas. It crisscrosses, rises up, sweeps low, an extraordinary feat for an aircraft of its size.

"We're shocked when we get there," Greg says. "Many of us

still half believed this would be another false alarm. We are at a vast, empty expanse of heaving sea—hard to tell at first, where the sea ends and the sky begins—but it's all lit up. It's like, hey, we've just had Christmas; then we get here and it's like having it all over again."

Strobe lights from life rafts illuminate the furious ocean. This is definitely no false alarm; rather, it is a devastatingly real and tragic incident: people are in the water. Several "vessels of opportunity" (any craft in the area that can offer assistance), still more than a hundred miles distant and plowing toward the scene, beam across the ocean. The scene is surreal: the night is black, and dawn is obscured by rain, wind and snow. Menacing walls of water ten to thirty feet in height raise themselves up, then thrash down in fury.

Over and over, the pilot brings the aircraft low over the water. It sweeps back and forth, severely buffeted. At the window, Greg cranes his neck, straining his eyes to find life, to find a glimpse of anything. If he spots something that might be a person, the crew will throw SKAD kits from the craft, kits that include ten-person life rafts that inflate, lights that activate as they hit the water, and bundles containing food, lights, radios, and warm clothes. Then the search and rescue technicians will immediately prepare to jump. But Greg explains that SAR technicians will only parachute out if there is a ship in proximity. "It's suicide to drop from an aircraft to people in the water, or even people in a life raft, without having a large vessel nearby," he says. "And still, we spot nothing on the ocean. We're frantic to throw out the life rafts, the SKAD kits. We have this overwhelming feeling of helplessness, not knowing if we should. it is wasteful if we can't see any people, but we feel desperate to do *something*. We have to assume that the ship's life raft lights were activated when they hit the water, that the sailors saw them and swam toward them, that there are people now in the rafts. But we can't see them. We can only keep sweeping over in the Hercules not doing anything more, but badly wanting to. And then, there's always a thought in the back of your mind: you remember the Hercs that have crashed in the past, and here you are…you feel so helpless in face of Mother Nature. Puny. You think you're in control but you're not. You are, only to the extent that you've trained and prepared the very best you can; worked with your team, trained with them, relied on them…but you never know when Mother Nature is going to turn and grab you…"

The bridge of the *Sir Wilfrid Laurier*—the scene of massive coordinating efforts among the vessels and crew involved in a mission.

The aircraft crew knows that it will take days before the Coast Guard search and rescue ship arrives, but they don't know that it will be twenty-four hours before another aircraft comes on the scene to assist in the search. They are always reluctant to leave a scene to refuel and recharge without handing over to another aircraft crew. They consider it is their duty, until relieved, to continue unceasingly to sweep over the ocean in search of signs of life.

Meanwhile, the forces of nature are doing their best to grab the Coast Guard ship as it ploughs its lonely path, one day after another, across the trackless surface of the sea. They, like the Armed Forces crew, are bruised and worn out when they arrive at the area where the freighter has sunk, three-and-a-half days after their departure from St. John's. They, too, are stunned at the scene that meets their eyes: Hercules and Aurora aircraft crisscrossing low over the water while merchant vessels conduct a search of the seas. These vessels include the *Freja Svea*, the *Thorgasa*, and two Russian container ships, *Khudoznik Pakhomov* and *Khudoznik Romas*. The *Sea-Land Atlantic* also attempts to help, but cannot alter course because of the severe sea conditions; it continues on its easterly course through the search area.

Captain Bergeron, the commanding officer of the *Sir Wilfred Grenfell*, has been given status as on-scene commander, taking over from the *Freja Svea*. Two other vessels now join the effort: the *Companion Express* and the *Cast Beaver*. Captain Bergeron has the thankless task of coordinating the efforts of all the other vessels in the area. His own ship begins searching on a grid pattern, a task requiring intense concentration. The crew hangs on, safety harnesses attached, while scanning the swells, hour after long hour.

"Each of us in our hearts, hopes for the best, but is prepared for the worst," says Dave. "We begin to understand what it must be like to hold on for dear life in a raft in seas this mountainous, day after day, night after night. The ocean might be somewhat warmer than the waters off Newfoundland, but the seas are just ferocious. We just keep searching while we're being pounded and tossed, searching and searching..."

It has been approximately sixteen hours since the Hercules aircraft crew departed St. John's. They are reluctant to leave the scene, but it is a mandatory requirement that they return to shore to re-fuel, and for the crew to rest and recharge. Rather than head home to Newfoundland, it makes sense to head toward the Azores, just two hundred miles distant; it means a quick passage and a quick return.

Unfortunately, a head wind prevents the approach to the island. "A strong wind, a big aircraft, and a short runway—no way we could do it," says Greg. The crew is forced to make the long journey back to St. John's, where the crew remains for the required eight hours. Then they climb back on board the craft, and fly back to the scene to continue their search. Search patterns are repeated, with the pilot flying low, back and forth, back and forth..."I'm straining my eyes to see, craning my neck, beginning to lose hope, like all of us," Greg says.

But suddenly he gives a shout: he has spotted something in the water. The pilot wheels the Hercules about and flies it as low as he dares. Greg has glimpsed fragments of life rafts below. "We're flying right over, can just make them out with the help of our strobe lights...all we can see are these life rafts that peak on the swells, then roll down the other side," he says. "Great mountains of water looking like they will swallow up the rafts, huge white caps, and the shadows of the life rafts." He pauses, then adds, "nobody could possibly survive in these seas."

The crew feels extremely frustrated. They have years of training, they have the tools and technology, and an aircraft that can fly around the world, yet they can do nothing.

The pilot of the Hercules radios the location of the life rafts to *Sir Wilfred Grenfell*'s captain, who immediately heads there. The crew is up on deck, safety harnesses attached, straining their eyes to penetrate the foaming green swells. Suddenly they see signs of life as the life rafts peak momentarily on the crest of a swell; Captain Bergeron maneuvers the ship alongside as best he can, "a phenomenal job of ship handling in the circumstances," says Dave Griffiths. "We're down now, in the rescue zone of the boat. The decks are awash and there's water cascading over the gunnels; you have your safety lines on and you're just trying to hang on, but also trying to grab onto the life raft."

The crew finds that the cover of the first raft is ripped away, revealing nothing but black tubing. They see immediately that there are no survivors aboard. They come alongside the second raft with its covering intact, and hope rises that there are people inside. Anticipation is keen: the raft is pulled aboard the ship, the covering ripped off, but it is washed clean and empty. The disappointment is intense. The crew continues to search the seas in the hope of finding possible survivors, or at least the bodies of the men thrown into the sea.

The search is eventually put on reduced status, and on January 21 the crew of the *Sir Wilfred Grenfell* is stood down. It has been almost two weeks from the time they left their home shores. The ship needs refuelling because fuel is also used as ballast, and its crew needs relief from the pounding they have endured without respite. They face the almost eight hundred mile trek across still savage seas to St. John's, or they can make for the Azores. The captain elects to head his ship to Ponce, or to Ponta DelGata.

The loss of the freighter *Marika* and all thirty-six hands on board has received international media attention, and the crew arrives in the Azores to a hero's welcome. That these Canadians have voyaged so far at considerable expense, and put themselves in jeopardy to search for another nation's sailors, is keenly appreciated.

"If it were my father, my brother, I would want to know that someone was doing everything in their power, anything, to try to rescue them. We do it for ourselves, so we can sleep well at night," says Dave.

Media representatives come on board the *Sir Wilfred Grenfell* to interview Captain Bergeron and to inspect the life rafts. The crew goes ashore to do what visitors to another country usually do: look around, enjoy the landscape, buy souvenirs, make phone calls home. It's not difficult to spot them as sailors—they walk with a peculiar, staggering gait as though they are expecting the earth to move at a forty-five degree angle, not yet having found their 'land legs.' They are recognized, too, as the sailors from the Canadian search and rescue ship, not least because, unlike the locals, the crew wear short sleeves.

"It's summer to us," says Dave. "When we left home, the temperature was minus twenty degrees, and fierce winds were blowing. It was all a little unsettling too, because we'd been conditioned to twenty-four hour pounding and mountainous seas; now we're walking on a flat surface and the ground doesn't move!"

Ponta DelGata is very clean, and its people friendly. The crew's reception is warm indeed; when they enter a crowded bar, waiters rush to find additional tables to seat their honoured guests and proceed to treat them as celebrities. All the while, the crew remain on a half-hour standby with its attendant responsibilities.

On the return home, the ship is again thrashed mercilessly as it struggles through furious seas at six to ten knots; winds are still close to one hundred kilometres an hour. Hope is gone, replaced with despondent knowledge that thirty-six men have perished at sea.

"We go home with nothing but empty life rafts, nothing to show for two or more weeks of effort and absence," says Dave with a deep sigh. The crew deals with the knowledge that so many families will be grieving the death of a member. They identify with the heartache, having witnessed it so many times before.

The sea, and ships that sail it, will become Dave Griffiths' destiny, although he did not know this in his third year at university, where he was a science major. He considered journalism, law, and teaching, but was not passionate about any of them. In 1984, he joined the naval reserves. It was a watershed year: he discovered he loved to go to sea, enjoyed working on boats and ships, and found pleasure in all aspects of marine life. Still, something was missing. He needed more, but what? The answers eluded him.

In 1986, Dave left the navy and returned to his studies. He remembers someone asking if he would be interested in joining the Coast Guard, explaining that it was all about boats, ships, and the sea. Dave was intrigued, and that summer he joined the government-run inshore lifesaving program that provided summer work for university students and others. Dave jumped right in.

The young people accepted in the program had already been involved in life-saving and life-guarding programs and had already achieved certificates in first-aid and CPR, pleasure craft operation, and radio phone operation. All were required to have a bronze cross in swimming. They were stationed in areas where pleasure boats and other boat traffic, particularly fishing boats, were concentrated. If, at any time they found themselves in trouble, the Coast Guard's fast rescue boat would be made available to them. As part of this program, Dave responded to about thirty calls each year.

At the end of the summer, Dave Griffiths realized that he didn't want search and rescue work as a summer job; he wanted it permanently. He graduated from university in 1988 as a science major, and immediately signed up with the Coast Guard's inshore rescue program.

In 1989, a position opened up on the *John Cabot*, a cable ship involved in laying submarine fibre optic cable, among other duties. Dave's travels with the ship brought him to the Caribbean and the eastern coast of the United States. When this vessel was decommissioned, he was offered a position on the *Sir Wilfred Grenfell*. He had already begun his rescue specialist program, and everything started to come together for him. Dave flew through the courses required for this program: St. John ambulance advanced level first-aid, and courses in medic-aid specifically designed for the Coast Guard, including how to hand over a critically ill or injured person to the SARTECHS who flew critical casualties to shore.

"I was completely happy then," Dave says, "not just being a crewman on a ship, but now being able to give immediate first-aid to seriously ill and injured people as a rescue specialist—there was tremendous satisfaction in doing that. At the end of my time off—we had twenty-eight days on, and twenty-eight off—I couldn't wait to get back to work. I liked everything, especially seeing the relief in people's faces, their gratitude..."

Today, Dave Griffiths is Rescue Specialist Coordinator for the Coast Guard in St. John's. For someone who enjoys the outdoor world of boats and ships and the sea, it might seem surprising that he has chosen this area of Coast Guard work. But to those who know him, it makes sense. Dave appreciates the opportunity to offer additional help, not just to rush out to sea to rescue someone, but to be able to offer skilled first-aid on the spot. He believes deeply in a highly-trained Coast Guard force and has worked hard on improving training programs for crew members.

"Put your money where your mouth is, Dave," he was told lightheartedly when he debated whether or not to take the position. He knew he would enjoy it, but he knew also that it would be a job that would take him away from direct involvement in ships and the sea. In this position, his life changed; Dave now organizes and coordinates the training program, including education of the instructors.

"It's a very demanding job trying to get everybody into the appropriate training programs they need when they're free or available, when they're off their shifts," he says. And yes, he misses the camaraderie of shipboard life. To satisfy this need, he remains on call for rescue missions, and gives first-aid when it is required. But his first passion is being able to teach new skills, to know that knowledge gained by those on board the ships might mean the safety of their own lives, as well as the lives of others.

Dave, like many of his counterparts, is known for a humanitarianism that extends well beyond the hours of his official duties. He is often seen going to the hospital at St. John's to visit a shipwrecked sailor from Russia, from the Philippines, or elsewhere, taking with him a book in the language the patient speaks to help mitigate the loneliness and isolation. He is also known, as are many in search and rescue work, for his fierce loyalty to his mates. Regardless of the work he does, this loyalty will remain.

Greg Smit, too, likes to be where things happen, but in the skies flying above the seas, rather than sailing upon it. He has worked for sixteen years for the Canadian Armed Forces, the first years as a medic at the army base. Like Dave Griffith, he too searched for something else, something more...work that would satisfy him.

"I liked to be out on the street and in the ditches," he says. "Becoming a doctor and working in hospitals never really interested me...I loved the outdoors, parachuting, diving, those sort of things. I was in Trenton, Ontario one year and saw the search and rescue technicians there. I thought, these guys do these things for a living—parachuting out of planes. They get paid to practice all these neat medical skills that help save people's lives."

"He needs to do this like we all need to breathe," his wife, Donna, says. "This is the man he is: born to do this kind of work. Sure I worry. Once, these calls spelled crisis, and I wouldn't sleep the remainder of the night. But I'm used to them now: a phone ringing in the small hours of the morning, my husband rolling out of bed and rushing out into the night. I never know what it's about, or for how long. But Greg and I have a pact: he will not do anything crazy because he knows the kids and I are waiting at home, and he will call me the minute he's back on the ground— no matter the hour.

"I tell myself that if anything were to happen to him, I would know that his last minutes have been spent doing the things he loves to do. I love him to the ends of the earth, but I understand that he must do this work to be himself, to be the man I love."

Greg learned that to become a SAR technician, he had to be a member of the Armed Forces for a minimum of four to five years and pass one of the toughest physical fitness tests in the forces, and he had to write a paper explaining why he wanted to be a SAR technician. Other screening included the ability to function on his own and to participate as a member of a team. He passed the lengthy and comprehensive screening process and has been working in this capacity for the past seven years. Greg and Dave Griffiths became good friends after their search for the *Marika*; for both men, this is an occupation about which they are passionate, and they would do no other.

Fishermen
to the Rescue

Wreck Cove, Newfoundland

I t has often been said of Newfoundlanders that their destinies are intertwined with the mighty ocean that surrounds the island's rugged shores. A quick glance at a map shows that little of the massive rock's interior has been claimed by its inhabitants; they apparently have little identification with the rock-strewn and largely treeless landscape a short distance from the water's edge. The sea that swells around these shores has a vital, living presence, and gives an unsettling feeling of sentience as it laps gently, or breaks furiously, upon the deeply-indented coasts. For the people on these shores, the sea is often the only, and ultimate, reality: those who live by it, and take their living from it, know that they will never master it—this sea that gives life also takes it away.

Russel Cox knows about the fury of the ocean; just one year ago, the sea came close to taking his own life. "Nearly dead, I was, they told me in the hospital," he says. "Another hour or two, and I wouldn't've been here."

Russel, his brother, and two friends had gone scallop trawling in their fishing boat, the *Valerie Brothers II*, heading for Taylor and Olde Bays. They left their home at Wreck Cove on Friday, March 17, 2000, planning to return home on Sunday evening. Nights were to be spent warm and cozy in a friend's cabin in the woods.

Late afternoon saw them returning from the fishing fields, but as they trudged to the cabin to get a wood fire blazing in the stove, bitter winds began to moan outside the cabin walls, and the heavens opened, sending rain in drenching sheets to the earth, and especially to Wreck Cove. By evening, winds were driving freezing rain and snow to obscure both land and sea.

As darkness deepened and the storm thundered in from the sea, the men feared for their fishing vessels. Russel's brother Dwayne went outside to check that they were still securely anchored out from shore.

Today, his voice remains seared in Russel's memory: "You'll have to hurry up if you wants to save your boat because she's drifting away."

The fishing vessel had been purchased new just eight months previously; feeling anxious, the men got up and trudged through the woods to the shores. They reached cliffs and beach, and stared out across the water. Horrified, they saw that anchor lines had broken, both boats and had been driven onto the cliffs and rocks. The men scrambled out into boisterous surf and large breakers in an attempt to save the ships, but the motor on Dwayne's boat stalled, and high winds drove the boats toward each other. They swung out of control and collided, the anchor line of one wrapping around the blades of the other.

Dwayne's boat swamped and began to sink rapidly; the men tried furiously to row to the other boat, with only one paddle. Northeast winds were gusting seventy kilometres an hour, and fog was creeping over the seas.

Russel managed to board his boat, while the others made for shore. By this time, they had drifted far from the area of the cabin. In his attempts to get aboard his vessel, Russel slipped and fell, injuring his groin and tearing several ligaments in his leg. Paralyzed by pain, he was unable to get off the boat. His mates returned to help him, but could not extricate him to carry him out. Russel's engines now failed; his boat began to fill with water and to break apart.

Russel dropped to the cabin floor, not able to get up. As his boat continued to swamp and disintegrate, his mates' rescue attempts became perilous to them. Chilled, drenched with sea-water that surged over the cliffs, in danger of drowning if they did not immediately leave the sinking vessel, the three men crawled off the boat and made for the cabin in the woods, facing a walk of an hour-and-a-half.

Russel Cox was left behind on the floor of his boat. His only hope of survival lay with the Coast Guard: he had put out a Mayday call over his VHF radio, but knew that his antenna was small and crusted with ice. He was not certain, as he lay there, that his message had been received. And if it had, would a rescue boat come in time? Would it be able to get into a shore where surf heaved violently in great swells against the cliffs?

Cox's companions, freezing and exhausted, struggled through the bush toward the cabin. Cox's brother, all three hundred pounds of him, soon dropped into the snow and lay there, unable to continue. He insisted the others were to leave him there and save themselves. They would do no such thing; they heaved, struggled, and half dragged the big man over rough ground until they reached the cabin.

Arthur Pierce's fishing boat, *Stephen & Jayde*. As part of the Coast Guard Auxiliary, Pierce and other fishermen respond willingly to requests for help from the Coast Guard.

On board the sinking fishing boat, Cox lay immobile and in severe pain.

"I was sitting on the floor in ice cold water, unable to move because of the pain in my legs," he says. "The water kept coming in through the cabin door and splashing in my face. I tried to stick the handle of the mop against the door to keep it shut..." Russel trails off. He recalls how he found himself rapidly sinking into a state of hypothermia, but struggling all the while to continue to try and make contact with the Coast Guard, or with any vessel that might be in the area.

Miraculously, the maritime regional subcentre in St. John's did receive a weak signal from the *Valerie Brothers II*. They immediately tasked to Wreck Cove all their tremendous resources: a Hercules aircraft, search and rescue vessels, the crew of three fishing vessels in the area, and the Coast Guard Auxiliary.

Arthur Pierce and Wesley Snook Senior were among those who struggled to reach the shipwrecked men off Wreck Cove that violent March day. They know about the fragility of life: as fishermen, they have been in jeopardy themselves, faced hardship and frequent danger. And as members of the Coast Guard Auxiliary, they have added to this risk and inconvenience by making themselves available to go to the rescue of others.

Saturday morning, March 18. Snook Senior is already down at his shed among the fishing nets. Pierce, having finished his breakfast, is about to get into his truck and drive down the hill to his shed above his dock, to spend the day repairing his fishing nets in preparation for the upcoming lobster season. He whistles as he gets into his jacket. This is his life, hard but decent, a life inherited from his grandfather and his father before him. All have taken a living from these seas that wash upon the rocky southwest coasts of Newfoundland and his home village of Harbour Breton. Pierce has just shrugged himself into coat and pulled on his boots when his pager goes off.

Before this summons comes, neither man has been concerned about the weather because they do not intend to be out on the sea—unless, of course, the Coast Guard calls them to a rescue mission, always a possibility. As members of the auxiliary, they respond to search and rescue calls when requested by the Coast Guard.

This call is from the maritime regional subcentre in St. John's, tasking both men, together with Reuben Rose in his boat, to go the rescue of the *Valerie Brothers II*, a vessel capsized and sinking in Wreck Cove. The one man remaining on board is severely hypothermic and injured, in need of evacuation and medical care, they are told. The call is urgent: a man's life is in danger, and his mates are also in need of rescue.

"We just got onto our boats and went out there as fast as we could," Pierce says. "When we get there, we see that the *Valerie Brothers II* is stuck on the beach among a pile of rocks. It's a blizzard of a day and we can't quite see how we can get our boats close in. The surf is crashing in against the cliffs something fierce."

Sam Stowbridge, who had been in the area, has attempted to help in his small boat. Reuben Rose Junior, in his boat *Jayne and Brothers*, has also been out to see what he could do, but has had to turn back because of the severe ice that has built up on the decks and railings. It is a smaller boat, and there is increased risk for it to be out in the stormy conditions.

"You do your best when someone's life is in danger; you watch your own life, and do what you have to do," Pierce says.

The men on board the two fishing vessels quickly size up the situation and conclude that they cannot safely pull the *Valerie Brothers II* off the rocks and tow her to safety; they cannot even get their own vessels into shore without extreme risk. They confer with one another, then decide that they must somehow get the small lifeboat off *Trina and Sons*, float it to the stricken boat, and evacuate the injured man.

Arthur Pierce, taking Rod Pierce with him, leaves two of his men aboard his own boat and climbs aboard *Trina and Sons* to help get the small lifeboat off.

"None of us is too keen to get out in that little boat and take it to the pounding shores," says Pierce. "It doesn't look too good in there. We're wearing survival suits and both of us are good swimmers; young Rod Pierce, he's a scuba diver with lots of experience."

Each man stares toward shore. It is like a canvas, hanging on a living room wall in a seafarer's home: a boat lying on its side, low in the water, the tide out but spray washing over and almost filling the vessel, seawater raging against jutting rocks and surging up the jagged cliffs.

The men in the two fishing boats study the scene, and worry about how they can rescue the injured man in the menacing sea.

The little lifeboat is the only answer, but who is willing to navigate it to the foot of the cliffs? It is a serious risk.

It is Arthur and Rod in the end who climb into the lifeboat. A towline is attached to it from *Trina and Sons* and the two men paddle

Wesley Snook's boat *Trina & Sons*, one of the fishing boats to offer assistance at Wreck Cove—at considerable risk to the lives of master and crew.

furiously to keep the boat's bow heading into the wind so it will not be swamped. Wesley Snook Senior holds the *Trina and Sons'* stern to the heavy wind and seas while the remaining crew members—Wesley Snook Junior, Gary Snook Senior, and Tim Stoodley—slack the boat all the way to the beach. The sea sweeps the little life raft right up on the beach, close to where the stricken *Valerie Brothers II* lies.

The two men manage to get aboard the half-submerged vessel only to find a deep silence within it. The door to the cabin is locked or stuck but one man breaks it down. There on the floor lies Russel Cox, as silent and immobile as an iceman, frozen into awful stillness. Rod sees that he is close to succumbing to hypothermia. The two men struggle to move him but this proves difficult because he is not able to help himself at all. They struggle to get Russel out and to another location so he can be placed safely in the lifeboat. Once this is managed, they yell to the crew on *Trina and Sons* to pull them in.

Once on the fishing vessel, the two men carry Cox down to the cabin and immediately get to work with a knife cutting his frozen overalls and heavy jacket off him; a propane heater is turned on to blow warm air about him. Arthur, absorbed in his work, hears a sudden burst of laughter and looks about him to discover that the back of his trousers are alight, having caught fire from the propane heater—a wonderful release of tension for the watching crew. He laughs too, as he beats out the flames.

As master of *Trina and Sons*, Wesley Snook Senior makes with all possible speed to Harbour Breton where the severely ill and injured Cox can receive urgent medical attention. Cox has spent five hours in the frigid ocean waters, and it is the opinion of the attending physician that he was very near death when he arrived at the hospital. Arthur Pierce and his crew return to the seas to tow Sam Stowbridge, who suffered engine trouble during his rescue attempts, back to Wreck Cove.

The men who put themselves at such extreme risk have since received official recognition from the Department of Fisheries and Oceans in the form of certificates for valour and bravery: Wesley Snook Sr. (Master), Gary Snook Jr., Tim Snoodley, and Wesley Snook Jr. of *Trina & Sons*; Arthur Piercey (Master), Rod Pierce, Todd Piercey, and Glen Jarvis of *Stephen & Jade*; Reuben Rose Jr. (Master) and Robert Rose of *Jane & Brothers*.

While these men flirted with death, Russel Cox came closest to it.

"I had some thoughts about going out for some while after that," he says. "But I got no choice for a living. Still in my mind, I can never forget it: it haunts you. Rough weather—it gives you a bad feeling, sitting in cabin, a bad storm..." his voice trails off.

Ordeal
by Ice

Pointe Riche, Newfoundland

long the coasts of Newfoundland, bitter winds blow, shift, and alter the movement of ice. Intrepid men still go to the fishing grounds to hunt seals on ice at the beginning of spring. In blinding snow and freezing spray, still the men go to the sealing grounds. They face danger and the risk of death, and the knowledge that none of the Coast Guard's enormous and sophisticated resources are a guarantee of rescue.

It is March 17, 2001, when Larry Plowman gets up; "a real nice morning," he says. He thinks how the seals are having their pups early this year because of a warm spell, and thinks that he might go and take a look. If the pups are still in white coats, Larry can do nothing. But if any have reached the "raggedy jacket" stage—where they begin to take to the water and when the dark fur of the adult coat begins to appear—he can legally take them. Larry, who owns a landsman's seal hunting license and a lobster and ground fishing license, gets in touch with his friend Maurice Rumbold. Together they haul Larry's twenty-foot fibreglass boat through the snow from behind his house, and attach the ski-doos to it so they can get it to the shore and into the water.

"We thought we would just go out for an hour or two, take a look, and come home," Larry explains afterwards. "I took my gun to shoot the pups, if there were any I could take, and nothing else, for we weren't planning to stay out."

The two men set off in the fibreglass boat, without radio, cell phone, flashlights, distress flares, food, or blankets.

As the men steam out from shore, winds pick up from the northwest. Larry makes for Pointe Riche and just beyond, a distance of about five miles. "But as we go out, the ice comes in,"

Larry says. "The wind has shifted a bit to the east and there's a lot of ice—black polar ice, we think. Next thing, it becomes a solid jam, and it's coming straight for us."

Larry steers through a gap in the ice to a point where he can see the seals, but they are still in their white coats. It is early afternoon and the men are a mile off land when ice starts driving toward them. They make for open water, steaming through slob ice that Larry explains is first-year ice made in the gulf, ice that freezes over in February.

In northerly seas, where gusting winds cause ice to shift and jam quickly, Coast Guard ice-breakers are called upon to free ships from their icy traps.

"We steam through it for about half an hour, but couldn't do nothing with it," he says. "We see one big ice pan and we shove the boat up on it— you don't want to damage your motor with the ice. And then, it might crush your boat. Ice is pressing hard up against us because the wind is pushing it. We couldn't see any water when we got ourselves up on the pan, but we see ski-dooers on the shore watching us through binoculars, like, what are we doing?"

By late afternoon, the men in their small boat stuck up on the ice pan get very cold. The wind now shifts to the north and rain begins to fall. With ingenuity, Larry yanks up planks from the wooden flooring of his fibreglass boat and nails two of them to the bow, to act as a windbreak, while two more are kept for use as firewood. Darkness falls, Larry figures it must be about nine in the evening.

Larry takes the one object he does have in his boat—an aluminum shovel—fastens it to the head of the vessel, and places a coke can atop it. He then takes some tissue paper soaked in gasoline, lights it with a match, and burns two to three small splinters from the floor boards in the can. The floorboards burn slowly, the shovel acting as a barrier between the flames and the boat. He keeps this fire burning until about four in the morning. In spite of the small fire, Maurice, wearing only a hunting jacket, gets very cold; Larry, in his survival jacket, fares much better.

"We got miserable with smoke in our eyes and our feet cold because our socks are wet," Larry says. "We take the socks off to dry them in front of the fire. Maurice goes to sleep and I have to wake him up. I'm awake because I have to watch the fire when a north wind comes onto us."

Larry expects that, with a northwest wind, the ice will open up; he watches for it all night. It doesn't happen. Both men now can only hope that search and rescue will come, as they have always come for them before.

Unknown to the men, their families have already contacted the Coast Guard. Ski-dooers from shore, having seen a small fire on the distant ice about nine in the evening, called the marine subcentre in St. John's. The moment these calls are received, all the tremendous resources available to the Coast Guard are activated: a Labrador helicopter is tasked to the area and the RCMP at Port Saunders, once contacted, immediately sends a snowmobile to Pointe Riche to sight the boat. Personnel at the Ice Operations desk in St. John's, who have access to reports forecasting that the ice will not move off soon, judge that it is too dangerous for the men to try walking across the ice to shore. They task the Coast Guard ice-breaking ship *Ann Harvey* to the rescue. Provincial Emergency Measures Organization is contacted and asked to send a helicopter, and a marine urgency broadcast by the St. Anthony Coast Guard radio calls for any vessels in the area to assist.

The resources are many, and there is enormous capability to respond to an incident of this nature. But the natural world holds sway over the most sophisticated efforts of humans to protect and save themselves, and it is often the elements that determine the fates of people. The pilot from 103 Rescue Squadron reports he cannot fly because of freezing precipitation (the helicopters have no de-icing capability). The ice-breaking ship is 120 nautical miles down the south coast at Corner Brook, and she has also been tasked to the rescue of men in two snowmobiles who have gone through the ice in the Bay of Islands. The Provincial Emergency Measures Organization says they have no helicopters in the area.

"The ice that day was drifting at two knots," explains Brian Stone, controller at the subcentre. "It was not packed in tight—it was about five-tenths of an inch thick, and the chunks not big and breaking up all the time into smaller pieces, moving with the shifting winds. It blocked their return to port."

The two men wait in an open boat that is stuck up on an ice floe out on the sea in zero degree temperatures, not knowing if help will come. It is in the early hours of the morning when Larry sees pinpoints of lights through the snow squalls that seem to be coming toward them. "Looks like search and rescue," he says, his voice rising, and Maurice, who has become despondent, rouses himself, thinking that he will, after all, see more days of his life. Happily, he begins recounting memories of his hunting days.

The lights disappear, and gloom settles once again on the men. About an hour later, lights re-appear. Larry grabs the shovel with its burning wood attached, and holds it aloft. Peter Frost, captain of the *Ann Harvey*, sees sparks from the small fire in the darkness as he steams his ship toward Point Riche. It is now about four in the morning. His vessel, crunching the ice in its path, reaches the ice pan at last, and comes alongside the small boat. The men cheer, grab the rope thrown them, attach it to the boat, and watch as they are pulled through slivers of open water. Crew from the *Ann Harvey* pull it in, throw down straps to the men, and pull them up.

"The captain gives us a good breakfast," says Larry. "And cigarettes to Maurice. We discussed where he will put us ashore. He says he would like to avoid Port Saunders because he doesn't want to break up the ice; ski-dooers are still using it."

It is ten in the morning when the men are taken ashore at Gargamelle, where their families are waiting for them. The ski-dooers on the beach attach lines to the boat and pull it up the beach; the families express their profound relief that once again their men have come back from the sea.

Larry Plowman, the fisherman caught out on the ice unprepared, is also a university graduate with a major in history from Memorial University in St. John's. He thought he might teach, but during holidays went shrimp and lobster fishing with his father, who eventually transferred one of his lobster licenses to his son. Larry does teach when he's not fishing. "You won't believe it, but I teach safety courses on the sea," he says. "I like teaching. Been fishing since I was in grade seven, and just kept on doing it—you can make good money with the shrimp. But I like the teaching, too."

The jeopardy in which he found himself that day on the ice was unfortunate. "A spur of the moment decision just to go out and take a look and come back home," he says. "I just took paddles and gas, and nothing else. I never expected to get caught like that—never again."

What's a Seaman without a Ship?

St. John's, Newfoundland

As a young lad, Wayne Connelly grew up at the battery in St. John's, watching the moods of the ocean. Often, he gazed out on its mighty vastness, awed when it thundered to the shores on days when the wind blew from the east, contented when it lapped gently against cliffs that ran steeply right down to meet it. Best of all was the satisfaction of studying the boats and ships; Wayne never tired of seeing vessels large and small ply the shipping lanes along the coasts, and steam in and out of the harbour at St. John's. His special fascination was reserved for the Coast Guard ships: mighty ice breakers like the *Labrador* and *Sir John A. MacDonald*; smaller ones such as the *Sir Humphrey Gilbert*—all magnificent, three-foot-steel-hulled creatures rising up and over the surface of the ice. Sturdy Coast Guard multi-purpose vessels, rescue cutters, and powerful little tugs. To Wayne they were living, breathing things.

In high school, his dreams were of a seaman's life, out on water that was forever all around him, trackless paths to some unknown place. His pleasure was studying the face of the sea, its constantly changing moods that registered no permanence, no passage of time, an ocean with an immutable existence. After school, his dreams flowered in a specific direction: he would be a ship's captain, sail his vessel across the seas and up and down the coasts. To him, a ship was a living thing that he admired and respected. He must be on, or near them, for it was the only interest he really had in life outside his family, and nothing, it seemed, would change this.

Three weeks into navigational school Wayne was out the door, failed because of his eyesight. Intense disappointment flooded him: what would he do now? The powerful and all-encompassing dream of his youth had been dashed.

"Then it dawned on me: this didn't mean I couldn't live and work on ships," he says. But it would be a long and circuitous route to the position where he would wake up every morning and want to go work, enjoy what he was doing, experience deep-felt satisfaction from it.

Today, Wayne spends his days in a spare little office in the marine subcentre in St. John's, down in the harbour. He is seated at a desk, on the phone, surrounded by files and little else. People walk past his desk from one office to the next as though his space was a public walkway. Five years now he has been here, not on a ship sailing the oceans, but staffing all the Coast Guard vessels, big and small, that are engaged in their many different functions. His responsibility is to make sure that the required number of appropriately trained and experienced staff are placed on all the ships when they sail.

"It took me a long time to get here, to this work," he says. "Right after high school, I worked on the salvage tugs out of Halifax, doing mechanical work in the engine room, one of the most interesting and demanding jobs I've ever had." He glances out the window where he can glimpse the tops of the ships anchored in the harbour. "Salvage tugs go out when all other vessels have come back in. I liked that we used the tugs to go to the rescue of people in trouble, used them as vessels of opportunity to go racing out to help people."

Wayne tells how, after a period of time, he returned to St. John's and worked for Canadian National Marine as fireman, oil-man, and junior engineer. He enjoyed it, except for one serious drawback: he was supposed to be replaced, after his months at sea, by another crew member. For some reason, there never did seem to be a person to relieve him, and he found himself stuck on board ship for months at a time on numerous occasions.

"Enough was enough; I quit." But Wayne did not have another job to go to. It was September 1966. A friend working for the CBC recommended him for a position there; he applied, accepting an accountant's job, but he was unhappy without quite knowing why.

It was time for a decision, and the one he made surprised even himself: Wayne decided to go to university. Perhaps this would lead him to find out what it was exactly that he wanted. Accepted at Memorial University of Newfoundland, he studied North American history. In five years, Wayne Connelly earned a bachelor of arts (Honours), and a bachelor of education. He graduated from university, a history major with a minor in English, only to go to work with Canada Customs, once more engaged in

CCGS *Henry Larsen*, transiting in ice.

accounting. It was not long before he found himself unhappy once more, not wanting to go to work. Once again, he quit, after having applied and been accepted for a teaching position at the Placentia-St Mary's Roman Catholic School Board.

By the age of thirty-two, Wayne Connelly had tried navigation school, life aboard commercial ships in the engine room, work on salvage tugs, accounting for the CBC and with Canada Customs, and teaching high school—none of it satisfied him.

One month after handing in his resignation to the school board, Wayne was again working around ships as the District Operations Supervisor for a large offshore oil and gas supply company. Eight years of pleasure in this work came to an end with the slump in offshore oil exploration. Wayne was told that the options were a job in western Canada, or alternate employment.

Landlocked western Canada? The choice was simple: quit, and find another job that would keep him near the sea. He heard that the Canadian Coast Guard was looking for stewards. Who better than him, with his experience on ships and oil rigs.

"I found myself on board the CCGS *John Cabot*. It was off the eastern seaboard of the United States, and I was working on the very first trans-Atlantic fibre-optic cable. Within a short time, I became the storekeeper and then, the logistics officer." After a number of transfers, he found himself on the *Sir John Franklin*. At the time, there were no lay days (twenty-eight day cycles of work and leave as exist now); crew were at sea for up to six months at a stretch.

He found it tough to be away from family and friends for this length of time. It was wrenching for him to be on duty, to have his ship stationed during the winter on the northeast coast of Newfoundland escorting boats and ships in and out of the harbour, yet be unable to get off or communicate.

"It was so close to home, yet so far away because there was no contact," he explains. "There was no shipboard telephone for crew to use; we felt so isolated. You could wave to your family from the ship, but rarely could you get on the land. Sometimes, the captain would tell us we had three hours to go ashore for supplies. If we were lucky, we would find a phone booth and make a quick call home. It was very stressful to be in a situation like that."

Today, Wayne Connelly is content in the position of crewing officer for the Coast Guard. It is a job he truly enjoys; it doesn't often take him out on the ocean aboard ships, but it is all to do with the sea, and he wakes up each morning happy to go to work.

"We have one dedicated ice breaker, the *Henry Larsen*. She's placed on the west coast during the winter, but moves to wherever she might be needed. During the summer, she's up in the Arctic. Three ships in the 1100 class generally do all the buoy tending and supply work, and are also available for other tasks such as ice-breaking. There are three search and rescue ships, two engaged in fisheries patrol, three used for scientific research, and two lifeboats; staffing for all these vessels is my responsibility.

"If the vessel is on primary SAR duty, you look for people who are qualified in SAR," he continues. "For those doing navigational aid work, you choose people who have a strong background in this type of work. Sometimes it's tough to find appropriate people who are available."

Juggling crew can be a thankless job. Wayne has to know who has what background and what experience, who has just come off shift, who is due to go on, and who is due for vacation. He has to understand how today's requirements and needs might shift, and to foresee the urgent needs in situations that might arise. It is Wayne who calls a crew member to come on duty unexpectedly, he who sends them out on a ship for twenty-eight days, perhaps when they have not long been off a twenty-eight day cycle. It is he who faces their ire, disappointment, objections. Wayne is a gentle and compassionate man, and he commiserates with crew because he knows what it's like. But in the end, he must staff the ships.

A Cliffhanger

Burin, Newfoundland

"Have I said no to a rescue job, stood it down?" asks Darryl Taylor of the Burin lifeboat station on the southwest coast of Newfoundland. "I tell you, I couldn't turn my back on a person, even if I'm having to ask myself, can I get in, and get out again, safe? We don't say no to a person. But there was a time I said no to a cow; three years ago it was I said no to a cow that fell over a cliff."

The few animals kept during the spring and summer in Burin and Port aux Bras are grazed on fields around the houses, land that wanders out to the edge of steep and jagged cliffs. Some people tether their beasts while others have someone keep an eye on them to see that the animals don't wander far. The cows are slaughtered in the fall to provide the winter's meat supply.

One day, a cow falls over the cliff, sixty feet below onto rocks that jut above the shoreline. Miraculously, the animal appears to be alive, and the owners are anxious to retrieve her. Not being able to do this themselves, or not knowing how, they ask the Coast Guard crew to go out in their cutter to get her.

The crew fires up their inflatable zodiac fast rescue boat and takes it the short distance around the bays to Port aux Bras. They study the scene and consider what it will take to rescue the animal, and at what risk to themselves. It is not an inviting scene: rocks, sharp as shrapnel, jut out at the foot of sheer cliffs. Seas sweep around and rise above them with intermittent fury, and winds blow spray up the cliffs and fling it far in the air. A cow weighing three hundred pounds or more is stuck on rocks that are perilous for them to approach. Alive, she will not fit into their zodiac. Even if she did fit, she can hardly be dragged on board the cutter in these violent conditions—the hazards are considerable.

"Sorry, we can't take no risks for a cow," they say. "We'll go back tomorrow if the conditions improve."

That evening, someone from the village walks along the road and down the slope to the lifeboat station to argue with the

Coast Guard crew about why they won't rescue the cow. 'It's your job,' he says. 'Don't you care that some people in the village are crying because their cow fell over the cliff?'

A standard fast rescue craft, used mainly for inshore rescue operations where speed and manoeuvrability are key.

"I have to explain myself," says Darryl. "I tell him absolutely that I will risk myself and the crew to go into the cliffs for a child, for an adult, but not for an animal. For people, I would stay out all night, would do anything." He pauses, then adds, "Would they be crying if the guy that owns her had her slaughtered for his winter supply of meat when it came her time, and stuck her head on the gate post? She just died a little bit earlier, that's all. But if it was a youngster...I would have stayed out all night.... Sometimes you have to bite your tongue and say nothing, turn your back and walk away."

People feed the cow by throwing hay over the edge of the cliff, some of which lands close enough for her to munch. The crew at the lifeboat station advises the owners about how they might try to retrieve their cow. "Wait until the seas are calm," they say. "Then take out a flat-bottomed boat; tow a dory behind it. Go in, tie her legs, and see if she can be hauled into the boat." The owners do retrieve their cow, feeding her until the fall when they have her slaughtered, as is the custom.

"Sometimes, some of the people make fun of us, that we sit here all day and do nothing," Darryl says. "I say to them: when you see this fella here move fast, someone out there is in trouble, and it could be you, or your father."

Darryl Taylor is the rescue specialist at the Coast Guard lifeboat station in Burin, southeastern Newfoundland.

"I never knew anything else since I was fifteen years old," he says about his maritime work experiences. "I saw people get lost and drown, die alongside me, never saw them again...saw lots more death than if I had worked on shore. You always have it in the back of your mind that it might happen to you—that you might get lost, go overboard, get drowned."

Darryl got into the Coast Guard around the time of the fish moratorium. He had worked for the Department of Fisheries back in 1988, but the money was poor compared to what he made fishing, and so he returned to a fisherman's life.

"I did fishing, buoy tending, research," he says. "I really like the search and rescue work. Fishing is just fishing, but SAR—you don't know what you're going to face, what you're going to do, until you get there. Every day is different, and that's what I like—not ever being bored.

"And then there are experiences like this," he continues. "About two years ago, two guys in a speedboat went missing one night in Conception Bay. A helicopter pilot spotted the boat the next morning, but the SAR technician on board wouldn't go in and do a drop." Darryl explains that it was too dangerous because of the weather, and because the boat was mostly submerged. The Coast Guard fast rescue boat was dispatched. When it got close, Darryl, as the rescue specialist, put out his hand to help the guy into the rescue boat.

"He said it was the best thing he'd seen since yesterday. The look in his eyes—I'll never forget that look, the expression on his face. When we got the two of them in our boat, one said to the other, 'I told you we was going to make it. I told you, didn't I?'

"Deep down inside, if I can't help someone today, I can't let myself get down about it," Darryl says. "I know I'll be helping someone tomorrow."

Captain Newell's Legacy

Clark's Harbour, Cape Sable Island, Nova Scotia

Cape Sable Island is a low-lying stretch of rock, sand, and scrubby grass connected to the southern tip of Nova Scotia by a causeway. It is a place where distinction between sea and sky is often obliterated, the land a faint, shrouded silhouette. Winds sweep along an unprotected shoreline to scour the terrain and bend the stunted trees. For days at a stretch, the island might lie shrouded in fog, a cold and forbidding place where an icy chill settles deep in the bones. Winter wind and freezing rain snap power line poles and wires, while fine salt spray obscures vision by creating an eerie, frosted gloom.

But the island shows another profile in summer when gentle warmth spreads across the savanna grass, and the sea sparkles in soft sunshine. Hundreds of brightly-coloured boats crowd the wharves and jetties

Coast Guard vessels are often moved from station to station, depending on where they are needed most.

that extend into the water like arms of the land. Other vessels scatter themselves across the sea.

Clark's Harbour is on Cape Sable Island's west coast near the approach to the southern promontory, called the Hawk Peninsula. Hulking, rain-soaked buildings that house fish-processing plants and storage sheds line harbour wharves. Along those wharves fishermen work on nets, traps, ropes, and buoys. Down on the wharves among the fish plants and storage sheds is a small trailer; just beyond it, along the wharf, a red and white cutter swings on its moorings, proudly announcing itself as "Canadian Coast Guard/Garde Côtière Canadienne Recherche et Sauvetage."

In 1966, the Coast Guard positioned the trailer as a search and rescue base in Clark's Harbour, in the heart of the fishing industry, a location chosen as the most appropriate to respond to the needs of the huge inshore and offshore fishing industry that provides almost the sole source of income to the people of Cape Sable. Built to the requirements of the class known as the forty-four-foot self-righting MLB (motor lifeboat) and named CCG 101, the cutter was the first boat in Canada providing dedicated inshore and offshore rescue service.

The search and rescue crew, a tough group oblivious to cold and discomfort, came to the Coast Guard from the fishing fields. Most are locals, descendants of the hardy pioneers who emigrated from France and England—Acadians who named the island "Cap Sablon," meaning "sandy cape," and English who arrived from New England in the late 1750s.

It is January 17, 1856, and Cape Sable is still an island, separated from the mainland by a short stretch of water known as Barrington Passage. On this day, Captain Thomas Newell of Newelton has crossed to the mainland to conduct some business. He goes down to the landing at Knowles Point to get a return ferry ride across to Cape Sable Island. His eyes search the water, then he turns to the ferry master and says, "If the conditions are too rough to make the crossing, I'm willing to spend the night in Barrington Passage as there's more business I can do."

He's told not to worry, that the small skiff that serves as a ferry is prepared for the crossing. A strong ebb tide runs directly against the winds, making the water choppy. Snow begins to fall. The ferry is nearly across the strait and not far from the island when a sudden rogue wave strikes, swamps the small boat, and overturns it.

A strong swimmer, Captain Newell strikes out for the shore, but the tide sweeps him out beyond the point. He turns and swims back to a boat that appears to be drifting toward Gunning Ledge and climbs inside. But the boat floats right past the ledge, and Newell decides that he has to abandon it to try to swim to the rocky ledge. With effort, he struggles out of his jacket and slips into the chilly water. One arm thrusting in front of the other Newell struggles on. Numb with cold and hindered by the strong tide and the now-heavy snow, he finally succeeds in reaching his goal: he grasps the rocky ledge. But climbing higher beyond the surging waves is an ordeal; the rocks are sharp and icy, the wind cutting, salt spray flies in his face.

Time stands still for Newell as he clings to the rock. He feels totally alone. Gradually, as the snow becomes lighter, he catches a glimpse of Mr. Kenny at work in the lee of his barn. Newell shouts, and shouts again until he is hoarse. At last, the farmer lifts a puzzled face toward him.

Mr. Kenny sees a man clinging for his life to a rock; he turns and runs from his barn, disappearing from sight. Shortly after, Captain Newell sees two men stride to the beach, approach an overturned skiff that is beached there, turn it upright, and throw themselves into it. They launch it toward the ledge to which Newell clings.

Captain Newell rubs himself vigorously with hands he can scarcely feel, wriggling about on the narrow ledge as best he can, to try to keep himself warm. The two men in the skiff have reached him; they maneuver the skiff close, reach out and haul the soaked and frozen man into the boat, then paddle furiously to a nearby house. Warmed blankets and hot irons are placed around Newell. Over the following hours, Newell's core temperature rises slowly, and by about midday, he begins to feel warm. The following day, feeling largely recovered, he gets up from his bed to walk the five miles home in the cold and blowing snow. The skiff that had acted as a ferry, and the bodies of the crew, have never been found.

The ferry, such as it was, was operated entirely without safety or communication systems, and there was no Coast Guard to come to the rescue. Safety in general was ignored, perhaps because there was no assistance available, government or otherwise, regardless of need.

"It was a very ill wind that set in motion the efforts to obtain a Coast Guard station at Clark's Harbour," wrote Ethel Swim, "a tragedy that caused many tears to flow, and much heartache on the Island."[1]

[1] *The Islands Look Back*, produced by the Archelaus Smith Historical Society, Nova Scotia, from which this story has been adapted.

November 30, 1964 is the opening day of District 34's lobster season, a region that stretches from Baccaro Point to Shelburne County to Burns Point in Digby County. More than one hundred years have passed since the 1856 sinking of the ferryboat. Navigation is still by means of a compass and a stopwatch for most fishermen; perhaps one in ten owns a Loran C, the occasional fishing boat is equipped with a marine radio. The Coast Guard rescue vessel is not readily accessible.

Captain Stillman Quinlan and his helper, James Smith, have been setting their lobster traps. Darkness has settled over the sea, but at 6:30 in the evening, Captain Quinlan has still not returned to his Stoney Island Port. Worried now, Mervin Atkinson, his son-in-law, begins calling all the local fishermen to ask if they had seen Stillman as they made their approach to port.

"We saw him still at it, setting the traps after the dark had fallen," they say. Mervin waits. He calls around again at 8:30 PM to say that Stillman is still not in. All the time the wind increases, howling across a sullen landscape. Some of the local fishermen struggle to get one of the long liner vessels out of Clark's Harbour to where they think Stillman might be. In the darkness, lobster traps and buoys create obstacles, and navigation is difficult because it is impossible to see anything; the fishermen feel helpless and frustrated.

During the night, the wind continues to increase to more than eighty miles an hour and the seas surge high and wild in the East Bay area. Nobody goes to bed. Around 9:00 the next morning, Hirtle Smith at the Hawk says that he saw a lobster boat anchored about a mile from the beach, and that it looked like it was in much danger.

"I'll call search and rescue for a rescue boat or helicopter to go out for them," she says. "They tell me the nearest Coast Guard ship is in Saint John, New Brunswick, and that the winds are too strong for a helicopter to fly in."

Quinlan is one of their own: husband, father, uncle, brother. It could be any one of them out there, and the local fishermen cannot stand about and do nothing. They attempt once more to go to the rescue in a fishing boat, but eventually they have to abandon the effort. The seas are too rough, and the men face almost certain shipwreck themselves if they try to navigate around Baccaro Point.

By early afternoon, winds are from the northeast and blowing at more than one hundred miles an hour. By mid-afternoon, Quinlan's boat is seen to have broken its anchor rope. The last glimpse the local people have is of a doomed vessel being blown out to very rough seas, its two helpless men on board.

Ronald Newell, first captain of Clark's Harbour lifeboat station, and his son, Jim Newell, currently one of the coxswains at the station.

The boat is found several days later, in two parts—its bow is discovered off Seal Island, the stern off Pubnico. Rope is wound around the propeller, explaining why the men were unable to reach shore. The bodies were never found.

This is one tragedy too many for the people of Clark's Harbour; a meeting is called in the Legion Hall. All the fishermen and concerned citizens from Shelburne to Yarmouth attend, for it is their common desire to get a Coast Guard lifeboat station built at Clark's Harbour.

A group of local fishermen meets with the Minister of Transport, Pickersgill, and with various officials from the different branches of his department. The fishermen make a formal request that a rescue boat be stationed in Clark's Harbour, suggesting the class of surf boat being tried in the United States to service the southwestern Nova Scotia fishing fleet. They say that the deaths that have occurred over the years will continue unless formalized search and rescue assistance is provided.

Clark's Harbour lifeboat station.

A Coast Guard cutter breaks ice in Clark's Harbour on Cape Sable Island's west coast.

"Hundreds of inshore and offshore fishing boats will not, cannot, cease their voyages out on the seas and in the elements, because fishing is our livelihood, our way of life."

The meeting is successful. A rescue boat is built and stationed at Clark's Harbour on Cape Sable Island. A class 101 vessel, it is forty feet in length and practically unsinkable. It arrives in Clark's Harbour in 1966. Twelve men apply for the position of crew, and prior to the arrival of the new craft, those accepted take courses in preparation for their life-saving mission.

Thirty-odd years later, in 2000, the people of Clark's Harbour continue to live off and by the sea in much the same manner as their forebears. Processing plants have been built to make Irish moss or seaweed harvested from the sea, into an emulsifying agent used in products such as cold cream, ice cream, and pectin; welders work on boats and boat-building enterprises. The ship and yacht building on the island serves the entire Canadian east coast, as well as the United States; it is a big industry.

But some things have changed: The fishers now have advanced navigational aids and means of communication, and the Canadian Coast Guard provides search and rescue lifeboat stations and crew in locations best suited for fast response to maritime emergencies. Crew members now have sophisticated equipment and technology to help them in their search and rescue work, augmented by Hercules aircraft and helicopters from the Department of National Defence.

In October, Jimmy Newell is at home with his family. He's on duty, but because he lives a short distance from the Coast Guard base, he goes home after four each day. Shouldn't have any trouble tonight, he thinks. The boats are in; the night is mild with a gentle swell on the sea.

It seems, sometimes, that a mantle has been thrown upon one generation of Newells, then another, then another: one that is to do with rescue operations at sea. Jimmy Newell's father, Ronald Newell, descends from Captain Thomas Newell who survived the ferry crossing in 1856. Ronald himself was the first captain of the Clark's Harbour lifeboat station when it was established in 1966, devoting his life to it until the day he retired. His son Jimmy is one more Newell in this long line of family members dedicated to rescue missions on the vast Atlantic.

Newell relaxes with his family in front of the television when trouble booms into his living room across the VHF radio and from the Joint Rescue Coordination Centre in Halifax (JRCC). Newell and his crew are tasked to go to the aid of the fishing boat *Flying Swan*, rapidly sinking on the German banks. Would they take a chainsaw with them? The vessel, loaded with fish, has rolled over, and it is believed that one of the crew is trapped inside.

Newell learns that most of the fishermen had been working aft; as the boat started to list, they hurried to the high side, except for one man who was working forward. He went around the bow to join the others, and somehow became trapped inside the boat.

Newell and his crew are in the cutter in a matter of minutes, racing to the aid of the stricken boat. It is approximately 11:30 in the evening, and conditions are favourable, with just a light swell on the ocean.

But before they arrive at the sinking boat, the man inside is washed out by the rocking motion of the sinking vessel and is picked up by another fishing vessel in the vicinity. The crew immediately start cardio-pulmonary resuscitation as the captain heads south for Yarmouth. Newell makes a rendez-vous with the boat shortly after midnight. He knows that the surviving fishermen from the sinking boat have been picked up by two other fishing vessels. All the while, a Hercules aircraft circles overhead, where two search and rescue technicians are preparing to make a jump onto the boat carrying the unconscious man. In the dark, it's a risky maneuver. Newell sends a rescue specialist on board to

Old and new Coast Guard cutters sit side by side in the fog.

examine the stricken man. A doctor on shore is appraised of the man's condition and the decision is made not to risk a night-time parachute into the water to help a man who cannot be revived.

"We escort the boat into Yarmouth where the guy is pronounced dead after he's assessed," Newell says. "It's pretty rough for the rescue specialist; he'd had lunch with this man just the week before; now he pulls him, dead, out of the water. We give him the name of a counselling service out of Halifax in case he needs help, thinking he might be traumatized...he didn't use the service."

"It's a winter evening and I'm sitting home with the scanner on, the VHF, listening to the boats coming in," says Jimmy Newell, coxswain of Clark's Harbour lifeboat station. "Lots of times I sit until one or two in the morning, listening, listening, especially during winter fishing when the conditions are bad, like high winds and freezing spray. I think to myself that I must stay up and awake until all the boats are in; if I hear their call for help come in, I'll be better prepared when we're tasked to assist them. And if there's one still out there, sure enough I'll be up and out on the sea to get it."

It's getting late, but he remains glued to the VHF, listening to the boats coming in to Clark's Harbour.

"I know the boats are having a very tough time," he says. "The fishermen are struggling in this storm. Some stop their engines while the crew beats the ice off decks and railings; others slow their speed to three knots instead of the usual eight while they do it."

Radars and windows are iced up, and it's difficult for the crew to see the whereabouts of other vessels. In fact, they have trouble seeing anything at all. Fierce gales blow from the northwest; freezing spray and squalls of wet snow obliterate the seascape and build up on the vessels.

It is eleven in the evening now, and the last fisherman to come in is Roger Atwood on *Danny and Chrissy*. He radios that he's getting close to Pubnico.

"He'd been fishing fifty miles out from there," says Newell. "I'd been listening to him coming in from six that evening. He tells me that he's mostly in the lee of the land, but that his two-foot-high safety rails are iced from the top wire right down to the deck. He's the last guy, I say to myself; I'll go to bed now."

Newell, a lifeboat station veteran of twenty years, says that now, and during the past few years, he has not had to worry as much as he once did about the fishing boats out in the winter storms because the boats are generally well maintained. Because of the fishing quota system enforced during the 1990s, a boat might lie idle for a few months, giving a fisherman time to get it in good shape. But there are still those who continue to use their boats everyday, regardless of the weather.

"I think tonight is going to be a good night's sleep for me, because all the boats are in, and I can go to bed," he says again.

But there is little rest for Jimmy Newell this night. At twelve-twenty in the morning his pager startles him awake. "Now what's this all about?" he mutters. "I saw all the boats come in...but there's always some guy out there who doesn't listen to the weather, thinks he will stay an extra few hours, another day, to get a few more fish. He gets in trouble, and we're the ones that get up out of bed and go out into the storm to get him."

The call is from a controller from the JRCC in Halifax. He tells Newell that an EPIRB from the *Cape Aspy* has been received, and they are tasking him to head out in the direction of the sinking ship.

"Mother of all Holies," Newell says. "I jump out of bed, call my crew, and run down to the wharf."

This is one wicked night in a thousand, a night when a fisherman or sailor stuck out on the seas will plead with the Almighty to spare his life, just this once. Giant waves crash right over the wharf beyond the lifeboat station, and Newell cannot even get his vehicle down to the docks to where the Coast Guard cutter is moored.

"It's very, very cold," he says. "We bend our heads against the blowing ice and spray, get into the truck, put the windshield wipers on high, but still we can scarcely see anything in front of us. The sea comes over the wharf in swells, covering us, the truck, and the wharf so we can't make out anything at all. It's all just a blur of wind and rain and water. Because of the high winds and the tide, our cutter is out from the wharf about twelve to fifteen feet. We take the rope that ties the boat to the wharf and hook it up to the truck, and rev the truck, using its engines to pull the cutter into the wharf."

The truck engines roar. The cutter tugs at its moorings, but does not budge. Heavy ice has accumulated on the boat, and the tide and wind keep pushing it outward. Newell continues revving the engines of his truck while his crew struggle, pulling on the ropes that tie the cutter. Finally, Newell jumps from the truck, thrusts it into four-wheel drive, and revs it again. The engines roar and, slowly, the cutter is drawn in to thump against the wharf. In angry seas and blinding rain, the crew climbs aboard and steams it out of the harbour.

"Severe weather and very cold temperatures like this happen only about every two to three years," Newell says. "As we go out, snow squalls and freezing spray blow on to us; the conditions are terrible. We plough out into the gale in the worst possible weather, knowing that there might not be much we can do when, and if, we get there. But the task has been given to us and we will not give up." After a pause he adds, "We would risk ourselves to go out for anyone, but the fishermen in the *Cape Aspy*, they are our brothers."

Newell and his crew struggle in the heaving seas, the snow and freezing spray to try to get to the area where they believe the *Cape Aspy* has sunk, a distance of about sixty miles. Their cutter is the *Bickerton*, a 52-foot Arun class boat launched a few years earlier and on loan to Clark's Harbour to cover off the winter season.

Newell and his crew are just two nautical miles from base when one of the cutter's water-intake pipes freezes up because of the frigid temperatures. The crew shuts one of the engines down to cool it, and the coxswain turns the vessel around and returns it to the wharf to get it fixed. They work all through the night to get the cutter running. It is not until 6:00 in the morning that they leave the harbour once more.

Passage is rough for the sturdy little cutter, but eventually the wind dies down as a weak sun begins to peep through the clouds. The cutter arrives at 10:00 AM at the stretch of empty sea now being searched for survivors or bodies from the sunken *Cape Aspy*. All hands have not been accounted for (see "*Cape Aspy's* Last Run," p.54). The exhausted crew from Clark's Harbour refuses to give up. They search all day, until ten in the evening. At one point during the day, the lookout person exclaims that he can see something orange in the water. Apprehension grips the crew at the possibility that they might find someone, alive or dead, in the water.

"A funny sort of a feeling comes over the whole boat, like an eerie calm, because no one is sure what to expect," Newell says. "Some begin getting first-aid equipment ready in case it's needed, and others prepare themselves to actually recover what's there...We've never recovered a body, but we've recovered survivors out of the water. All we find is an orange balloon used to mark a string of lobster pots—nothing else."

Darkness falls, and it seems to the crew—none of whom have slept in thirty-six hours—that the task this night is hopeless. With heavy hearts, knowing their brothers are lost to the sea, they begin the long, slow journey back to base. They may catch a few hours sleep before they have another call, or they may not.

"I have total faith in my crew, and do not put myself or them at undue risk," says Newell. "But we have done things that are not written about in books because they are not textbook ways of doing things. When you arrive on scene, there are only four people who know what you're up against: me and the other three guys on the crew. Nobody can sit behind a desk and tell you what you should do. If you're not there, you cannot possibly understand what the conditions are like.

"If I think there's a certain degree of risk, I'll get the guys together and I'll say, this is what the job is. Here are the possible ways of doing it and these are the possible hazards if we do it this way. What it comes down to is one or two people putting themselves at more risk than the rest of the crew."

Speaking with a crew member who has volunteered to put himself at greater risk, Newell never downplays the risks. They discuss strategies. "I say, this is what you will have to do. Are you comfortable with it?" If his crew says yes, and there is good justification to do it, the plan is implemented. We never do anything just to be able to say afterwards that we did it." If the crew is not comfortable with what has been decided upon, Newell would not go ahead with it.

"But it's never happened," he says. He sits silent for a moment. "One thing about this job, you have to have the best equipment there is available, like navigational tools and communication systems, all well maintained. And the crew must be very well trained. There's another thing: it's ideal to work with the same crew all the time. You know what their skills are, even for the simplest jobs. Actually, it's more than ideal, I would say it's critical. You have to have confidence in the people you work with. About our boats: we have to have the best—and we do."

Newell describes another incident; the crew receives a call from someone who radioed to say that he had seen an abandoned boat still under power and steaming around, half-submerged, and in bad weather. "It's out there in beyond the harbour, steaming around and around, and it will probably sink."

Although it is not within the Coast Guard rescue workers' mandate to salvage boats, they discuss what, if anything, they should do about it. They agree that they should go out and tow it to shore. If they leave it there, it will pollute some of the most lucrative fishing grounds in the world. More than that, it is a hazard to other boats in the water.

"We're given the autonomy to make these judgements," Newell says. "The rules are that the Coast Guard is not in the business of salvaging boats, but we are trusted to do whatever seems the most appropriate action to take, according to all the circumstances—it's up to a coxswain and his crew to make such judgements.

"We are out on the sea in terrible conditions, towing a boat in to dock," he says. "But we don't just tow by attaching the boat and dragging it along behind us; we bring it alongside in a maneuver called a "saddletow." To do this is difficult and time-consuming, especially in heavy rain and wind and cold…but there's less possible damage to the boat we tow if we do it this way. Our rescue operations are about saving the boat, as well as its people."

Jimmy Newell lives with his wife and two children just a short distance from the Coast Guard base. His house nestled among a group of others facing out to the street, and then to the sea beyond, and the rough trailer at the wharf are his two homes. In this second home there is no fresh water; seawater is used for cooking and cleaning, and a portable cooler provides drinking water. Today, rain lashes against the windows so that it is hard to see out across the piers where fishing boats strain against their moorings in the wind. The odour of salt, fish and seaweed, of old rope and nets and oil, tell a casual visitor that this is a busy and profitable industry.

While still in high school, Jimmy simultaneously applied for Coast Guard college and university. He obtained an engineering scholarship and made arrangements to begin in the fall. Three days before he was to leave, he decided that perhaps university was not for him; the call of the sea—the wish to go fishing, to live a life out on the water—was too powerful.

"The call of the sea—you think of an old salt with seawater flowing through his veins," Newell says. "I spent my childhood bouncing around the wharves, jumping ice pans in the harbour and doing anything I could that was remotely associated with salt water. The feeling never seemed to go away. I just couldn't see myself doing anything not related to the sea, harbours, boats, and wharves.

"I don't do it for money," he adds. "It's a sense of accomplishment, a way of life that's hard to beat. When my pager goes off, I have an instant rush. At that moment, I have no idea what the call is about, no idea what's in store for me." But there are those who don't share this philosophy; they come in to the station to do shifts on a contractual basis, and don't care for it.

"They don't like the commitment, because this is your life until your cycle ends," Newell says. "They have a hard time getting their heads around the fact that they are here for the whole cycle. It's about loss of freedom. One guy said to me that he didn't realize what a sense of relief it was to take the pager off his belt when his cycle was over, didn't understand what a tie that little electronic box was until he'd taken it off."

In the community there is tremendous respect for the search and rescue workers. If they need extra people or an extra boat, they are never refused.

"People are very respectful of us, our boats and equipment," Newell says. "They might steal from each other, but never from us. They might come and take some of our fuel when we're out on a call. We come back to find them re-fuelling our tanks. But it's also because they never know when they might need us.

"It's not just sinking boats and getting people out of the water," he says. "Lots of people go missing, like the two men who went out for the day to harvest Irish moss. They get into a small skiff and go off in it, south off Cape Sable. It's not a bad day when they set out, but a thick fog comes down and a moderate swell develops. We get a report from the wife of one of them about mid-evening that they have not come home. She asks if the Coast Guard will go out and find him."

Newell makes phone calls to other fishermen who have also been out fishing that day. They say that they saw the two men still out there, raking, and that they had a boat full already.

"In our fast rescue boat, we go along the shore where they have last been seen, using flashlights to look for the rakes. One of the crew shines his light on the sea bottom; it's shallow water, and he sees what looks like the shape of a small boat covered in Irish moss, and something else, something bright, like someone's oil pants. It sure makes our hearts jump. One of the crew is a good friend of one of the missing guys, and he's really upset when he sees this."

The crew member focuses the flashlight on these underwater objects. After some time, he realizes that what at first appeared as a sunken boat and a piece of clothing is just an oddly-shaped rock. The crew has been shaken up, especially the friend of the missing man.

Farther along the shore, the Coast Guard crew comes across the skiff belonging to the missing men. It is washed up on the shore and there is no evidence of life anywhere about. Again, there is a collective sinking of hearts. They search the shorelines and beyond. Darkness has fallen when they reach a small island. They are determined to search all of it. Without warning, they stumble upon two men lying in long grass up from the shore. The two fishermen had given up trying to return home, and had settled themselves in for a night on the island.

Newell loves his life as a search and rescue worker for the Coast Guard and wouldn't do anything else. He loves the smell of salt, the fresh air, the sun and wind in his face. He stands outdoors in wind, rain, and blowing snow and takes a deep breath, savouring it. He appreciates the cooperation between himself and the coxswain on the other shift, how they work for each other in a way he finds extraordinary, believing it is seldom seen elsewhere. The risks of the job do not bother him, nor does the lack of comfort, convenience, or the isolation. He is at home with the fact that he and his crew may be out on a call for eighteen or even thirty-six hours at a stretch in difficult conditions, thumped about only to come home exhausted, not to sleep, nor even to rest, before he is out once again on another rescue mission.

"The day when I get up in the morning and say, geez, why the hell am I going to the station to work today? Then it's time for me to do something else," he says.

Cape Aspy's Last Run

Lunenburg, Nova Scotia

lthough a Coast Guard vessel pushes past the fishing boats in the blue-green swells of the sea, Captain Don McKay of the *Alert* is not on patrol or responding to a call for help. Instead, he carries on board his ship the survivors of a sunken fishing trawler, the *Cape Aspy*, along with their families and those of the dead. They are on a pilgrimage to cast flowers upon the sea. On the slopes of Lunenburg, a town that rises steeply from the water, people watch as Don steams his ship slowly out of the harbour to the watery graveyard of five Lunenburg fishermen.

The Coast Guard crew has offered the use of its vessel to take the mourners to the burial ground, welcoming them aboard with solemn dignity, having warmed the ship's accommodation in preparation. The aroma of steaming hot food and drinks floats out from the galley on this cold February day.

The captain's destination is an empty sea off the southwestern tip of Nova Scotia near Cross Island. He anchors the ship, has his crew bring the flowers and wreaths to the top deck, then invites the mourners to leave the warmth of the cabin to cast them on the water. In the frigid wind that howls across the decks each family member and surviving fisherman grips the railings with one hand, takes a floral wreath with the other, and throws it into the heaving swells of the sea. Except for the low hum of the boat's engines, there is silence on deck.

It is the evening of Thursday, January 29, 1993. Dusk has fallen on Lunenburg, the two-hundred-year-old, picturesque fishing village on Nova Scotia's southeast coast. Snow blankets its steep slopes to the sea. Albert Eisner, captain of the fishing trawler *Cape Aspy*, convenes a meeting of the fishermen scheduled to sail the next day for twelve days of scallop trawling. The weather is harsh: high winds blow freezing spray and snow, and the air is cold—minus six degrees Celsius and expected to drop to minus fifteen or twenty during the night.

If the men will lay over Friday, the captain asks, will they agree to go out early on Saturday? He needs their concurrence, as union rules stipulate that members cannot have their weekends pre-empted without their consent. The men agree to go, in spite of the cold and the near gale-force strength of the wind. The *Cape Aspy*, one of Scotia Trawler's fleet of scallop draggers, departs from Lunenburg harbour at 9:30 in the morning of January 30, heading for the rich fishing area of Georges Banks, some 320 miles southwest of Halifax. This is its last run to the fishing grounds.

The sixteen men who have agreed to go out that day understand the risks of a life at sea, and they know about winter fishing. Of the more than one hundred ships and the six hundred and fifty sailors lost over the years from the Port of Lunenburg, more have died during this season than any other. Many of the ships, and the bodies of the men, have never been found. Over the past century, just one year has passed when a Lunenburg ship or fishing boat has not been lost and men drowned in the North Atlantic. But still the young men go to the sea.

When young Randy Feener told his mother he intended to be a fisherman, she groaned and tried to persuade him to do something, anything, else. She tried once more after his near-drowning in a capsized boat nine years later.

"How can I work on the land?" he had asked. "You might as well put me in jail." This is a common attitude among fishermen. Even for the sake of his family, Carmen Laffin, one of the *Cape Aspy* crew, could not endure a job on dry land. Bob Berringer too, although not a young man, had gotten out of bed leaving behind his wife and three daughters, to head for the *Cape Aspy*. "You couldn't put me in an office, or anywhere on land," he says. "This is my life, and nothing will take me from it."

Some of the men say, afterwards, that while they were not particularly concerned about the weather that day, they would have preferred not to go out. But if they had not, they say, someone else would have, and they would be the losers. Scallop fishing is a business conducted year-round. It is a hard and rough job in the winter: the land can be white to the horizon with winds that come mostly from the northeast, blowing snow and freezing spray across the shores and crusting up the fishing vessels. The cold is bitter, the winds fierce, and the work long and back-breaking. The men stand, bent over, shucking scallops for countless hours at a stretch, hauling heavy nets on icy decks. Sleep, such as it is, is intermittent and never enough to sustain them for the work that has to be done. There is something else, never spoken aloud. It isn't, as the Reverend Fred Hiltz explained at the funeral services, that the men are fatalistic, but they are ever mindful of the danger inherent in what they do.

After meeting with the skipper, the fishermen had gone home for the last night in their own beds, prepared to sail the next morning and hoping that the weather would improve. January 30 dawned white and cold. On their way to the doomed ship, the men listen to a forecast that promises gale-force winds and snow. Perhaps they are comforted by their training—they have practised getting into their survival suits, and inflating and lowering the lifeboats. They may be comforted too, knowing the Coast Guard is always near to rescue them. They are aware that the Joint Rescue Coordination Centre in Halifax is staffed year-round with skilled and experienced people who, with their sophisticated technology, are able to pinpoint the location of vessels in distress and immediately activate their tremendous resources: people, vessels, and aircraft. They are aware too of the lifeboat stations along the coasts.

The *Cape Aspy* leaves port that morning for a seventeen-hour voyage to the fishing grounds in temperatures already frigid, and promising to drop much further to a projected minus-fifteen to minus-twenty later that day. Snow and freezing spray blow across her bows, although at first she is sheltered in the lee of the land. The captain maintains a speed of about thirteen knots in a south-westerly direction, gradually diverging from the protection of the coast. The seas worsen and the wind speed increases to near gale force. About twenty-five miles southeast of Cape Sable Island at the southern tip of Nova Scotia, the *Cape Aspy* is exposed to the full force of the weather, and is shipping water, sea spray ice building up on her decks.

The men are in their oilskins, heavy boots, and seaman's gloves. The captain continues to plough the *Cape Aspy* through giant swells that break across the decks. Freezing spray flies in their faces, and it's not long before a thick crust has formed on the decks and railings. The boat lists to starboard.

Bob Berringer is in the galley, cooking for the men. "It's a bit tough to stay upright, and keep anything on a surface," he says afterwards. "But I've done it all before. The wind, she's blowing

The knowledge that vessels like the CCGS *Sprindrift* are positioned at stations along Nova Scotia's coasts give fishermen venturing out in rough seas some comfort.

hard and cold like you never see it here. Before we're even out of Lunenburg harbour we're getting ice onto us. Are we worried? At about five or six that night we get worried. We have to go out and mark the warps—mark the depths so you know how far to leave them out when you put out the rakes. We see the wind is making a lot of ice. Except for me, because I'm the cook, everyone has to take turns at wheel watch for two hours each, until you shoot away—put the rakes in the water."

Bob Berringer cleans up and turns in about six in the evening. Is he concerned when he goes to bed? "We all figured we would have to beat the ice off the boat. Yeah, we're surprised that the captain doesn't get us to do it. The fellas are concerned now about the ice; it's building up and the boat lists pretty bad. For us to beat it off, the skipper will have to slow the boat down and head it up into the wind or run off the wind, then it will be no problem to beat it off. We don't get much sleep, all tossing and turning because of the weather."

About 8:00 in the evening there is a further increase in wind speed and wave height, and two hours later a starboard list of eight degrees has developed. The vessel rolls twenty degrees and ships water on deck. The captain alters course to southerly. Still no attempt is made to physically remove the ice. Subsequently, in the Transportation Safety Board Report, it is estimated that about twenty tonnes of it have accumulated, predominantly on the starboard side, and the vessel heels further.

At about 11:15 PM, the vessel rolls heavily to starboard, partially returns to the upright, then rolls further to starboard. The list suddenly increases to about 45 degrees and the vessel seems to be 'settled by the head,' as sailors say.

A deckhand rushes into the room where Bob and Randy Feener are trying to sleep. "Get up! Get your survival suits on!" he yells. "The boat's rolling over!"

"One of the guys flings survival suits at us as we crawl into the galley, and all I remember is getting my legs into it," Bob says.

By now seawater is flooding the starboard shucking house and surging to the level of the galley portholes. It roars into the engine room and the lights go out. The men struggle to get to the life rafts along the steeply sloping wheelhouse side of a deck encrusted with ice, and have difficulty staying upright. The two inflatable life rafts are positioned on either side of the poop deck. "The starboard list is so bad," explains Bob, "you couldn't get at the one [raft] on that side at all. Lights go out until the emergency, battery-powered ones come on."

Randy Feener asks the captain if he's sent out any Maydays. The captain says yes, but he's not got any response. "Get into your survival suit and I'll send the Maydays," Feener says, but then he sees that the aerial is all crusted up with ice, and, with a sinking feeling, realizes that they most likely have not been received.

"I'm the last to come out of the wheelhouse," Berringer says. "We're all in the dark for a while. I can hear the fellas shifting about trying to get the raft out, but it's hard because of the listing. It is heavy, and they have to get it over the railing, which is raised up high." The *Cape Aspy* is sinking fast. Amid the towering waves and blowing snow, the men inflate the life raft right there on the deck.

As it inflates, a wave washes over the deck and sweeps the raft right over the side of the boat. It floats off the stern, an empty life raft in a monstrous sea. Most of the men are swept overboard with it. Larry Wentzer, thirty-two years old, makes a desperate leap from the portside railing and lands on the canopy. He struggles and eventually manages to crawl into it. It takes Bob Berringer, who flails about in the water, only a matter of minutes before he himself makes "a swipe for the raft," as he describes it. He grabs hold of its sides, but Larry is unable to pull him in. Another mate crawls into the raft and together they haul Bob inside. The men who manage to cling to its sides are pulled in, one by one, by those inside it.

On the sinking boat, Leonard Clarke is struck in the head by a dory jarred loose in the gale. Dazed, he is swept over the side with the rest. "All I was thinking was, don't panic, you gotta keep a steady nerve," he says later. He describes frantic minutes when he swims for the life raft and hauls himself aboard. He grabs his mate, Neil Halliday, and the two begin nabbing their shipmates. "There's quite a bit of hollering, and lots of sea...some fellas, we couldn't do nothing for."

Eleven men make it into the life raft, but Randy Feener and four other men not so fortunate are swept away by wind and wave. The men in the raft paddle furiously toward the bodies in the water but within moments the paddle snaps, and the crew is at the mercy of the elements. Randy Feener and the others in the water are swallowed up by the seas.

In their fear and confusion, none of the men had thought to grab one of the ship's new Emergency Position-Indicating Radio Beacons (EPIRBS) to take with them into the life raft. But the one EPIRB that does not require manual activation happens to float free of the sunken vessel. Once it struck the water, its signal activated automatically and was picked up.

"We're all huddling in the life raft," says Bob Berringer. "It's sturdy, and we distribute the weight around evenly, but we get tossed around pretty bad. I knew we were in for a dirty and cold night. That's all I was concerned about, not if we would be rescued, but about the damned cold."

Some of the men in the raft remember that when they last saw the captain, he was standing in the doorway of the wheelhouse and not wearing a survival suit. They know Randy Feener is somewhere in the water. He is glimpsed for brief moments riding the crests of the waves, one lone man inside a survival suit out in the stormy seas.

Feener does not know if the plight of their ship has been signalled, does not know if help will ever come. He struggles to stay alive, feeling very alone in the universe. Suddenly he catches sight of a figure rising on the crest of a wave and recognizes it as that of the ship's chief engineer. He struggles toward him, hoping they can hook up, but the engineer disappears into the trough and Randy does not see him again until later when his body is hauled out of the water, an expression of horror frozen on his face.

Hang on, just hang on, he thinks now as his eyes rove over the world about him. He sees nothing but giant walls of water and, beyond the swells, an eerie silence, a stillness, as though nobody else exists in heaven or on earth. He forces himself to maintain an upright position, knowing that it will help keep him awake. His mind moves over many subjects, but keeps returning to his wife, his mother, his family, and his small son. He sees his house nestled among the trees on the banks of La Have River, the latest addition to it not yet finished...remembers his mother's pleading with him to do anything but go to the sea. At this moment, Feener believes he is by now far from the raft and alone in an empty sea, when in fact some of his mates are out there with him, bobbing about in the hostile Atlantic.

Jim Mosher, owner of the *Cape Aspy* and seven other fishing trawlers, went to bed early that frigid and blustery night of January 30. Before retiring, he listened to the weather forecasts, and wondered, briefly, if the *Cape Aspy*'s captain would take his boat out in the violent conditions that raged outside. He reminded himself with a flash of comfort that he and his father had recently upgraded their boats to include new modern survival suits,[1] life rafts, and class 406 MHz Emergency Position-Indicating Radio Beacons (EPIRBS). These latter devices, registered and approved by the Coast Guard just seven days earlier, had been purchased and installed on the *Cape Aspy* only a short time before she sailed.

"It was just two months ago that I had been with my father at a trade show." Mosher says. "I said, 'Look at these new EPIRBS.' They were a fairly new technology then, and he said, 'What do you think?' I said, 'Let's do it, let's not wait around,' and we had the installation done within about six weeks."

"It was a very good move, as it turns out," he adds. "A little costly, I suppose, but safety, how can you argue with that?"

---

[1] Survival suits are expensive, bulky dry suits. Each has a waterproof outer layer made of flame-retardant, bright reddish-orange material; a face spray shield; an inflatable collar to keep the head above the water and to improve over-all buoyancy; a three-finger mitt for grip and hand movement; zip-up legs to make the suit easy to wear; and escape valves for trapped water or air. Each suit has a water-activated distress light, conforming to Coast Guard requirements, a buddy line that can be attached to a boat or other person, and light-reflecting patches for increased visibility in the water.

Mike Voigt, Search and Rescue Marine Controller at the Joint Rescue Coordination Centre, drives along the waterside streets into Halifax at 6:30 the morning of January 31. The streets near the long, low-slung government buildings are quiet, near empty. He feels the tension in the control room from the moment he walks through the door.

"The two officers on the night shift look pretty glad to see me, and one of them immediately briefs me on a search and rescue mission in full swing," Mike says. "It is the sinking of the *Cape Aspy* off the southeastern coast of the province.

"It's like having cold water thrown on my face," he says. "My heart rate goes up, and soon it's pumping a million miles a minute as I think of all the things I have to do." He explains that to walk in on an operation once it's already started is the worst possible time to do so. "At the beginning of an alert there is an entire system one goes through from the moment a Mayday is received. The controller knows what, and where, all the resources are." The *Cape Aspy* incident is a few hours old when Mike comes in to the JRCC, where a full-scale search and rescue operation is being mounted.

For the purposes of a national coordinated search and rescue program, there are three rescue coordination regions across the country—an Eastern region located in Halifax, a Central and Arctic region in Trenton, a western region in Victoria. Mike Voigt shoulders the responsibility to deploy personnel, equipment, communication systems—whatever is considered necessary—for a rescue operation in the Eastern region.

He takes his usual position at his desk and the information hits him cold. Mike knows that he will have to organize a coherent search plan, appoint an on-scene commander, and task resources to search the different areas. There is as yet no formal search plan worked out at the JRCC for the rescue of the *Cape Aspy*.

The night-shift staff has activated whatever resources they could to get to the scene to locate the raft and find the crew.

What Mike learns in those first few minutes of his shift is that the *Cape Aspy* has gone down off Cape Sable Island, and the only knowledge the rescue centre has of it is a signal emitted from an EPIRB. There have been no Mayday calls. The night-shift officers have immediately tasked to the area a Coast Guard ship on search and rescue standby in Shelburne, as well as Hercules air-craft and all other boats in the area. And Coast Guard crew in the small cutter from Clark's Harbour have set out for a long and treacherous trek across the water to help the rescue effort.

The *Cape Aspy* life raft has just been found when Mike takes over. Not all the men are in it. During hectic periods at the JRCC, a shift-handover can take up to two hours, as the activity does not stop. He will have to write up a search plan using the CANSARP (Canadian Search and Rescue Planning Program), a sophisticated program that takes into account wind, tide, and current. Based on available information, the computer deter-mines the position of search objects, taking into account the rate of drift and direction, and using models of men in the water.

"How to define the marine search area is difficult," Mike says. "It's very different from a plane that crashes on land or a hiker who goes missing in the woods. Everything stays put. But for us, the ocean current is always moving and everything pans out-wards. Over time, the search area increases exponentially in size. As well, things don't just drift straight downwind but sail off the wind a little, spreading out very quickly on the surface of the water. We send out our aircraft, but for the crew, looking for a person whose head is just sticking out of the water from a thou-sand feet up is truly like looking for the needle in the proverbial haystack."

The *Edward Cornwallis* pounded through rough seas for over six hours to reach the last known location of the *Cape Aspy*.

Captain Larry Meisner leaves the Canadian Coast Guard ship *Edward Cornwallis* to buy a newspaper after dinner on the night of January 30. The wind howls down the deserted streets that run parallel to the sea in the little town of Shelburne, on Nova Scotia's southeast coast. The captain turns right around and goes back to his ship: he's not going to walk anywhere in this weather. Before retiring for the evening, he visits the bridge, as is his custom, to meet with the officer of the watch and the quartermaster.

"Lousy conditions," he says. "Glad we're not in the gale that's blowing out there, for this sure is one really mean night." He requests that his officers keep a good listening watch on the distress radio frequencies, gives them their orders for the night, wishes them a good evening, and goes below.

The *Edward Cornwallis* is moored in this small fishing village on what is called "search and rescue stand-by." It has just returned from supply missions and buoy tending, and in one week's time is due in the mouth of the St. Lawrence to begin ice-breaking duties. For this week of dedicated search and rescue work, Larry Meisner has chosen Shelburne as a strategic location to berth his ship. His choice is based on the weather forecasts, fishing traffic and seasons, marine traffic, and the fact that it is a good, central location allowing a fast response time to a distress call. The search and rescue area tonight encompasses Halifax westward to Yarmouth, and all offshore adjacent waters.

"Stand-by periods generally involve the towing of boats with engine or other trouble, and finding vessels that are lost," Larry explains. "It's not often that a full-scale search and rescue mission is required for a sinking boat."

Larry Meisner remains warm and cozy in his cabin for just a few short hours until he is awakened abruptly by the officer of the watch, who has received a call from the JRCC in Halifax. The captain is tasked to take the *Edward Cornwallis* to search for a fishing trawler in trouble off the southeast coast toward Georges Banks. No Mayday call has been received, he is told, but the control centre has been alerted by an EPIRB emitting from this area. Larry Meisner gets up, looks at the night outside, and alerts his crew to prepare the ship for search and rescue work in the stormy Atlantic on one of the coldest and meanest nights on record.

"Yes, I was concerned about ice accumulation as we went out," Larry says. "I said to the officers of the watch, let's get out there with the best possible speed, but let me know at once of any icing on the superstructure. That's something you don't want to have to worry about when you get to a rescue scene—keeping ice off. It's dangerous and it accumulates very fast in these cold temperatures. Every drop of water that comes aboard forms ice immediately. Once it's on, it's difficult to get it off. And it's not just a matter of taking an axe or mallet to it—sometimes you have to use steam. This ship can handle three hundred tonnes of ice before I get concerned about its stability, which means the centre of gravity is altered and raised. When ice builds up, the ship will roll, and roll further and further, until she goes right over."

The *Edward Cornwallis* pounds through rough seas for over six hours to reach the area identified by the EPIRB as the last known location of the *Cape Aspy*. Larry's destination is a stretch of tumultuous ocean, empty save for two fishing vessels already searching the area, the *T. K. Pierce* and the *Ernest Pierce*. Both were within a radius of about twenty-five miles from the *Cape Aspy* when they were contacted by the JRCC in Halifax. They immediately hauled in their fishing gear, turned their boats about, and, in near-blizzard conditions, headed for the missing vessel. The captain of the *T. K. Pierce* had identified the probable area where the fishing vessel had gone down in accordance with the EPIRB information he had been given, and had begun a methodical search, together with the *Ernest Pierce*.

Larry Meisner is commander at the scene of the tragedy. As soon as his ship enters the area, the captains of the two fishing vessels connect with him. "Tell us what you want us to do, and we'll do it," they say. "We'll go where you want us to go." Larry appreciates the cooperation but is not surprised by it; the Coast Guard is held in deep respect by all fishermen, and by communities along the coasts. Larry cannot see the faces of the men in the fishing vessels, but he can hear the pain in their voices. He knows that they may well be searching for friends, brothers or sons out on this lonely sea.

Larry asks that the two fishing vessels expand their search and he himself will take his vessel either upwind or downwind. The Hercules aircraft, dispatched at the same time as the *Edward Cornwallis*, circles overhead. Meisner thinks it will have difficulty locating anything in the semi-darkness of the early morning. Even with the ship's powerful searchlights, Larry has picked up nothing but an oil slick and some debris.

Although the rescuers cannot see any part of the *Cape Aspy*, they keep combing an empty sea in growing winds and reduced visibility. Four quadrants have been marked off as the search area, and now other fishing vessels arrive to help, including the *Ryan Atlantic*, the *Cape Blomidon* and the *Cape Rouge*. A Canadian Forces aircraft from CFB Greenwood sweeps overhead for four hours straight before the pilot sights the flares and strobe lights set off by the men in the lifeboat, and he directs the *T. K. Pierce* to the lone raft bobbing about in the sea.

The raft itself is not visible, but the men's survival suits retain some of their original bright hue. Patches of colour are glimpsed as the men in their raft rise and fall in the swells of the sea driven by winds up to forty and fifty knots. As the *T.K. Pierce* draws close, her crew hears the voices of the fishermen in the raft singing "Amazing Grace," over and over.

The men in the life raft catch sight of the fishing vessel heading toward them and begin screaming. The seemingly impossible has happened: someone has come for them at last, and they will be rescued. "We yell yahoo and everything else, and we're all pumped up," one says. "The *T.K.*, to us she was like a knight in shining armour."

The fishing vessel struggles to come alongside the lifeboat, and one by one the crew manages to pluck the men from the raft and pull them up into their trawler. Some men are yelling, some scream and sob, while others keep singing.

"There are five more out there," they cry. "Feener, he's in the water, and Charlie Hancock and some others."

"Old Charlie, no, he was froze up and never made it off the boat," someone says. "Last I saw him, he was sitting in his bunk with his head in his hands."

"And the captain, he never left the wheelhouse," said another.

Meanwhile, Randy Feener is alone in the dark Atlantic. Icy water splashes over him. He gazes up at the stars and yells, "Why don't you cut me a little break, eh, why don't you?"

"I got thrown over the side," he says. "I was gasping with water in my mouth, all disoriented. I was looking around when another wave came over me and pushed me farther away from the raft. I to swim to it, but got no closer. Then I just waited and waited, thinking all the time about my wife, Mary, and my boy, Cody. Suddenly a light appeared across the water and I saw that it was the powerful beam of a searchlight. I swam frantically up the crest of a wave to try to get into the circle of that light, hoping it would pick up the reflector tape on the arms of my survival suit. I washed up on top of a wave and crossed my arms, but the light passed by me. Then I despaired. My last chance was gone and I didn't know how long I had left. Suddenly the light came back on me and picked me up. A boat came toward me, but now I couldn't move—my hands were all frozen up. It was the *Ernest Pierce* fishing trawler and its captain, Harold Moore, who came for me and hauled me out of the water. I was flipped face down on the deck. I stared at those oak planks all iced over, and a wave of pure happiness flooded over me. I'd punched in some more time for myself."

Jim Mosher and his father, owners of the sunken fishing trawler, are in the company's offices down by the water. It is now 5:00 in the afternoon on January 31, and they have been here since 2:30 this morning, awaiting the grim news about their employees—the survivors, the missing, and the dead—and answering the phones that never stop shrilling into the empty rooms.

Out on the water, the Coast Guard's *Edward Cornwallis* and the two fishing boats have been joined in the search by other fishing trawlers, some of whom are Scotia Trawler's competitors. The *T. K. Pierce* now has most men from the life raft safely on board, but she and her sister ship continue searching for the men who are missing. Hour after hour slips away. Late in the afternoon, three lifeless bodies are sighted and plucked from the ocean by one of the fishing trawlers. Doggedly the fishermen continue searching for the remaining missing men.

"It was outstanding, the courage and expertise of the captain of the *T. K. Pierce*," says Captain Larry Meisner. "I was impressed with his knowledge and the degree of cooperation with the Coast Guard; he and his crew rescued most of the men in the life raft." Larry guesses that the captain must have had some training in search and rescue patterns when he wrote for his fishing certificate. "I didn't have to explain much to him," he says. "I just said, this is what I want you to do, how I want you to do it, and he jumped right on the bandwagon, and did an excellent job."

Because Albert Eisner and Charlie Hancock are still missing, the fishing boat's captain is reluctant to leave the area, even after a full day's exhausting search; he wants to continue looking. Larry says, "Look, you have some people, both living and dead, on board. You need to get back to shore.

"I understood his sorrow," he says. "He was haunted by knowing there were still men in the sea, perhaps a good friend, or cousin, a brother. But there was really little value to remaining."

The two fishing vessels, now heavily crusted with ice, turn about and head back to shore, to a Lunenburg that has once again gathered together to mourn the loss of her men to the sea. The Labrador helicopter and two Hercules aircraft from the military's 413 Squadron make another sweep of the search area, sixty nautical miles south of Cape Sable Island. They return three hours later, having sighted nothing.

The *Edward Cornwallis* alone remains at the place where the *Cape Aspy* went down, a vast expanse of empty sea. The Hercules aircraft has had to turn back because of blinding snow and poor visibility. Larry gets on the phone to the JRCC. He says that since his ship is not required for its ice-breaking duties for another few days, could he not stay and continue looking, even though there is little chance they will find anything? "You never know," he says. He and his crew search tirelessly throughout the long night, together with two stern trawlers from National Sea Products.

The people of Lunenburg trudge down steeply sloping streets to attend burial services for their dead. Hundreds fill the two churches, while others linger in the freezing cold to bid farewell to those who will never again sail the seas. The ritual of mass mourning is not new to this rugged place. Since its origins in 1753, the inhabitants have regularly trudged the streets in sorrow. Today, once more, the town is draped in sombre silence. In one of the churches, a small choir lifts its voice to sing "Amazing Grace," echoing the prayerful singing of the men in their small life raft.

"While it is true to say that the days of the wooden ships are for the most part gone, the days of iron men are not," says Reverend Fred Hiltz from the altar of St. John's. "Nor shall they ever be, so long as men brave the elements and endure the dangers of the deep to reap the harvest of the sea. Lunenburg has both prospered and suffered from the sea—prospered by the abundant harvest of fish, while suffering the cost of the fish in terms of human life."

The Reverend Mawhinney speaks of the sinking of the *Cape Aspy* as a painful reminder of the harsh realities of life in a fishing community, and the Reverend Andrew Crowell, of the people who live with their families by the sea. "And, in the end, the sea cannot strip us of our memories," he says. "These deaths are a reminder of the dangers and risks to the men who reap the silver harvest of the sea. The Atlantic is a harsh place on which to work, and there is a tremendous price paid to be involved in the fishing industry. We pay tribute to the courage of those who go to sea, that they continue to do so."

The community, struck by grief, mourns together. "Fishing is not just a hard life where men are absent from home and out on the ships for so much of the time; there is inherent risk in what they do for a livelihood," says one of the clergymen. "Death is a constant companion, and it is always like a knife in the back of the community when it occurs to a sailor or fisherman, or any man of the sea. The people, the community, depend for their livelihood on the men who are out on the ocean."

"Fishing is your job," says Bob Berringer. "What else will you do around these parts? But it's more than a job, more that a means of earning a living; it's your way of life. Sure, there's risk, like there is in most things. In winter especially, you know you can get in trouble, but you take the chance, and you don't really think anything's going to happen to you."

"When I walked out at the end of my shift, I was disoriented; it was like a surprise that there was another whole world out there," Mike Voigt says. "It's like that sometimes at the JRCC. The sun may have been shining, there's fresh air, a real world with cars driving by on the street, and you don't know it. It dawns on you that it's your world that's bizarre. You're pumped up and into doing this case, and you think of nothing else; this becomes your universe. Your adrenaline is flowing and you become completely focused on the tasks you're working on."

Mike and other controllers speak of the stress inherent in the job they do, but say that knowing about the degree of power they have in their positions in the Joint Rescue Centre is itself a stress reliever. Unlike many positions in the public and private commercial worlds, they are given the tools to do their job.

"This must be one of the few places in the world where you are told to do something—here it happens to be saving people—and are given the tools to do it," says Voigt. "It's like, 'and, by the way, you have the full legal authority under the Shipping Act to do so; you can task whatever you need to get the job done.' You have authority to use whatever is at your disposal—you can request a big commercial airliner and send it to wherever you need it, you can task a cruise ship to go to a rescue. The power you have is awesome.

"If things go wrong, as long as you can show you were acting in the best interests of the people out there, and can prove it, from the top down you will be supported; you won't be questioned. Cost is not a factor if someone is in distress. But," he adds, "we still have to be careful of the public purse—if someone is frivolous, uses a false alarm, if there are non-distress incidents like broken-down boats, we have to be careful. Guys put their neck on the chopping block sometimes, deciding what is a hoax, and what is serious.

"You have to make sudden shifts in your thinking and communication," he says. "You're on the phone one minute to the captain of a commercial ship, ordering him to do what you need him to do, maybe exercising your authority under the Canada Shipping Act. You might have to say, look, let's be clear here, you are being ordered to do this. The next call you make you're telling relatives about the death of a family member, or you are on the phone to the media. You have to be an expert in everybody's business."

Voigt says that an active search was continued for the missing men from the *Cape Aspy* until three in the afternoon on Monday, January 31. The Department of Fisheries and Oceans helicopter returned to Yarmouth and the *Edward Cornwallis* left the scene to take up its ice-breaking duties in the St. Lawrence. But as Lt. Commander Agnew explains, a search is never called off; it is simply scaled down by levels and degrees.

"We will still advise people in the area to keep a look-out," Agnew says.

People remain on watch for the dead, for the bodies of friends and relatives.

Larry Meisner remains today as captain of the Canadian Coast Guard ship *Edward Cornwallis*. It has been a long association. He was the very first commanding officer assigned to the ship after it was built in 1986, and has continued in this position for twelve years, interrupted only by two short stints as commander of other Coast Guard vessels, the *Terry Fox* and the *Sir William Alexander*.

Larry speaks of himself as a person driven to be on ships and at sea ever since his high school days. His career on the water began on a research ship that circumnavigated the globe. Since then, with the exception of three years as executive officer at the Maritimes headquarters, the remainder of his career has been spent with the Canadian Coast Guard's Maritimes Fleet. If he were go back in time and choose again, he would not have it otherwise.

Mike Voigt, one of the controllers during the *Cape Aspy* search on behalf of the Coast Guard, is now in Ottawa in the position of chief of rescue coordination. The seemingly never-ending shift in the control room in Halifax on January 31, 1993 is burned forever in his memory. It heightened his respect for the work of the departments of National Defence, the Joint Rescue Coordination Centre and the Canadian Coast Guard—for the combined efforts and cooperation, the extent of the sophisticated technology, and the authority given to those whose task it was and is to save people's lives.

"To me, this rescue was the epitome of what the Coast Guard, the Canadian Forces, and volunteers, can do," Mike says. "The whole system of technology we have, the resources that are so quickly available, and the dedication of the people to make it all work."

Jim Mosher, owner of the sunken fishing trawler, remains as president of Scotia Trawler Equipment but is a changed man. He speaks of how he left Lunenburg to study business management, not intending to return, but was drawn home by the pull of the sea and a family tradition: Jim's grandfather was a sea captain and fisherman, and his father was the founder and owner of a fleet of scallop boats.

"I was more interested in the business side, in profit, when I was younger," Jim says of his pre-*Cape Aspy* days. "Not anymore; I only care about the people. It was a profound shock to me that some of our people drowned, and I will never be the same."

Bob Berringer is home now, with his wife and three daughters in a comfortable house on the banks overlooking First Peninsula, just north of Lunenburg. The air is fresh with a breeze that blows in from the water, the land green and sloping up to the tree line that shelters the deer. Bob and his brother own a fishing license and continue to work as fishermen, as they have since both were very young; Bob goes off-shore fishing while his brother fishes inshore.

"We fish up to the first of January and then we lay our traps," Bob says. "Water freezes up so that even the scallop draggers have trouble getting in and out of the harbour and the Coast Guard does the ice breaking. We put down lobster traps before the water freezes up, and land them in before the water gets so cold that they don't crawl, some time in January. After that, I go out scalloping. My brother sets the traps again in the spring, and when I'm home again, we go out together. It's an off-and-on business. In spite of the *Cape Aspy*, I keep going out. What else will I do, for you won't get me working on dry land."

Randy Feener's fervor for the fishing life remains undimmed, in spite of his near drowning twice within a few years, and in spite of his mother's opposition. Young Larry Wentzell went back out on the boats, but not for long. He turned his back on a life on the sea in the end, and found himself work on more solid ground.

Sambro's Strategic Station

Sambro, Nova Scotia

Sambro is an old fishing village on the east coast of Nova Scotia, southwest of Halifax. The people who came early to its shores settled themselves about its low-lying hills, close to the sea, sustaining themselves by its bounty: swordfish, mackerel, haddock, and cod. They salted it and took it to Halifax by boat, as no roads existed at the time, and returned with flour, salt, cabbages and turnip for the winter. Other boats came in to pick up crates of lobster to take directly south to American markets. This was the way of life: boats and fish and the sea.

Life in the village has changed and evolved; many people living in Sambro now work in Halifax, a distance of twenty kilometres by winding road. But at heart, Sambro remains a fishing village. While the sword fishing for which it was once famous is greatly reduced and much of the industry has moved offshore, still many of the people fish, and most families own two boats— a small one for inshore fishing and a larger one for offshore— although the boats are on the water for fewer days of the year because of fishing quotas introduced in the 1990s. The industry is highly competitive, so they often go out when the weather is bad, or refuse to come in early because they're afraid others will be catching the fish and that they'll miss out. Today, when not out on the water, fishers spend their time repairing and servicing their boats and gear.

"Many of the people here *live* for fishing," says Steve Beasely, as he gazes out over the harbour from the equipment room at Sambro's lifeboat station. Years of seascape shine in his eyes. "My life is a hand-me-down, sort of passed on to me from generations of forebears, all old salt dogs of the sea."

Steve lives in Portuguese Cove among rocks, trees, and the small hills of this rugged coast along the eastern shores of Nova Scotia. From a young age, he fished with a family friend, continued throughout high school and after. When the fish became fewer and the living from fishing poorer, he tried carpentry. He was skilled but, like so many of his peers, he could not abide a life away from the sea, so he returned to fishing. Steve now makes his living from the sea, though not exactly in the manner of his Newfoundland forebears—he is coxswain at the Sambro lifeboat station.

"I was going to be on the ocean, some way," he says. "Once you've been out on the water, you miss it always when you're away from it." His first job was as deckhand on another's boat while he worked to build his own, in Portuguese Cove. Hours were squeezed in to go handlining, and sometimes longlining—an old occupation where hooks are set on rope, rigged in such a way that they lie on the ocean bottom.

"This life, you have to experience it to understand," Steve says of both fishing and his work for the Coast Guard. "Like when you're doing a tow job. You're not just towing a boat; you're going along looking at the water and the birds swooping over-head, the porpoises, the whales breaking the surface of the water. You're sitting out there on a boat that's coming in on the land, and you think, my God, this is a peaceful place to be. All the con-fusion and rat race is on the land, and you're out on the water. And then, when you have a rescue job to do, you're it; there's no one else. It gives you a good feeling."

In 1979, Steve heard about a relief search and rescue position available at the Sambro lifeboat station while he was still doing carpentry. The idea struck him that this might be a chance to get back out on the water, to make a steady income, more important now that he had two children.

He applied. "You got hired by people you knew," he explains. "Those who employed you knew you could do the job, knew you could handle a boat and look after yourself. But you had to enter the competitions; if you won the position, you had things to learn and courses you had to take, such as first-aid, marine emer-gency duties (MED), radio frequencies and procedures, and how to speak on radio." Steve went beyond the required qualifications for the position of deckhand, undertaking a further seven-week course to qualify as coxswain. These courses included advanced first-aid, further marine emergency duties, simulated electronic navigation (SEN) courses involving knowledge and familiarity with radar and global positioning systems (GPS). Virtual naviga-tion meant he could actually watch himself navigate among rocks and shoals, along coasts and buoys and through channels.

Nowadays, when positions become available at the lifeboat station, it is still the local fishermen who are asked to join, but fewer fishermen are interested. The formal demands of the job are greater now than they once were. A strict series of courses leading to certification is required, the pay is less, and local fishermen do not like the idea of being committed to a station where they might have to sit by a phone waiting for a rescue call. They can earn better money out in a fishing boat when the season is good.

Steve agrees with his Coast Guard counterparts that, despite the lower pay, the total commitment required, and the occasional periods when they sit and wait for a call, it's a good job. For him, the rewards of the work are tremendous: it's a privilege to be able to help people; it gives a great feeling, even when there is sometimes no acknowledgement after a successful rescue. "I've literally pulled peoples' arses out of the water and many don't even say thank you," Steve says. When they do, it's an added bonus.

Today, Steve moves in and out of the main office area of the lifeboat station where his crew have gathered at the beginning of their shift. Beyond the large window facing east up the harbour, the sea is quiet, serene even, just the faintest ripple disturbing its surface. The road falls away below the house and leads a short distance to a building on one side of the dock containing the station's supplies and equipment, with the Coast Guard cutter *Sambro* moored on the other. The station, which has been open since 1976, averages between seventy and ninety calls each year. The *Sambro,* which has been involved in more than two thousand missions since arriving at the station, participates in exercises with the RCMP, the Department of National Defence and

Five SAR vessels in the Maritime Region.

other organizations, in fisheries conservation and protection boardings, and in regular crew training. One of nine such "Arun class" vessels in Coast Guard search and rescue service in Canada, it is equipped with the latest electronic, navigation, communications, safety and first-aid equipment, and can carry twenty-two seated survivors, with a small boat for operations in shallow water.

Steve's crew includes Donny Morris, Dwayne Symes (the *Sambro*'s engineer), and Bruce Flemming, all inheritors of a love of ships and being on the water. "We're sort of stuck in here by ourselves, a small operation," Steve says. "But we communicate with other stations all around the Maritimes at least once a week. It's peaceful, and we do our own thing: water, boats, training."

"The night we got the Mayday call, it was one of those black and filthy nights when nobody wants to be out," said one of the crew at Sambro. "We thought there might be fishing boats still out beyond the harbour, and couldn't see how they could get back in. We hoped they wouldn't try because they would have been safer had they stayed out in the open waters beyond the harbour." The Coast Guard lifeboat crew got up and began a nightmare journey up a harbour whose rough contours and rocky obstacles could not be seen in the driving rain and heavy seas.

"It was hazardous to us," admitted one of the crew members. "We couldn't pick up the land or nothing on radar."

The crew was halfway up the harbour when the fishermen changed their minds, radioing to say they were all right, but the lifeboat crew continued on through the storm. They explained that they figured things were worse for the fishermen than they knew or were saying; if they had taken in sea, blacked out, lost all their power and stalled the engines, then considerable damage must have been sustained. The Coast Guard crew surmised that the fishing boat must have temporarily re-gained power, that the lights had come back on and the engines had started up again.

"We kept on going because we figured they would need us in the end, and besides, there were two other small fishing boats like this one out there that night, too. We didn't think any of them were going to get in because it just wasn't fit to come through the harbour."

"There was another reason we kept on going," explains the coxswain. "I really didn't want to go out the harbour again that night, struggle a second time with all we had just been through to get there. And I knew I would probably have to. I'll be honest…it was too rough and really dangerous in the mouth of the harbour—you're trying to navigate between shoals in heavy rain, with seas breaking on the rocks. We still couldn't see anything on radar. It was safer to stay out beyond the harbour. What we reckoned was that if the fishing boat had been hit hard enough to stall the engines and knock out all their power, they would be hit again and need our help."

The fishing boat and its crew were not all right; they were hit by another rogue wave, which struck the wheelhouse and cleared it out—a big hit and a big problem. The little Coast Guard cutter reached the stricken boat, drew alongside, and took the fishermen off their boat. They never saw their boat again and were grateful that the lifeboat crew had not listened to them.

In this region, fog does not creep across land as the storybooks say; it descends out of nowhere to obliterate the world. That's what happened in St. Margaret's Bay along the shores southwest of Halifax one windless August day.

Beyond the lifeboat station at Sambro, the harbour waters lie still, just a gentle swell on the ocean, the barest of ripples near the shore. A weak sun tries to break through the low-lying cloud and the air feels thick and still. No drills or training exercises have been scheduled, and vessels expect little trouble. Steve Beasely and his crew retire in the evening, relaxed, hopeful that the night will be undisturbed. At 4:00 AM the pager goes off: a man is missing in St. Margaret's Bay, believed to be lost in the fog. The controller from the Joint Rescue Coordination Centre in Halifax says he is a young man, all alone in a small sailing boat. His folks say he has been out all day and all evening, and has not returned.

"We're out there in the cutter within a few minutes, speeding up the harbour and along the coast to get to the bay by daylight," says Steve. The sweep of St. Margaret's Bay is large and the fog very thick; the crew's vision is limited to about one hundred feet as they begin a methodical search pattern using radar that will pick up the smallest object on the water.

"Back and forth, back and forth we go for about five hours, running out our search pattern lines," says Steve. "By calculating the wind direction and the tides, this guy should have been blown in, or drifted in close to the bay."

By 11:00 in the morning, the cutter is in the middle of the bay; a pale sun pierces the clouds at brief moments, and the fog slowly begins to burn off. The late-summer water temperature is about sixty-four degrees. The crew work their way in closer to the shore, passing quietly, ghost-like, through the remaining fog. Suddenly they find they have passed through it, and now the bay is wide open to them for half a mile or more.

"Going through to the other side of the fog is like waking up in the morning and opening your eyes," Steve says. "We spot a tiny white object that looks like a fish box, and I yell out to the others. We make straight for it to see what it is. But we have to get really close before we can make out that it's a small boat on its side, its mast and sail in the water."

Getting closer still, the crew sees the figure of a man hanging from its side, his arms folded like a coat hanger in front of him, chin resting on the folded hands, a stance that suggests he has said goodbye. Foot-high waves wash right over his head and he remains unmoving. The crew believes he is dead and possibly in rigor mortis until they are within four feet of him. The noise of their engines disturbs him; he turns his head and looks at them with a look they will never forget.

"His eyes were like silver dollars, huge and black," says Steve. "A haunted look." Steve maneuvers the boat close against the clinging figure and hovers about a foot distant. The crew reach out and grab the man. At the touch of hands upon him, the young man in the water closes his eyes, suggesting that he knows now that he is going to be all right. He is wearing one sneaker, a pair of shorts and a T-shirt. His wristwatch has stopped at the hour of 3:30. He has been on or in the water since 10:00 the morning before, over twenty-four hours. They maintain him in a horizontal position, cover him with blankets, and phone an ambulance. He is taken to a hospital where he remains unconscious for two days, having suffered from hypothermia. Once again, the Coast Guard crew has the satisfaction of knowing they saved a life.

"What's the big deal?" asked the lone sailor as he was plucked off his sinking boat. "Everybody does it. I just had bad luck." There was a momentary silence on board the Coast Guard cutter.

"Hey man, we just rescued you and your dog from a sinking boat in the middle of the Atlantic," said one of the deckhands. "Bad luck, be damned. You were out in fifty mile-an-hour winds and in hurricane season. Did you think you were crossing a pond?"

It seems to the crew at the Sambro lifeboat station that it must be a popularly-held belief that anyone can sail from Canada's East Coast across the Atlantic to Europe, no sweat. No different from walking to the corner store, so frequent are the calls for rescue of people trying to make the crossing. Would-be ocean trotters set off in sailing vessels and small rowboats; they take no heed of the weather, no precautions, nor proper provisions. Some have few navigational tools and little knowledge of the sea.

"This guy and his dog set out in a thirty-four-foot sailing boat to sail to Europe," says Donny Morris. "It was late October and he was out there in forty to fifty-mile-an-hour winds. His engines failed, and we saw that they were poorly maintained, partly because he was using bad fuel. He got into rough weather and his engines conked out, so he hauled in his sails. The seas washed over him and the fog rolled across his path. He gets on the radio and calls us to come out and get him."

The man with the dog paid no heed to the advice and the warnings, setting sail a second time in early November.

"He got buried in fog, crossed the path of a freighter steaming north, and nearly got himself run down," said the deckhand. "Another vessel close by struggled to get to him and pass him a line, but missed. Here was this guy, a second time, alone and trying to keep his sinking boat afloat. We get a Mayday call at three in the morning."

The passing vessel, unable to get a towline attached, stayed alongside, sheltering the sailboat on his lee side, and putting out the Mayday call. The Coast Guard ship *Riverton*, on standby near Sable Island, monitored the situation while the Sambro station cutter steamed out to the rescue.

"It was rough for us getting out there, and we didn't make it until six," says Morris. "We told the guy we were going pass him a line and tow him into Halifax. We managed it, but it was one long, hard tow: the winds slowed us down to just under four knots. We towed him from about 7:00 that morning until 8:00 in the evening, right into Halifax. Then we had to get ourselves back to the station."

A few days later, this same man tried yet again. On this occasion, he got as far as Bickerton before he got into trouble and this time it was the Coast Guard vessel from the Bickerton lifeboat station and its crew who had to go out and rescue him. He was approached by the RCMP and told that his escapades could cost him his life and that he was costing the taxpayers too much money. It was at this point he decided to sail south around to Panama and go through the canal to get to Europe.

It is the practice of either the RCMP or officers from the safety division of the Coast Guard to become involved with those who require repeat rescue. The offender is approached, and the seaworthiness of the boat, and the extent of the sailor's knowledge are investigated. The authorities try to convince such offenders that they can't continue to expect the taxpayers to pay for their rescue.

"It's not just the guys in their sailboats," says the crew from the lifeboat station, "Once there was a woman in a row boat, thinking she could row across the Atlantic. Luckily for her, a container ship from Newfoundland came across her seven days after she had left. They asked her if she was all right, if she needed food or water.

"No," she said. "I'm okay, and my family knows where I am. But please tell them I'm okay."

"She'd been gone a week, needed to cross 2,600 miles of water, and had gone 350. She thought she had it all figured out. But she was low on food and water because she should have gone much further than she had in one week. "We figured she had faced an easterly wind of a kind that could almost make a row boat—or small boat—go backwards," says one of the Sambro crew.

Where's My Father?
A Boy's First Rescue
Mission

Ketch Harbour and Sambro, Nova Scotia

The big man strides down the hill to the sea, his small boy running after him as a faint light spreads across the sky. Young Chris Flemming, roused out of his bunk bed and still rubbing the sleep from his eyes, marvels each morning at the creeping resurrection of sea, sky, and the slope of the distant hills. The grass-covered rocky and indented shoreline around Ketch Harbour, Nova Scotia is his place on God's earth. He is a member of yet another generation of the Flemming family that has inhabited this part of the world in such numbers that it is sometimes called Flemming's place. Halifax might lie about a half-hour drive directly north, but one would never know it here. A stillness breathes across a landscape of dips, valleys, and sudden views of the sea; of houses and buildings nestled among small trees, or perched on rocky outcrops as though to keep a vigilant eye on the sweep of both land and ocean.

The "Big Man," as he is sometimes called for his six-foot-seven height and not-so-skinny frame, and his young son Chris have this ritual on both school days and weekends: they get up with the sun and go out to fish.

"Come on, my boy!" The cheerful booming voice would come from the doorway of Chris's small bedroom. "Time for us to go out there and pull in some traps before you go to school; we'll get out and back before dawn's quite got itself all over the sky."

Father and son are buddies in this business of inshore fishing. The boy follows his father, watching and learning from him, the "Big Man" who is hero to his son. For the rest of his life, anything Chris knows that anything he believes he has learned from his father. He curls up in the bow of the boat, half dozing, finishing his night's sleep to the *chug, chug, chug* of the motor.

This morning, a benign pale sky arches over a tranquil ocean.

For the next two hours, man and boy concentrate on pulling lobster traps and salmon nets into the bottom of the boat. It is a world of fish and fishy smells, bait, lines and nets, and the caressing waves of the sea. Flemming returns his boat to shore in time for Chris to run up the hill to get ready for school. The boy stands on one foot in the doorway of his home, looks at his mother who is busy in the kitchen, and says to her, "This is what I want to do with my life, just this." As he speaks, he gazes out to the sea.

The ritual of early-morning fishing and hauling in traps remains a pattern for Chris until he is sixteen years old and goes to work. At this time, a small, wiry old man known simply as Musty took his place as his father's partner in the small-time fishing business.

"Musty just loved fishing with my dad," Chris says. "He didn't know how to handle the boat they went out in, didn't know anything about engines—he had never driven it, or any boat. He set the nets while my Dad looked after the boat. And neither of them could swim. Around here, unless you learn by the age of fourteen, you never learn, because by the time you're fifteen, you're out on the water, fishing."

Saturday in late summer is time for fishermen to get ready for the lobster fishing in the fall. Musty, having completed his part-time maintenance work at the yacht club, goes out for a day's fishing with Mr. Flemming. The day dawns as any other and as the first light streaks into the sky and the dew lies heavy on the grass, the odd-looking pair treks down the hill to the boat. Chris gets up a little later to help his sister and brother-in-law build a house not far from the family home.

The young people are busy, but Chris's gaze strays out to sea from time to time. He cannot see his father's boat, although the water is calm and quiet and the sky is clear. The builders quit their labours about 5:30 PM and return home. Chris notices that his father's boat is still not in, and is surprised, perturbed. He jumps on his bicycle and rides furiously down to the heads to gaze out to sea, squinting against a blood-red sun that dips low in the sky. He can see the boat now, but what's it doing way off at Bell Rock?

"What on earth is it doing out there?" he asks out loud. "That's way far out from where they usually go; this is weird." He bikes back and waits anxiously until he can see the boat coming past the point. Then he rides swiftly down the hill and onto the wharf as the boat comes closer. He sees Musty at the wheel. "This is *very* weird," he thinks. He watches him circle about out in the bay, but Musty doesn't come in. Even from the distance, Chris can see that he's nervous.

Chris leaps into a small skiff that's tied up to the dock and rows out, straining at the oars, fearful and puzzled, knowing Musty is alone in the boat. The skiff comes close, and angles to get alongside the boat. Chris watches for his chance, and makes a leap aboard. Musty is sweating and agitated and will not look Chris in the eye.

"Where's my father?"

"Down at Chebucto Head. He—he fell overboard, and—and I couldn't get him back in." Musty is close to stammering.

"What's he doing down there? Musty, what on earth's happened?"

Musty describes how the "Big Man" was just going past the wheelhouse on his way back from hauling in mackerel when he suddenly clutched his chest, lurched, and, with a shout, fell overboard into the water.

"I couldn't haul him back in; he was too big for me. He floated out there, and then he disappeared under the water…I—I didn't know what to do—I managed to get the fishing nets clear; guess I figured how to get the boat in gear to bring it back home. I can't say nothing more. I couldn't do nothing to help him."

His father had fallen out of his boat! But the day is as calm and clear as the most perfect summer day on the sea. Images flood Chris's brain. He remembers the incident three months ago when his father and mother went out shopping in Spryfield, his father in the back seat of the car. He was quiet for a time, but suddenly clutched his chest, groaned, and collapsed. Afterwards, nothing was found wrong.

Chris stares at the small man in his father's boat. Then, with a calm presence of mind that is already his hallmark, he begins his first search and rescue mission: to find his father who is floating somewhere out in the vast Atlantic. Chris attaches a towline to the skiff, puts his father's boat in gear, and brings it alongside the wharf. Musty climbs out. By this time, Chris's older brother and cousin, having seen Chris's actions, run down to the wharf to find out what the commotion is about. They jump aboard Flemming's boat and roar it up the harbour.

"This was the first time I had ever operated the boat by myself," Chris says. "My father always did that. We raced it out to Bell Rock where my Dad and Musty had been fishing. It's now late in the day, starting to get dark, but we found the net that Musty had cut, floating in the water. We strained our eyes until mine felt as though they were going to pop out of my head. None of us could see anything else out there and we figured we had about an hour of daylight left to look for Dad."

His eyes restlessly search the surface of a sea that he knows and loves, trying to penetrate its depths, willing it to give up his father, not yet accepting that the ocean has claimed yet another life—that of his very own father. His overwhelming drive at this moment is to find him and bring him home.

Soon the three are joined in their lonely search by Joe Flemming. The old man has driven his fishing boat at full throttle to help them. But darkness is falling. Reluctantly, and in great sorrow, three teenagers and an older man slowly head their boats back to shore and tie up at the wharf.

It is a family's worst nightmare: a fisherman goes out to sea and does not come back. Chris has a sudden image of his mother in the kitchen up on the hill; of her trudging the paths along the cliffs, creating tracks in the grass at its rocky edge, eyes scanned out to sea in the way that women did in the days of old: widow's walks.

"We went out again the next morning," he is saying. "The sea was quiet, a pale blue, and clear. We were all alone as it was the early sixties and there was no Coast Guard to help us then."

It is true: there were few aids for shipwrecked sailors and fishermen in the years between 1946 and the early 1960s. If this mishap had occurred only a year or two later, there might have been help. Crew from the one of the new search and rescue Coast Guard cutters—vessels able to carry twelve crew members, with a range of fifteen hundred miles at sea and a cruising speed of seventeen knots—might have been able to help.

"Later, at home, we're sitting around, my Mom and the rest of us, and none of us can believe what's happened," Chris Flemming says. "Then the Royal Canadian Mounted Police (RCMP) come up to the wharf in their cutter, the *Kingfisher*. They tie up, walk up to the house, ask me to go out with them and show them where the accident happened. There was this look in my poor mother's face as I went out the door."

Chris jumps in the police cruiser, and once more goes out to the empty sea to look for his father. He shows the constable where the grapple hooks and lines had been thrown overboard.

The police cruiser marks out a search pattern and begins to comb the area. Chris stares into the depths of the blue-green waves, willing himself to catch sight of his Dad, at the same time, still not really believing that's he's down there. Suddenly a voice booms out the wheelhouse, startling the group in the boat.

"This young fellow shouldn't be here. What if we hook his father and grapple him up? It's not the kind of thing a boy should see." There is silence, then the commanding officer abruptly turns the boat about and Chris is brought back to shore. As he drags himself slowly up the hill, he sees his mother's silhouette in the doorway of their home: she's turned, staring out to sea. The officers return to continue to sweep the ocean, but the "Big Man," Chris's father, will never be found.

Chris now gets up at dawn by himself. There is no booming voice in the doorway of his bedroom to tell him, "Come on, my boy! Time to go out there and get the fish." He does some fishing in a desultory fashion with an older man called Bernie Gray, but there is an ache within him that begins whenever he goes out on the water. Subconsciously he never ceases to search the seas that have entombed his father. The "Big Man" lies somewhere at the bottom of the ocean and Chris can never find him. He keeps searching; thinks he sees him everywhere, and is haunted by a vision of him floating, or being dragged along the ocean bottom by the currents, while he, Chris, is on top of it.

He has nightmares. He feels he must get away from the water, do something else, anything else. To his mother's nodding approval, he tries vocational school. Chris now has his feet on dry land, stuck beneath a desk in a classroom. He stares out the window, walks back and forth to catch a glimpse of the sea. He's restless; he yearns for the sights, sounds, and smells of the ocean.

"I couldn't hack life on the land, or work that didn't have to do with fish and boats and the sea," he says. "I had to be on the water, or beside it, to do something with it. I tried to get away, but I guess it's in my blood." Chris went fishing on a 65-foot dragger with Bernie Gray for three years, just the two of them.

"I loved it, just loved it," he says. "But of course, once you get into the fisheries, it's feast or famine. You have to be big to survive, and if you are small, the business often just dwindles and falls by the wayside over the years. We were small."

One day, Chris and Bernie Gray are out on the dragger when the engines fail. The boat tosses helplessly on the swells. In vain, Bernie attempts to extricate it from its entanglement in the lines and nets cast out on the water. Hour after hour passes as he and Chris struggle. The sun climbs from its zenith and begins its long descent. The fishermen look at each other. Bernie shrugs, picks up the marine phone and radios the Coast Guard for help. Twenty minutes after the call is made, a Coast Guard cutter is cruising toward them. With speed and efficiency, a line is hooked to the dragger and the cutter tows the dragger in to shore.

Chris looks at the search and rescue workers in their blue and navy uniforms, the faces of the men whose lives are dedicated to saving the lives of others. Something swells within him; he turns to Bernie Gray and says, "What if there were no Coast Guard?"

Bernie shrugs.

"I want to do that someday," Chris declares. "That's the kind of job I want to do: to rescue people. Yeah, I think I could do it for the rest of my life."

In winter, the seas are frozen over. Few boats go out, little fishing is done, and many people are unemployed. Chris Flemming is nineteen and has nothing to do. He has energy and ambition and cannot see himself sitting around unemployed all winter. On December 20, he strides off to the Dartmouth base to ask for a Captain Armstrong, having heard that he was hiring.

"I'm looking for work," Chris says simply. "The boats are all tied up and I don't want to sit around with nothing to do; I want to work." He is told to go and register with Manpower.

"Yeah, yeah, yeah," Chris thinks, but he goes off and registers. He stops on his way back for a drink with his friends. It is mid-afternoon when he arrives home. His mother meets him at the door with the message that Captain Armstrong had called to tell him to be on board the *Sir William Alexander* by noon the next day.

"Wow! Just like that! He phones up before he knows that I've gone and registered. I didn't have a clue what I would have to do, what kind of ship this was, what it was going out for, where it was going. I just stuffed my duffel bag full and took off for Dartmouth base...I had the world by the tail, that's how I felt."

Chris walks up the gangway onto the ship. There are a bunch of guys there, all in their forties and fifties.

"They just stare at me, and I guess I seemed to them like a snotty-nosed teenager coming up the gangway," he says. He tells

When not involved in actual rescue missions, search and rescue crew participate in training exercises with other Coast Guard vessels, auxiliary craft and air support from the Department of National Defence.

them awkwardly that Captain Armstrong told him to come and see Amish Moorash, the mate.

"Upstairs—his room's on the right," one of them says indifferently, assuming Chris knows where to go. Chris gets lost. He wanders all over the ship as it is loaded with supplies and equipment for Sable Island, the ship's destination. Chris learns that he is needed because some of the sailors believed they would not be home in time for Christmas and have called in "sick."

Chris is excited: here is his chance to see the fabled island, a desolate place haunted by tales of shipwrecks and the ghosts of lost, wandering sailors; a place of sand and rock and shaggy ponies roaming the savanna grass that blows on the dunes.

Chris spends two days on the shores of the lonely island before returning on the *Sir William Alexander* that arrives back in port on December 24. In January, he works as a deckhand on an ice-breaking ship up the coasts; at the end of it, declares that he is hooked on this life.

"Why did I want to work for the Coast Guard? I'll tell you: you have to have your shit together to do the Coast Guard job. You have to go out in weather when no one else is out, when no one else will go out. So, like I say, you have to have yourself together. The work appealed to me because it seemed challenging, and you get to help people. When you're out fishing and you hear of a storm, you get yourself home. But with the Coast Guard, that's when you head out. It's an awesome job, but I knew I could do it; I have no fear of the weather, and if the boat is in good shape, what's there to fear? I liked the whole picture, in spite of the brutal cold, the wind, the aching muscles and the lack of sleep," he says. "The old salts from years ago took me under their wing and taught me all I needed to know in a couple of days, just so I could survive on board. Anything I didn't know, I just asked them, and they just took me along."

There were ten deckhands on board when Chris began his marine career with the Coast Guard. When the sailor he was relieving returned to his job, Chris expected to be laid off. He waited, and nobody said anything to him. He was puzzled, but learned later that, one by one, the older men took leave so that he could stay. For six months they rotated, each booking time off so that Chris could stay. Chris was valued by the sailors because he knew his stuff, he was good at his job, and took his responsibilities seriously. And they believed that if he were let go, they might never get him back. Today, the young boy whose first search and rescue operation was the search for his own father is now coxswain of the Coast Guard cutter at the lifeboat station at Sambro. The station is his home away from home, and his crew members are his mates. Sometimes it's a hard life, but never dull or routine. And there's nothing else in the world he would want to do. For him, the Coast Guard is it.

If It's Not One Thing, It's Another

Sambro, Nova Scotia

Sambro was chosen for the establishment of a Coast Guard lifeboat station because it is near Halifax and the large pleasure-boating population that sails and cruises the harbour and the coast along the eastern shore of the province. Sambro is also near the coastal waters where the inshore and offshore fishing boats come and go. Its 125-mile patrol radius allows the station a reasonable response time to all boaters. Pleasure craft sail locally from bay to bay, as well as along the entire United States and Canadian east coasts. Fishermen sail the waters from near and far, and commercial vessels traverse shipping channels up and down the coasts.

About half of all the calls to this lifeboat station are from fishing vessels experiencing engine failure, perhaps a prop failure, or a bad clutch. Other common distress calls are for boats that drift untended because the owners have fallen asleep or are drunk, and for aircraft flare sightings. Occasionally the crew rush to the aid of rescue divers in trouble. On bright days in the summer, calls for help come from sail boats de-masted or becalmed. The increase in the number of pleasure boaters has meant more work for crew at the lifeboat station.

—

"Two rescue calls, and some dumb stuff," Steve Beasely says. "Would you believe that the man with the dogs tried to get out to the island—again?"

The crew laughs. The story of the rich businessman, his dozens of dogs on Devil's Island, and the man he employs to train them, is like a soap opera, a tune-in-tomorrow-tale. The fellow tells the Coast Guard that he urgently needs to get food to the dogs, that the seas have been rough for two or three days, preventing him from getting there, even though the island is only a quarter mile from the mainland. At first try, rough waves seized the dory and capsized it; dog food scattered all over the water. Someone contacted the Coast Guard—as well as the RCMP—because they thought the man was drunk.

"The guy tried a second time," Steve says, "but the surf smashed his dory on the rocks, and once again he lost all his dog food.

"The third time, getting desperate, thinking how his dogs must be starving, he bought a rubber dinghy, once more filled it with dog food, got himself some fins and flippers, and pushed the dinghy out. He swam behind it, trying to push it to the island. But once more he got shipwrecked in the surf near the island.

"We had to go out and bring him in," says Steve. "Three times now we've had to rescue him. It's not funny anymore. The RCMP say they will tell him he's costing the taxpayers too much. Poor fellow, he was just worried about his dogs."

Chris Flemming smiles. There are always crazy people out on the sea doing crazy things, and he remembers the time he and his crew went out to the rescue the American man with his wife, children, and a dog who were setting sail for home—down the coast, they thought.

They family set sail off shore at the south end of Nova Scotia in the fog. They drifted about for a day or two and on the third day, the man was quite sure that he heard the wind roaring across the water. It seemed to him that it was off in a southerly direction. He started up his engines and headed toward it. To his horror and that of his family, he sailed instead straight onto the rocks at the southern tip of Cape Sable Island. He had headed north in the direction from which he had just come, and the noise he had heard was surf thundering on rocks. There was a crash and the sound of splintering; the sailboat shuddered and was thrown upside down in the water. Fortunately, the family and their dog all washed up on a beach, safe and sound.

"They're standing on the beach, soaking wet and wondering what to do, and they hear a vehicle," says Chris. "They see the headlights, and a four wheel vehicle comes out of the fog. The license plate says 'Mobile Oil, Texas.' They see a guy wearing a sombrero, and he's looking at them. He gets out of the truck and the family sees that he has a dark complexion. The man from the sailing boat says to himself, 'Geesus, how did I get to Texas when I left from Halifax and was heading for New York?'

"When told where he is, he says, 'Holy...my placemat didn't have Sable Island on it.'"

A Tough Decision

Peggy's Cove, Nova Scotia

Peggy's Cove sits at the very edge of the Atlantic, where its ocean currents surge restlessly upon the rocks, its granite boulders as ubiquitous as pebbles on a beach. A handful of small houses are dotted among the rocks, and here and there, one sits boldly squared on a rocky outcrop to face the Atlantic. Tourists tramp about the rocks and winding roads to peer into what they perceive as a quaint way of life, hoping, perhaps, to extract something from this timeless, idyllic, and isolated place.

The young couple jumping about the boulders down to where the tide sweeps in seem to have deliberately to have ignored the sign that warns them of rogue waves that can wash over the rocks and sweep people away or dash them against the rocky shore. The carefree pair are like so many people who pay no attention to these attempts to preserve their lives—the water today, after all, is breaking gently about these boulders, even while the air is sharp and remnants of snow lie among the rocky crevices. But it is December, a time when the tides are particularly unpredictable.

To jump from one rock to another above the swelling sea is a challenge, a risk—a game of one-upmanship. The girl is laughing, her long hair blowing about her freckled face as she calls to her companion in a voice that contains the hint of a dare: 'I've

The east coast of Nova Scotia, towards Peggy's Cove.

come out this far, see if you can catch me here.' And she dangles herself far out on the big boulder that sits slightly apart from the others. The waves break below.

Suddenly she hears his voice above the noise of the wind: "Cathy, watch it! Come back, you're too far out," and he begins the long climb down to the ocean toward her, the sea nymph on the rock. He's almost there, close to the rock above the one on which she's standing, a young man with concern on his face, entreaty in his voice. She taunts the waves, still seems to float beyond the reach of his grasp. A silence, then a shout is heard up on the cliffs, and another. Then there is silence.

Chris Flemming is bent over the rocks and boulders that crowd around his house, or perhaps it is his house that crowds onto the rocks at Ketch Harbour. A big, bright red house with patchy savanna grass that extends scarcely a few feet before reaching rocks and the sea, it is perched as close to the water as possible without being built right on it. Floor to ceiling windows open on a wide seascape that stretches out toward Sambro Harbour and the Atlantic Ocean beyond—a seascape of rocks and rocky pools created by the departing tide. Seals sun themselves on the bouldered seaweed, and ducks swim lazily in sheltered pools. Chris is acquainted with the ocean in all its moods—the fury of the complaining wind that whips the seas into moods of bitterness and cruelty, as well as its gentle lapping on the stones below his window on a summer's day. He sees, far out beyond the bay, the little red and white Coast Guard cutter plying the waters on a training exercise or patrol.

On this mid-December day, Chris is building a rock wall around his homestead. He's sweating, muscles tired and aching now. The sun is high in the sky. He should leave this, and get ready to go on duty; it's getting close to the time for the lifeboat changeover. Soon, he is in his car and on his way down the winding road to the Sambro lifeboat station fifteen minutes away. Chris is about to begin his tour of duty as search and rescue worker at the Coast Guard's lifeboat station at the mouth of this long and treacherous harbour.

The two-storey modern grey building that is the Coast Guard's base sits on a small hill above the docks where the *Sambro* is moored, above the buildings that contain their equipment and supplies. Steve Beasely, coxswain on the opposite shift, and his crew await them, and the hand-off begins from the crew that has just completed its one-week shift.

After the changeover, Chris is at the desk, establishing the schedule for the upcoming week: Thursday, joint exercises with the military where Squadron 422 helicopters and Hercules aircraft will drop targets—life rafts, pumps, SKAD, and survival kits—aiming for the Coast Guard cutter; Friday, the crew will practice lowering the rigid-hulled zodiac from the cutter; Sunday, they will practice simulated rescues in the fast rescue craft; Tuesday, if there are no rescue calls, they will practice shore-line rescues in the little boat, and practice boarding other craft from it.

Chris stares over the harbour, still with the mixture of love and angst left when his father disappeared beneath the waves all those years ago, when he was a boy of fifteen. His crew sits about the room where the desk curves in a semi-circle almost the length of the room, the far end facing the sea. The sudden shrill of the phone startles them all.

"Two people washed off the cliff at Peggy's Cove," says the radio operator from the Rescue Coordination Centre in Halifax. "The guy got his foot caught on a rock. When the sea left, the young man got himself back to shore, with help from others who were there, I believe. They say that when he last looked back out to the water, searching for his girlfriend, the last glimpse he had of her she was lying face-down in the water. He figured she was unconscious because she wasn't moving, and not responding to his calling."

"How long has she been in the water?" Chris asks, and is told about three-and-a-half hours.

Chris and his crew look at each other and then up the harbour. It is one of those December days that begins quietly, but blows up with gale-force winds and freezing spray. All craft have been warned to come in, and savvy fishing folk have long since pulled up anchor and headed for home.

"We'll go up the harbour, take a look at what it's like out there," Chris says, knowing that it is not a day for any vessel to be out on the water. The *Sambro* bucks wildly in the foaming swells as he navigates it upwind toward the mouth of the harbour. Freezing spray builds up quickly on the rails and deck, and tension builds in the crew as they look out on what Chris describes as a dead, white world. "Couldn't see nothing," he says.

"No lighthouse, no buoys, no way to tell where the shoals are. From one side of the harbour to the other—a six mile radius—we can't see nothing except the green seas coming over the bow, and it's coming on dark."

As the small cutter struggles up the harbour, a fisherman calls on the VHS radio and says, "where the hell are you guys goin'? Chris, there's nothin' on earth you guys are gonna be able to do. The wind's from the sou'east, comin' on shore. There are monstrous seas and freezin' spray. You'd best be getting' back."

"We're out of the harbour now, beyond the shoals," Chris says. "We've got all the way to the buoy beyond the harbour. Are we afraid? Well, our boat is a forty-four-foot self-righting fast boat, pretty safe. Sure, we're a bit worried. But you harness the fear, use it to do what you got to do. We get another couple of calls from other fishermen. They're asking us, 'Chris, where are you guys going?' Then the JRCC calls again to say this accident happened three hours ago. So this information becomes part of our evaluation about whether or not we should keep going."

The crew is still struggling to decide what they should do when they get a call from Halifax Harbour on channel fourteen. The operator says, 'Chris, for your own information, we've got a freezing spray warning out. It's twenty minutes to dark, and there's a fifty-five-mile-an-hour wind out there with gusts up to sixty-five. Just thought you should know.'

"It was snotty," says Chris with considerable understatement. "And cold as hell. The JRCC called back and told us, 'you decide on what you want to do, but the girl's already gone: she's dead.'"

Chris and his crew have gone up the treacherous harbour to look around, not liking at all like what they see. They discuss the possible options, and the risks there might be to themselves trying to find the body of someone they know is already dead.

"We know we will take more than two hours to get to the windward shore," Chris says. "Getting in and out of the harbour in this type of weather is extremely difficult and stressful." He explains how easy it is to misjudge a shoal, and go through a set of breakers. This is a very risky mission for them, one not to be undertaken without urgent need.

"What are we going to be able to do once we are there?" he asks. He calls the JRCC and says, "Look, we may be able to get there and look for the girl, and we may not. If we do make it, we won't be able to get back down the harbour. We'll have to stay the night somewhere along the coast."

This was a call to recover a body, and a mission the crew knows to be all but impossible, even suicidal. "But we always go, or we try to, even if it's to take a look at the conditions, even if we know it's hopeless," says Chris. "As coxswain, I decide if we will go out, but I always discuss it with the guys. This time, we stood down the job: we said no. We got out of the harbour and went back in, back to base.

"But it's hard. We are the Coast Guard. We rescue people," he adds. "You can't give up. You have to go all out to try to save the people from the sea." As he speaks, he remembers his old sorrow: his first mission years ago to search for his father. These crude attempts at recovery were but a precursor to the sophisticated efforts of the modern lifeboat station to rescue people.

Chris Flemming knows the feelings of a wife or a mother, who feels that unless the body of her loved one is recovered and buried, her hope will never die, but flicker in spurts forever. Chris knows.

The crew aboard the *Sambro* has managed the treacherous passage back to base. Chris goes home to his bright red house at the edge of the sea. He is one of those who lives within a thirty minute radius of the Coast Guard base and so is able to leave and go home.

"It's like this," says Steve. "You can't sit here in this station and say 'no,' you're not going out on a call. You always go out and look at the situation. Only a tornado would stop you going up the harbour. But once you get up out of [the harbour], you assess the situation and look at it from beyond the harbour and not from behind this desk."

"There's got to be a line where you say, you can't do that...sometimes the rescue coordination centre will make the decision for us and tell us to go home," says another crew member. "But this is our job, our mission: to rescue a person or many people, a boat, a cat or dog or any living, breathing thing. You can't sit around this station and say no."

QUEBEC, LABRADOR & HUDSON BAY

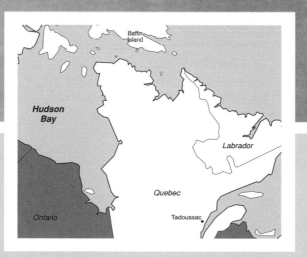

Baffin Island

Hudson Bay

Labrador

Ontario

Quebec

Tadoussac

L'Aigle's Last Voyage

Quebec, Labrador, and Hudson Bay

As they sailed past Killinek—old Port Burwell—the crew could not look upon the low-lying, sombre stretch of rock and the sheltered bay beyond without experiencing great sorrow, even goose bumps, at the memory of *L'Aigle d'Ocean*. It is here that the bones of the ancient coastal cargo ship and some of her crew lie scattered beneath a wintry sea, moved about the desolate shore by wind and currents.

It was enough to spook a person, thought Hubert Desgagnes as he stood on the deck of the Coast Guard's icebreaking ship and looked around. He had always enjoyed this indistinguishable greyish-white universe of sea and sky, distant mountain peaks and low-lying rocky shores. When sun burst through cloud, peaks of mountain ranges and sweeping glaciers on Baffin Island were cast in a surreal light that afterwards lingered on the rocky shores.

In 1975, Hubert was crew member on the *Norman McLeod Rogers* during its annual summer pilgrimage to Hudson, Ungava, and Frobisher bays, Canada's northern Arctic region that now encompasses its newest territory of Nunavut. Here, Hubert experienced life differently for a while, savouring the silence, the seeming absence of living things. But the barrenness was deceptive; if one's eyes and ears were attuned, one could detect myriad sounds of life that managed to exist among rocks and snowfields at these northeastern reaches of the Arctic.

The *Norman McLeod Rogers* was tagging polar bears on Apaktok Island in the Arctic when called to the aid of the *L'Aigle d'Ocean*.

"Coyotes, wolverine, bears, tundra wolves, lemmings, caribou, hares, and red foxes, among others," he said. "Seals, whales, and walruses:

it teems with life. And if the clouds lift, you will see all the plants that grow among the rocks." Hubert spoke of the lichen, moss, and tiny flowers that bloom in rocky crevices. This life exists, in spite of the inhospitable pre-Cambrian rock of the Canadian Shield, where permafrost exists for most of the year, and where small, low-lying plants struggle for existence. In the Arctic's brief summer, harebells, buttercups, whitebells, purple saxifrage, wintergreen, and the ubiquitous mountain aven bloom. The Arctic cotton flower, with its silky plumes, perfumes the polar desert, while in early fall, alpine bearberry, in early fall, lights up the landscape with bursts of scarlet.

"Such contrasts," Hubert said. "Mountains, and shores so low-lying that it's often hard to get a radar fix on them. In 1975, we had no global-positioning system. Up here, it's easy to feel you are alone in the universe, removed from the rest of the planet: no sounds, no lights at night. Sometimes, to break the feeling of isolation, we would listen to the radio on the HF band." Hubert paused, and then spoke of another Arctic that sprang to life when cargo ships approached Inuit villages, of local people racing out in canoes to greet the crew, looking to trade goods for cigarettes, Coke, 7-Up. Often, they sought the help of the trained nurse always present on the Coast Guard ship during long Arctic voyages. Inuit men in canoes spoke in English, and trading always began immediately: soapstone carvings, furs, sealskins, and Arctic char in return for the goods they required. On shore, women and children hovered about small houses built of granite, whalebone, and turf, conical skin tents erected alongside them for use during summer. Not far up from the riverbank stood the Hudson Bay store and a little wooden church.

"Living in tents reminds them of their nomadic inheritance," said Hubert. "They interrupt their summer and winter sealing to go on an annual inland caribou hunt, moving about a lot, but they always return to the village, to their traditional craft such as soapstone carvings." Hubert stood watching grey seas swelling gently about rocks, both jagged and smooth, that rose up from the foreshore to punctuate a desolate landscape, bleak only because of the absence of forms and structures of life familiar to him.

He thought now of how his cousin Julien Tremblay, had entered commercial maritime pursuits while he, Hubert, chose a career with the Canadian Coast Guard. They shared the same roots, family traditions, and a love of river, sea, and ships. Hubert remembered the happy times he and Julien had spent while in

Coast Guard College together. His cousin, at this very moment, was working aboard the small coastal ship *L'Aigle d'Ocean* on her very last run to the north before being sent to the scrap heap. He himself was aboard the Coast Guard's ice-breaker, patrolling and escorting ships as they passed through the ice fields. The cousins might see each other up there, a thought that gave Hubert much pleasure.

Each brief summer the Arctic sees ice melting enough to allow a few vessels safe navigation eastward to Europe or Africa. But shipping is infrequent and centred around Hudson Bay and the straits. A bulk carrier will pick up cargo in Deception Bay while another leaves the straits with a cargo of grain. Commercial freighters load shipments of iron ore and minerals from remote locations like Churchill, Manitoba, travelling eastward along the coasts of Greenland toward their destination on the other side of the world. Tankers travel north with furnace and other oil for the main Arctic settlements. In more recent years, occasional cruise ships risk traversing the Northwest Passage when ice conditions allow.

In addition to this small maritime traffic, sturdy little cargo ships such as *L'Aigle d'Ocean* ply the coasts of Labrador, bringing necessary supplies to numerous remote Inuit posts and villages dotted about Hudson and Frobisher bays. "And bringing them good money for their pay," said Hubert.

To make shipping possible during the Arctic's brief summer, the Canadian Coast Guard maintains an ice-breaking ship to assist passage of ships through the sometimes still-frozen seas. While there, crew engage in servicing navigation aids and in hydrographic and scientific surveys. This summer, the job was the tagging of polar bears on Apaktok Island.

Labrador—the name evokes images of things hidden and forbidding: pristine forests, jagged shores, with danger lurking in a secretive interior. It is a shoreline that Captain Lavoie, and all coastal pilots, avoid when sailing north. This summer, the captain kept his distance from the coast, as was his custom, pointing toward Greenland. All that was visible to the crew of the enigmatic shore were dark shapes of mountains looming high above rocky shores. Only when approaching the entrance to Hudson Strait did the captain turn east.

"Ships like to sail as far away as possible from the Labrador coast because of the powerful north-south currents," explained Hubert. "They are waters that carry much danger. Icebergs, too, can be a problem, even at this time of the year. Although most of the ice melts before it reaches the Straits of Belle Isle, there are 'bergy bits'—small tips of bergs raised above water, but hiding a large berg beneath—floating along the coast. Radar does not usually pick them up. That day we sailed north, we couldn't see much for the fog. Only when we got to the entrance to Hudson Strait could we begin to see land rising up.

"The crew is anxious at first. Then we get used to the conditions, especially when everything goes well."

As the Coast Guard ship entered Hudson Strait, the fog lifted sufficiently to allow a view of mountains on the south shores of Baffin Island. Hubert spoke of the lingering effect of ice ages and the movement of glaciers that had shaped the ranges—how the crew watched for a particular mountain peak known as the 'President's Seat' to greet them when they entered Frobisher Bay. For Hubert, the sights that most inspired him were three glaciers that swept their steep paths between Resolution Island and Frobisher Village. As the ice breaker steamed eastward, the desolate southern shores of Ungava Bay became visible at moments.

The *DesGroseilliers* on a research expedition in the Arctic.

For the crew aboard the old tug *L'Aigle d'Ocean*, that fateful last voyage had begun in pleasure and high hopes. This trip was to be the swan song of a faithful old cargo ship that had seen many seasons and endured much abuse from the elements. The crew's anticipation was dimmed only by their identification with their sturdy little ship. She lived among them, slept alongside them all winter in dry dock at the foot of their village, her bright blue hull gleaming among ice and snow piled along the riverbanks. During summers she carried them to the northern ends of the earth. But when they returned to Quebec, she would meet her end—this was her last run to the ice fields of the far north before being sent to the scrap heap.

"She belonged to us, and we to her," said Hubert. "When I was a kid, I called her 'Popeye, the sailorman's vessel,' after some crew member painted Popeye and his great love, Olive, on the forecastle!"

L'Aigle d'Ocean was built in 1919, originally a 43-metre, ocean-going tug, converted many years later to Coast Guard search and

L'Aigle d'Ocean in 1965—an ocean-going tug in her prime.

rescue cutter, eventually to be re-sold to the Desgagnes family in St. Joseph de la Rive. The family transformed her into a cargo ship and used her for trading on the St. Lawrence River and the Great Lakes, and for making occasional forays to the Arctic. In the north, she brought supplies to communities along the shores of Frobisher, Ungava, and Hudson bays.

Of the nine hardy members who sailed north that late summer most came from the small community of St. Joseph and adjacent areas; one came from Montreal. Each understood the risks of passage along the coast of Labrador and in the Arctic—even in summer. They were sailors grown tough through their gruelling work. Most knew each other, had grown up and worked together, and many were related. Each understood what he had to do, and no one grumbled.

St. Joseph de la Rive is a small village with a winter population of approximately three hundred people squeezed on an elongated strip of flat land just two thousand feet in width between the northern banks of the St. Lawrence River and the Laurentian Mountains. "A jewel between river and mountain," said Hubert. Quebec City lies over two hundred kilometres distant. From the windows of their homes, villagers look south to the glistening waters of the river as it flows swiftly by and the small island of Isle aux Coudres in its centre. Northward, mountains dressed in maples, pine and birch loom like towering shadows. The lifeblood of the village has always been the small shipyard at its feet and the host of small wooden schooners ranging in size from 90 to 130 feet.

"The river—it was always the way of living for the people," Hubert said. "Mariners, sailors, and shipbuilders...From about

1850 to the 1960s and 70s, there were many small villages all along its banks where men built boats and ships, repaired and sailed them. They transported cargo, and they traded. A captain here is also a carpenter who builds and repairs his own boat, sails with his sons, and with his family, trading all along the north shore. Mostly it's all family business."

"We knew that conditions were tough for *L'Aigle d'Ocean*," said one of her crew. "She was small and old, but she loved to dance in the rolling seas, and she would dance all the more on her trip home because she had no fuel to act as ballast, just enough to get her back home—and to the scrap heap." On this final trip, the men's fondness for their little vessel was such that they were happy for her to have this one last and glorious voyage to the north.

"When we went north," said Julien Tremblay, "we knew we were doing something useful and necessary by bringing supplies to the outposts. For ourselves, we carried everything we needed on board that little ship. In those distant places, there were no wharves where we could dock, so we had to anchor far out from shore. We also had fork lifts, a small work boat on board...you know, it was always very strenuous work."

The August run through the Straits of Belle Isle, up the coast of Labrador and across Hudson's Strait was uneventful. *L'Aigle d'Ocean*'s last port of call was to be Koartak at the extreme northwestern reaches of Ungava Bay. The sailors would then trek down the coasts once more and home to Quebec.

It was back-breaking work all that day for the crew at Koartak: in the cold and mist of early morning, they unloaded supplies onto the two barges from the hold, pushing them to shore in the work boat. Once there, they unloaded their cargo, trekked it up rocky walkways, returned to the barge and work boat, and back to a ship anchored far distant from the shore. The process was repeated again and again. By evening, the men had finished, stowed the barges back in the hold, and returned the forklift and work boat to their positions below. All felt exhausted. Captain Francouer maneuvered the old tug away from its moorings and headed east along Hudson Straits.

It was late evening as *L'Aigle d'Ocean* was steaming her way through gently rolling swells, when her captain first heard gale warnings, not something he wanted to hear. Gales, and the storms they throw up, can be particularly hazardous in the north, and the coast of Labrador is made all the more treacherous.

"Reverse polar currents exist when tide and wind oppose each other," explained Julien. "They are very swift and create waves that are high and vicious, making conditions very difficult for small cargo ships like *L'Aigle d'Ocean*—especially when she's empty."

On hearing the storm warnings, Captain Francoeur made the decision to head for shelter at Port Burwell until the storm was over. And so began a laborious journey through Hudson Straits, made increasingly slow as northwest winds increased.

"You have to have a strong heart to brave this weather, to sleep when it comes your turn and the gales are blowing," said Julien. He took to his quarters in the engine room of the tug to monitor the running of the engines, disturbed by the peculiar motion of the ship as it moved over high, rolling waves. At this same moment, the captain, also not liking the uneven rolling of his ship, sent the chief engineer to search for its cause. Suspecting that a barge had come detached, the engineer checked the interior of the hold and returned on deck, an unhappy expression on his face.

"The barges are still in place," he said quietly, "but there is more than a metre of water being displaced from one side to the other."

As he spoke, and the captain was coming about to make for port, a particularly large wave hit. The ship pitched violently. It returned to position; another wave hit, and it was thrust even further to starboard. This time, the severe list remained. Reasoning that something in the hold had to have come loose, the engineer went again to find out what was wrong. He opened a hatch to look below. Nothing in the hold was displaced, but he saw more water sloshing about.

"How on earth has it come in?" the engineer shouted as he joined Julien to frantically work the pumps so that all the compartments could be cleared. The two men worked furiously, but water seemed to pour in all the faster. Sweating and anxious, one of them leapt up on deck and to the bridge to inform the captain.

When he heard the news, Captain Francouer immediately understood that his ship was in imminent jeopardy. Quietly, and with no betrayal of emotion, he picked up the radio telephone and broadcast an appeal for help, comforted by the knowledge that the Coast Guard ice-breaker was anchored just eight miles distant at Port Burwell.

His words were terse: "Mayday! We're sinking fast. Come quickly!" He then ordered his crew to prepare to abandon a ship that now listed from twenty-five to forty degrees.

"Three thousand metres to land, and we can't make it." His voice had a sharp edge. "Put the starboard lifeboat into the sea at once."

A cold, hard rain had begun to fall, stinging the men's faces. A bitter wind whipped them as they silently prepared to lower one of the two lifeboats. As soon as the boat left its cradle on the starboard side, it lurched and rolled, and crew members struggling with the pulley cord could not control its descent. Mid-point from ship railing to water's surface, the lifeboat suddenly nose-dived into the sea. The moment it hit, it began rapidly to fill with water. Now it was every man for himself—one by one, the crew jumped. The lifeboat might be half-filled with water, but the men knew it would float because of its watertight pontoon. Six men half-fell into its interior, but their relief was short-lived. As the old cargo ship rolled, an extension of its hull struck the lifeboat, which capsized into Arctic seas that reached a summer temperature of just two degrees.

The men—Julien Tremblay, cook Marcel Tremblay, sailor Gilles Baril, third officer Pierre-Paul Bouchard and the two Parc cousins—were flung into the sea. Each knew they would survive for scarcely thirty minutes in the frigid waters. Marcel Tremblay seemed to hover at the surface of the water for a moment, and stared with beseeching eyes into those of Julien Tremblay, who clung to the side of the lifeboat. Julien willed himself to help his mate.

"My heart was willing my arms and legs to help him," Julien said. "But my legs wouldn't move, and my hands were frozen...I couldn't do anything with them; my arms, they didn't, they wouldn't, move..."

Marcel disappeared quietly beneath the water. His mates believed that he was wearing only an ordinary keyhole lifejacket, perhaps not fastened properly. Gilles Baril, deciding to swim for the rope ladder on the stern of the ship, was caught by ocean currents and never made it. Only the captain and first mate Jeannot Belley remained aboard, clinging to the doomed *L'Aigle d'Ocean* as she continued to roll.

"I just willed myself to stay alive," Julien said. "I was in love with my girlfriend, Sylvie, and engaged to be married to her. I saw her, smiling at me, heard her voice talking to me. Thinking about her gave me courage, gave me the power to do something more—I told myself it was not yet my time to die...the four men

L'Aigle d'Ocean: this is not the way she's supposed to sail.

who drowned, they had no woman in their lives, and perhaps that made a difference for them."

The Canadian Coast Guard ship *Norman McLeod Rogers* had been in the Arctic since June on its annual summer pilgrimage. It had many responsibilities, but its primary purpose was to escort vessels traversing northern seas: a search and rescue ship on standby. This was an unusual season of little ice, and the captain found his assistance not required. Not a problem, as he had many other jobs in the north. Some of these included hydrographic surveys, and on this particular afternoon he had steamed his ship out of Frobisher Bay to head for Akpatok Island, to begin tracking polar bears.

On this particular day, conditions were mild and the journey pleasant, but Captain Lavoie, like his counterpart on *L'Aigle d'Ocean*, also heard warnings of gale-force winds approaching and decided to find shelter until the storm had passed.

"Things will not be pretty along the coasts of Labrador," he said. "We should make for Port Burwell to wait for calmer seas."

"We called this place Cain Land—after Abel and Cain," said Hubert of their sheltering place. "Nothing here—just rock, smooth, because of the movement of the ice that acts like sandpaper on it. Nothing but a big antenna for marine radio communications and the Killinek radio. There had once been a small Inuit village at this spot, but the people were moved away. What it does have is a very small bay for shelter."

On arrival, the crew dropped anchor and settled in. An uneventful night passed. In the early dawn, as a grey light flickered across the sky, severe weather suddenly struck. The ship began swinging on her anchor line, still sheltered by the bay. The seas beyond the point rapidly grew into large swells and an ice-cold rain began to fall.

At the time the *Norman McLeod Rogers* first began swinging on her anchor line, Captain Lavoie received the urgent summons for help from *L'Aigle d'Ocean*. He stood, a lone figure on the bridge of his ship as the gale raged beyond the bay, thinking fast. He began issuing urgent orders to start up the ship's engines, heave the anchors, and prepare to depart. During the twenty minutes it took his crew to make these preparations, the captain summoned his helicopter pilot:

"Can you fly over and get the position of the sinking ship?" he asked. The pilot agreed, although his single-engine craft was designed only for reconnaissance and the carrying of personnel over short distances. It was not intended for search and rescue missions. Nonetheless, he flew in search of the cargo ship.

As the 295-foot *Norman McLeod Rogers* left Port Burwell for the straits, she began rolling from twenty-five to forty feet, not dangerous, but very unpleasant. Crew members were flung about and had difficulty performing their duties.

At this moment, Captain Lavoie lost radio communication with *L'Aigle d'Ocean* and wondered if the ship had already gone down. But moments later, the voice of its captain came, in broken sounds, over the radio waves: "lifeboat overturned and four men hanging onto it. Two missing."

Hearing this, Captain Lavoie radioed his helicopter pilot and requested he return. "Can you carry an inflatable raft aboard your aircraft?" he asked.

"Yes," said the pilot.

"I want you to carry one of my mates with you, so you can drop the life raft."

"Right," answered the pilot.

"No, don't do that," pleaded the flight engineer who was standing beside them. "Keep your officers with you, captain, you'll need them. I'll go with the pilot in the 'copter." The engineer didn't know it at the time, but this was a fateful request.

Without a moment's delay, the pilot and the ship's flight engineer flew together in rain and poor visibility toward *L'Aigle d'Ocean*, carrying a small, inflatable life raft, while the Coast Guard ship steamed toward the site as rapidly as it dared in the gale-force conditions. Because the *Rogers* remained in radio contact with his counterpart in the cargo ship, Lavoie knew it was still partially afloat, and he prayed that his helicopter pilot would manage to locate the sinking ship once more and drop the life raft to the men in the sea.

The sailors clutching the overturned lifeboat watched the inexorable sinking of their cargo ship, remembering at moments how this was supposed to be its last glorious run to the ice fields. None had entertained the thought that she would founder in frigid seas and storms far from home. At this moment, to the men, she still had claim to life: her main deck disappeared periodically under water but returned each time to the surface. The men in the sea swam back to her when she listed forty-five degrees and bulkwarks railings hit the water, clambering up her sides, and to the dry portside.

Captain Francoeur and second mate Jeannot Belley, who had clung to the outside of the hull, now found themselves joined by five of their crew. Pierre-Paul Bouchard looked at his mates, and—ignoring their protestations—forced two of the frost-bitten men to move about the sloping hull to try and prevent them from ending up as frozen corpses. Only Richard Pare, too cold and exhausted to join his friends, huddled in the interior of the hull, trying to warm himself.

"Radar contact thirty-five degrees off the starboard..." Gerard Belley, first officer aboard the *Norman McLeod Rogers*, saw an echo on the radar screen as the ice-breaker bucked its way through heavy seas, getting closer to the stricken ship. After what seemed like a lifetime to the *Rogers* crew, the dark specter of the doomed ship loomed out of rain and mist. It was twenty-five minutes after two in the afternoon. The crew began to make out dark figures on the portside. The ship's radar antenna veered, and lights flickered. The tired old tug listed at more than sixty degrees; they saw that she was doomed.

"She won't be coming back," said one of the men in a low voice.

Captain Lavoie, all the while, had been worrying about his helicopter pilot. As his ship approached the wrecked *L'Aigle d'Ocean*, the welcome sound of the pilot's voice came over the radio.

"Roger, this is Charlie Gulf Bravo Zulu. I seem to be having a little bit of a problem; I have to land," said the faint voice of the pilot, not sparing words to explain.

"I'll change course so you can land on deck," said Captain Lavoie.

"No, no, it'll just waste time." The pilot's voice was urgent. "They need you badly up there: some of the men are still in the water, and the old ship, she hasn't got long to go. Just give me some bearings, and I'll find somewhere to land. I'll wait for you."

Reluctantly, the captain gave him his bearings and the pilot flew off in wind and rain over hostile seas, toward shores that were only partially visible to him. Captain Lavoie knew that the little single-engine craft was outside its normal operations, flying in severe weather conditions over inhospitable terrain. Trying to put his concerns for the pilot out of his mind, he continued steering his ship toward *L'Aigle d'Ocean*, seeking to come near, but avoid a collision that would destroy the air bubble keeping the tug afloat. The voice of Captain Francoeur reached him as he circled.

"Send us a large life boat," was the terse request.

"We could see figures; we knew two men had been lost, but didn't know who. I kept thinking about my cousin Julien. All we could do was try and come closer, wave our hands in the air to tell them we were coming for them, encourage them. Even though the captain used full throttle to try to maintain his position, we kept drifting away. Our hearts were jumping in our chests, adrenaline pumping...We saw that their ship was capsizing fast, saw the figures huddled on deck, saw all the debris floating on the water—propane gas tanks, forty-five gallon drums, bits of food..."

Captain Lavoie's circling of the *L'Aigle d'Ocean* seemed the only way to prevent drifting caused by fierce winds and strong currents, the only means of remaining parallel to the cargo ship. His bosun took a gun and throwing apparatus and shot a line, with the lifeboat attached, to the men on the tug. The sound came like a violent clap of thunder as it shot out across the sky. At the same moment, a last puff of black smoke blew from the tug's chimney; its radar went blank, and the ancient cargo ship died.

The survivors managed to take the lifeboat-line that opened between the two ships and held it with frozen fingers until it was drawn against their vessel. But the length of rope connecting the lifeboat to the Coast Guard ship was too short to maintain sufficient distance between them to prevent collision. The crew on the *Norman McLeod Rogers*, satisfied that they would not lose the boat, cut the line.

Meanwhile, the captain of the Coast Guard ship struggled against wind and current to remain in position, the tug moving in one direction, the *Norman McLeod Rogers* in another, still in imminent danger of colliding. With the tug positioned ninety degrees toward the Coast Guard ship, the men on the hull began to jump, one by one, into the lifeboat. Seven men prepared to jump—no, six. Without a whisper, Richard Pare fell into the water and disappeared beneath its surface.

Hubert's cousin, Julien Tremblay, was the first to leap. Next came Pierre Hamel, who fell into the water. With superhuman effort, Julien struggled with hands stiffened with cold to pull Pierre into the raft. Andre Pare, cousin to Richard, made his jump, but he also fell into the sea; those already in the lifeboat shouted as they leaned far out, trying desperately to grasp him. But Andre, with frozen limbs, and weakened from the cold, could do nothing to help himself; he too, slipped quietly beneath the waves.

It was the chief engineer's turn to jump. Andre Pare was a heavy man, he was reluctant to throw himself into the boat because he feared he would injure the others in it. He made his decision to leap close to the lifeboat, but not in it, one arm outstretched so he could haul himself inside. He looked at the cold grey swells of the heaving sea, hesitated, then made his leap. At that very moment, a rolling wave thrust the lifeboat away from the tug and the engineer found himself about ten feet distant from it, rather than the one foot he had planned. He flailed about in the water, visible one minute, only to disappear the next: completely exhausted, he had not the energy to swim to the lifeboat. His mates watched in horror as the currents pushed him away. They watched him slip beneath the surface one last time. His mates searched the swells, but in vain. His cousin, assumed to be still inside the sinking ship, never did appear; his mates believed he had fallen into the water as *L'Aigle d'Ocean* sank on her side. Both cousins were lost in frigid Arctic waters.

"You don't accept that people are dead until you see them face down in the water," said Hubert. "It was a big shock—two dead and two missing—very hard to accept when you don't see them, and it was hard to see anything at all because of a heavy mist and rain."

Maintaining tradition, the captain of *L'Aigle d'Ocean* was the last to leave his stricken ship. He had been sitting on his upside down vessel, legs around the keel, encouraging his men as they leapt from the hull. He too made his jump. It was a confusion of men in a lifeboat, their shouts heard echoing across the sea. Euphoria erupted at first that there were five of them safely on board, but wild panic a moment later as they saw their lifeboat being drawn inexorably toward the sinking ship and its downward draft, bound to it by the towline. None carried a knife. The captain looked at the wild eyes of his men, grabbed the rope that held them fast, and bit into it with his false teeth, bit until it frayed and broke. With a shout of triumph, the men paddled furiously away from their doomed ship.

Like Lot's wife, at some safe distance, they turned to look back. The old cargo ship had rolled on her side more than 180 degrees, and, in final indignity, turned completely upside down. For a moment, a large part of her hull remained above the water. Its crew, and the men aboard the *Norman McLeod Rogers*, watched in awe and sorrow as she sank slowly by her stern, her bow lifted to a sullen sky. *L'Aigle d'Ocean* disappeared in a fury of white foam.

The crew from the Coast Guard ship, only five hundred feet away when the cargo ship sank, one by one rapidly pulled her crew from their lifeboat and on board ship. Crew with first-aid training immediately began treating the hypothermic and frostbitten men. Hubert's cousin Julien, one of the first to be pulled aboard the Coast Guard ship, stood bedraggled and haggard, then dropped to his knees and kissed the deck, giving thanks to an Almighty who had spared him his life—this time.

Captain Lavoie began maneuvering the ship in a search for the bodies of men who had slipped into the water. All the while, he was haunted by images of his helicopter pilot. He had received no further radio contact from him. His crew, too, were uneasy about the two men in the little single-engine helicopter. It did not return, and there was no communication from the pilot. Much as they worried, the crew's first responsibility was to search for possible survivors in the water. Their search located only two of the sailors, the Pare brothers, whose lifeless bodies were found in the wreckage. The focus then shifted to the helicopter pilot and flight engineer.

The crew studied the area indicated on the craft's distress signal and made for the shores of Port Burwell, where it seemed the helicopter pilot had headed. When darkness fell, the search, out of necessity, was put on hold, until the next morning.

As dawn broke, seven crew members left the Coast Guard ship to conduct a shoreline search. At ten, the bosun called his captain to tell him he had found wreckage of the helicopter, but not the men. Upon hearing this, the captain fainted; he had not lost a crew member in twenty-seven years. On board, a long silence prevailed. Eventually, with great sorrow in their hearts, the crew

Four ships at port in Quebec City.

on the *Norman McLeod Rogers* steamed away from the last resting place of the two brave men. The Coast Guard ice-breaker continued its responsibilities as a scientific survey ship, but the tracking of polar bears was abandoned, and the crew finally returned to Quebec City on October 3.

Among the factors that may have caused *L'Aigle d'Ocean* to sink was the possibility that the ship struck ice during the night. Or perhaps, during unloading, a barge struck the hull and punctured it. No definitive answer was ever provided.

The village of St. Joseph de la Rive has been forever altered by this tragedy. Captain Francoeur quit his job on disembarking and never returned to sea. He died seven years later. Julien Tremblay came back to his village and to his beloved Sylvie, married her, and remained largely on shore—not because he was afraid to make distant sea voyages, but because he did not want to be absent from his young wife for so many months of the year. He teaches technology at a local high school, works on shore, and makes short sea voyages during his vacation.

For Hubert, the legacy of the tragedy was a powerful wish to do something that would involve the saving of lives. Early in his career, he became interested in search and rescue activities because of a few tragic maritime misadventures near his home village in the mid 1960s. He was fascinated by the types of marine emergencies a mariner could meet, and how these could be prevented.

"If you have a fire in your house, you take your children and a few things if you can, and get out on the street," he said. "In a ship, you cannot walk away from the 'fire.' You must find its source and fight it. You are alone like this. I decided early that I should try to find a way to help mariners..."

Other survivors have returned to sea, but the blow to the village at the loss of its people was severe: survivors had been mates and friends of those who died. They had socialized with each other about the village, often meeting in the snack bar, with its jukebox, at the edge of the river, or at each other's homes during evenings. The sense of loss was pervasive and profound in a village sustained by

Hubert Desgagnes, commanding officer of the Quebec City Marine Rescue Centre.

blood ties, friendship, and family tradition—"with a little competition thrown in," added Hubert.

He speaks of men who have great pride in ships that are an extension of themselves; pride in the unique character of each ship's shape, design, and colours, pride in the manner in which the men care for them. Hubert explains how the owners of *L'Aigle d'Ocean* had wanted their ship to sail both winter and summer, but because she was an aging vessel, decided to sail her only during clement weather. And even though the summer of 1975 was to be the final run of her life, they had taken the trouble to remove winter rust and re-painted her, such was the pride in their ship. "It was about it being their own ship," he said. "and not someone else's."

Where the
Rivers Run Wild

Tadoussac, Quebec

The rivers hum with mid-summer maritime traffic. On the riverbanks, wild flowers bloom among the pine trees that occasionally crowd the shores. The population of the many small villages lining the river's course doubles every summer with visitors from near and far. They come to the place in the Gulf of St. Lawrence where three bodies of water meet: the mighty St. Lawrence River in its downstream flow toward the Atlantic Ocean, the Saguenay, and the estuary of the St. Lawrence.

Tadoussac is the chief attraction to those who are drawn here during the summer months, especially from Quebec, Montreal, and France. But by September, tour boats begin to call from the Far East. They come to this small village perched on the north shores of the St. Lawrence River at the juncture where its salty flow pauses to mingle with the cool, clear waters of the Saguenay. Tadoussac is old, quaint, and picturesque with a tall cliff rising up from the small bay on one side, while the more gentle slope on the other accommodates a marina, and the Canadian Coast Guard base. On the hills above, staring out across the gulf, old colonial buildings sit in languid elegance, their English owners often still in residence. Its one hotel is very old, and draws crowds largely from the upper echelons of local society.

On the waters surrounding Tadoussac, summer crowds imbibe the beauty of the place and clamber aboard tour boats to watch the blue and beluga whales disport themselves. They come to fish, sail, and picnic on the riverbanks. It is a corner of the world that is a little off the well-worn tourist paths, secluded, different. Boaters mingle with commercial traffic that plies the water routes to create a busy river scene.

At Levis, not far from Quebec City, two middle-aged couples are about to begin a nautical vacation. They work hard, and are anxious to make the most of their time off. They have prepared well by taking sailing classes. A leisurely trip has been planned, a slow sail down river making stops at Berthier-sur-Mer and l'Ile-aux-Coudres. Their ultimate destination is Tadoussac, where they will head the morning after their arrival at Rivière-du-Loup, just twenty-one nautical miles distant. It is the first boating foray of the season for all four, and on July 18 they sail downriver in a twenty-six-foot Contessa sailboat with keel, a single mast, and an inboard motor. Perhaps because of the short distance involved, they take with them only a compass and radio. They set out without life raft or dingy, without radar or GPS. Their flares are forgotten in the trunk of their car.

They arrive at Rivière-du-Loup in the evening where they stay the night. They hear a radio broadcast that warns of heavy rain for the next day, but prepare for departure anyway, against the advice of those at the yacht club who suggest they wait. At eight in the morning, visibility is excellent and winds are blowing at 10 to 15 knots. For these people, vacation time is short; they will not be deterred from a journey to the opposite riverbank downstream.

Perhaps they didn't know about the moods of the river, of the micro climate of this area, or of the extensive shoals that line the shore. Had they known, it should have given them pause. As well, there was evidence all around of the recent flooding of the Saguenay River that has spilled into the St. Lawrence. The rivers are littered with debris: wooden objects, docks, verandahs, roofs and lamp poles. But this day, a weak sun shines, and the atmosphere seems calm and clear. The vacationers are not to know that, following the severe flooding of the Saguenay River caused by the malfunction of its dam system, this region is about to suffer catastrophic rainstorms of such proportions that the provincial government will call it a disaster area.

The skipper's wife disembarks at Berthier-sur-Mer; perhaps she has premonitions of disaster. The remaining three in their sailboat begin their fateful river crossing around eleven in the morning. By noon, a heavy rain has begun to fall, fog envelops them, and winds become brisk. The ferry returning from Rivière-du-Loup reports overcast skies, visibility of half a mile, and winds that gust at 35 to 40 knots.

The change descends suddenly, violently, like a giant fist thrust in the face: by four in the afternoon, heavy rains and fog have obliterated the landscape, and boaters remaining on the river seem to sail, phantom-like, on an eerie sea.

The skipper in his sailboat finds himself with no visual reference. And without radar, GPS, or any electronic equipment but compass and radio, he feels lost and helpless in the thundering conditions. When a rock shoal looms out of the thick fog, he finds himself face-to-face with the dangers of continuing to try to cross, and he changes course, to head for Cap a L'Aigle, west along the St. Lawrence River. But, unknowingly, he has steered his boat inside the treacherous shoal area, and now its keel strikes hard rock. He loses his rudder and punctures the bottom of the boat. Above the noise of rain and wind is heard the ripping sound of fibreglass, like a fingernail run down a chalkboard. The boat will no longer respond; the skipper cannot steer. He issues a Mayday call just after two-thirty in the afternoon; he radios a message that he cannot see land, any of the navigation buoys, or the powerful beam from the Haut Fond Prince lighthouse that he supposes is nearby.

"We're hard aground on the reef, please hurry up."

The skipper has made the call on channel 16 VHF, where it is picked up by the Coast Guard radio operator in Quebec. The call is acknowledged at once and the operator alerts the Marine Rescue Subcentre (MRSC). Andre Hovington, SAR duty officer, at once issues an all-ship broadcast and immediately notifies the crew of the SAR cutter, the *Isle Rouge*.

Steven Neatt, the commanding officer on duty at the Coast Guard lifeboat station at Tadoussac, is mid-way through his three weeks on duty, and on half-hour standby. He's seated at his desk near the window in the base's small trailer—a mobile home on the banks of the Saguenay River. From this vantage point, he can see the old hotel, the church, and to the end of the wharf where the whale-watching tour boats tie up. But not this afternoon: it's beginning to seem that another flood of biblical proportions is upon them, although the source is different. Visibility is reported as being between zero and twelve hundred feet, the tide is rising, and winds are in excess of twenty-five knots. Steven and his crew know that some time before the day is over, they will be out on the rivers to pluck people from them. He hears that the ferry returning from the north shore of the river to Rivière-du-Loup is reporting an overcast sky, visibility of half a mile, rain, and North-easterly winds blowing up to 20 to 25 knots. By four in the afternoon, the rain is hard, insistent, and blinding. Wind gusts up to 35 to 45 knots. The pilot of the ferry that connects the riverbanks cancels the last crossing. But for one tour boat plying its way upbound, it is almost too late: weather conditions have sent its bow plunging into the sea; it loses all four life rafts and suffers structural damage.

As soon as the Mayday call is received, the Coast Guard activates the resources it has in the vicinity: the lifeboat crew in their cutter, the *Isle Rouge*, and the CCGS *George R. Pearkes*. Each is tasked to go to the aid of the distressed sailboat, to search the river and its banks until they find it. At this moment, the big buoy tender is seventy-five miles east and in the process of escorting another disabled sailboat upbound near Quebec City. It is requested immediately to change course and head in the direction of the sailboat.

The commanding officer of the *Isle Rouge* and his crew, aware of neither the hopelessness of their task, nor the seriousness of the call, nevertheless steam out from the dock within five minutes of receiving their summons.

"We're out in the river and it was like someone pulled this weather out of a hat," Steven Neatt says of that day. "Sudden gale-force winds and torrential rain and fog—just like soup. On radar, all we can see is a solid white image that blocks out all lights and buoys—very unusual weather conditions. All the small craft on the river are scurrying back to shore. But we have a big problem: we're out on the river, tasked to find a sailboat, but have no precise position for it. Eventually Quebec City radio station's direction finder (DF) antenna nabs an approximate location for us, and I get a second position on my own DF. Then we head up river to begin our search."

All through the long afternoon, Steven Neatt and his crew continue a methodical search along a five-metre depth line parallel to the shoal. Five rescue workers stand on the bridge, straining through fog and rain to find a sinking sailboat, or any part of it. The commanding officer navigates, the first mate is involved in communication, radar, and the DF, two seamen are on navigational look-out, and the chief engineer attends to the mechanical operation of the cutter and acts as additional look-out.

"Our last radio communication with the sailboat is at ten minutes after three," Steven says. "The skipper tells us that water is coming up in his boat; that he has no life raft or dingy, just life jackets...

"'Just hang on to the boat, stay with it as long as you can,'" Steven advises. "'We're doing our very best to find you and get to you.'"

"This area around here has had a nasty reputation ever since Jacques Cartier discovered it." Hubert Desgagnes, commanding officer of the Quebec City Marine Rescue Centre says afterwards. He explains that its sandbank, completely dry at low tide, extends two and a half miles off shore, and three and a half miles wide, giving a shoal line of nearly ten nautical miles. Inside it are rocks and shoals called Batture aux Alouettes. The sheer number of marine casualties prompted the government to position five navigation buoys and a lighthouse, considered to have the most powerful beam of any in the country, along this stretch of the river.

"Another thing: the Gulf of St. Lawrence has its own micro climate," Steven adds. "What applies elsewhere does not necessarily pertain here; this place has a life force all its own. Where the two rivers meet in the gulf, there is a mingling of warm salt water with cold, clear, river water. Then there is the estuary that has yet a different water temperature. It creates fog. You get three bodies of water meeting, tides going one way and winds another. Then you can get what's known as rip tides: one mass of water rises, another ebbs, winds change, and powerful currents rage at five to six knots...it can create whirlpools, and cause all kinds problems."

The *Isle Rouge* struggles on in the wind, rain, and clashing tides. Its five-man crew remains on the bridge, straining their eyes to catch a glimpse of something, anything. They fire flares, hoping that the people in the shipwrecked sailboat will see them. Nothing. Only the sound of wind and wave, the thunderous noise of rain on the deck, and on the water that heaves all about them.

Andre Hovington, Hubert Desgagnes, together with Marie Gagnon, who assists in the coordination of this rescue mission, are faced with three options: to assume that the sailboat is where they judge it to be, and that it is only poor visibility that prevents the cutter's crew from seeing it; assume that the boat has run aground on another reef six miles or more west of the position given, and nearer the middle of the river; or assume it is aground on a third reef east of the search area. Because the DF appears to be accurate, the third option is dismissed.

All craft in the river have now been requested to assist in the search for the hapless sailboat: among others, the *Famille Dufour ll,* the *Roman Star,* and the *Blue Moon* divert from their course to help search the river. They find nothing; the sailboat seems to have vanished off the face of the river. The *George R. Pearkes*, so far distant, has attempted to send the Bell 206-L helicopter it carries on board, have it fly low over rock and shoal and sandbank, but the small helicopter cannot get airborne in the gusting wind, fog, and torrential rain. Meanwhile, a Canadian Forces Griffon helicopter is tasked out of Bagotville to help. Its pilot valiantly searches for more than an hour in conditions that often exceed its safety margins, but locates nothing.

Conditions worsen. Parks Canada authorities have sent all vessels still out in the river and gulf to help in the search, but they have had to retreat to shore, in danger themselves in the furious tempest.

The crew in the *Isle Rouge* are cheered now to hear the sound of another aircraft. A Hercules fixed-wing military aircraft sweeps low in this foggy no-man's-land, hoping to catch a glimpse of the boat, or the people aboard it. But, all too soon, the noise of its engines are heard roaring off, diverted to another boat in distress on the north shore.

It's late afternoon now, and the dispirited crew aboard the *Isle Rouge* fear the worst for the people in the sailboat. Their own search has not turned up anything, and even if they were to come upon the three people now, it's likely too late: the lack of communication from them since mid-afternoon is ominous.

"We keep hoping that the helicopter will find something, because it flies low over the water, not much above the cargo ship that's trying to help," says Steven. "But the conditions make it much too dangerous for the helicopter, and it prepares to fly back."

Suddenly tensions rise in the cutter when one of the crew spots something in the water, floating near the five-metre depth line parallel to the shoal. They manage to hook it and get it aboard, only to find themselves in possession of a cockpit cushion. It's after five in the afternoon, and this is the first piece of wreckage discovered from the sailboat. About twenty minutes later, the crew picks up something else: a white life ring that bobs about among a pile of other objects, including a cockpit door, and pieces of fibreglass. Hope dies within the crew members that the three sailors will be recovered alive, and there is a sudden silence aboard the cutter. Crew members avoid each other's eyes, stare out over the river, each locked into his own thoughts, struggling with this knowledge.

Conditions on the river worsen suddenly, and Steven now

finds himself struggling for control of his cutter in wind, rain, and swirling tides. Water streams over the bridge, "like a sheet of white ice," he says. "It just hangs there, and it's like time is standing still. We're being knocked around, our cutter pitching up to our second radar antenna in water. When we submarine under, none of us believes we'll be coming up again. Waves are as high as five meters, and winds gust to thirty-five knots at water level, and to sixty knots at three hundred feet. We're moving very slowly.

"It's the only time in my fifteen-year marine career that I've felt worried that we might not make it" he pauses. "It's not often I worry about my ship. But I'm worried this night—worried about our safety. I hang on, but I'm weighing in my mind if I should call it quits. I drop an electronic marker in the water to track the drift. As I'm doing this, I see the *George R. Pearkes* steaming up to relieve us. We can go home, back to base."

Steven now attempts to turn his cutter and head northeast toward Tadoussac, but it's caught again in river currents that are in fierce turmoil swirling one hundred and eighty degrees. With the vessel listing close to forty-five degrees, he cannot steer the rudder and relies on his engines. The ship does not respond, and so begins another almost fatal roll.

The Coast Guard crew in their cutter arrives back at base close to midnight, only to be called out again to the rescue of a fishing boat that has broken from its moorings.

Out on the river, the Coast Guard buoytender has become the on-scene commander of the search effort. It remains searching all the long night, and continues following the electronic marker until the next morning. Eventually it locates other floating wreckage on the southern banks of the river, pin-pointed there by electronic software.

It is a very short night's rest for the Coast Guard crew from the *Isle Rouge*; they are up again at five the following morning to begin once more a search for the hapless sailboat and its occupants.

One day of severe rain is not enough: on Saturday, July 20, the storms continue unabated. Severe and catastrophic rainstorms devastate the Saguenay region, causing havoc and tragic loss of life on, and near, the river. All Coast Guard and other resources available are given over to the search for the three people in the sailboat. Hopes are not entirely dimmed that one of them might miraculously be alive. In rain, wind and fog, police officers from the Surete du Quebec, firemen from the nearby small village of Baie St. Catherine, and Parks Canada authorities comb the river banks up and downstream where it is judged that anything floating will have been pushed by wind and tide. In the air, a military Hercules plane from Greenwood flies as low as it dares, and a helicopter swoops low over rock and shoal. On the water, the *George R. Pearkes* searches a wide area of the shoreline that has been identified as being where wreckage has floated with wind and currents. The crew aboard the *Isle Rouge*, too, continues to comb the river and its banks.

Suddenly, the cutter's radio crackles to life; Mireille Samson, the helicopter pilot, tells them she has spotted the body of a man face down in the water, not far distant from the *Isle Rouge*.

As the *Isle Rouge* comes close to the body, Steven asks the commanding officer of the *George R. Pearkes*, if he should pick it up. The crew is told that the *George R. Pearkes* will be on scene within ten to fifteen minutes, and they will send their zodiac to retrieve it.

Before noon that second day, weather conditions force the suspension of all search efforts. There is even danger to those who toil on ground because it is no longer solid, but slips and moves beneath the feet of the rescuers.

Sunday dawns as yet another day of remorseless rain, and because of the emergencies in the Chicoutimi area, only the military aircraft Rescue 314, and the Coast Guard's light helicopter continue the air search. For the crew aboard the *Isle Rouge* and the *George R. Pearkes*, it is yet one more day of unremitting search efforts on the surface.

The search is put on reduced status at sunset that day, the whereabouts of the remaining two occupants of the sailboat still unknown.

On July 27, around noontime, a walker discovers the body of the woman who had been aboard the sailboat. She still wears her life jacket. It is not until September 3 that a third lifejacket from the sailboat is found adrift near les Escoumins, twenty-five miles west of the site where the accident occurred.

Hubert Desgagnes, commanding officer of the Quebec City Marine Rescue Centre, speaks about this attempted rescue and the toll it took on the Coast Guard crew who went without sleep, and feared, at times, for their own lives.

"But these were not the things that traumatized them the most," he said. "They are accustomed to danger and little sleep.

The most difficult thing was that they usually find people alive. It is hard to pull dead people from the water, to know that they were not able to save the life of that person. It takes its toll; often it's people they know, have just spoken to…they establish a relationship…they have hope that they can save this person."

There is further trauma for the crew of the *Isle Rouge*. The MRSC conducts an inquiry into the rescue effort. Questions are asked and accountability is demanded. As torrential rain continues to deluge the river and the earth about it, as lives are lost, homes destroyed, and unimaginable damage sustained, the search and rescue workers sit before a Coast Guard board of inquiry. They are required to listen to a tape-recording of the communication that had taken place during all the rescue efforts to remind them of all the details of the event. Steven cannot make it through the recording, so intense is the trauma he experiences as he re-lives that nightmare on the river.

"This job is often unforgiving," he says laconically.

The crew is found to be faultless in their conduct of the search, and counselling is offered to help them deal with the stress.

GREAT LAKES

Ontario

Quebec

Thunder Bay

Lake Superior

Lake Huron

Tobermory

Ottawa ✪

Kingston

Lake Ontario

Toronto

St. Catharines

Port Dover

Lake Michigan

Lake Erie

Amherstburg

Destruction
on Lake Erie

Port Dover, Ontario

Yesterday's hardy inhabitants once scattered themselves along the northern shores of Lake Erie from Port Dover to Point Pelee, in small villages among old forests bordering to the water's edge, building shipping centres at Ports Stanley and Burwell. Pilots sailing these inland seas in schooners and steamers suffered frequent and disastrous shipwreck, often as they approached the old ports. The waters of Lake Erie gained a reputation as treacherous. In the words of Dwight Boyer, author of *Strange Adventures of the Great Lakes*, "it is doubtful if any coast—westward from the desolate hook of Long Point—has claimed as many sailing craft over a relatively short span of years as the sixty mile stretch along the Ontario shore between Clear Creek and Point aux Pins."

In the first three centuries of sail by schooners, then by steamers, salvage companies played a pivotal role in the rescue and recovery of ships in distress. Before any government had organized lifeboat stations and systems of lighthouses, it was the vessels of opportunity—one ship coming to the aid of another that attempted rescue work. Ship's captains risked their schedules, the lives of passengers and crew, and, in the case of a private commercial ship, their profits, to do so.

The northern shores of Lake Erie sweep in a wide and gentle curve, as if to invite mariners toward its shores, presenting calm inland seas in the lee of the land, once rimmed by great forests of chestnut and oak. The lake then, as today, has a propensity for a sudden and violent shifting of northerly winds to the southwest and sometimes to the southeast, transforming benign waters into an unexpected death trap. It is said that scarcely one tenth of the time are the lake's waters calm. A wind might blow from the west causing lake waters to drop here dramatically, only to rise four feet or more at the eastern end of the lake. Winds change direction abruptly and frequently, to create confused seas that hit a vessel from every direction all at once. Sometimes there was no escape: a hostile shore almost upon them, mariners found themselves without sufficient sea room to claw their way out from the land. Seas that rose up abruptly in fury were a serious threat to captains of schooners attempting to haul around into the wind. Many vessels broached-to, capsized, and were lost.

Danger came not only from the punishing seas, but also from the land itself. Pretty to look upon, it was, in reality, a coastline of disaster. Sudden, violent, shifting winds blew an unwary vessel onto hidden sandbars, pounding it to death in thundering surf that thrashed itself halfway up the bluffs.

In this era of sail, there were only two significant ports along the dreaded coast: Port Burwell, twelve miles west of Long Point, and Port Stanely, almost the same distance west again, where Kettle Creek meets up with Lake Erie. These ports were busy with the shipping and receiving of coal, pig iron, fruit, general merchandise, and lumber. Subsequently, they became terminals for railroad car ferries.

In time, the focus shifted away from these old ports. Ships no longer call regularly and other centres of activity have sprung up at Port Dover and in Amherstburg. It is here, at these small villages, that the Coast Guard has placed lifeboat stations staffed by skilled search and rescue workers to serve the largely pleasure-boating public who crowd the waters of the lake. Early sailors could only have dreamed that such help might have been available to them.

Today, on the northern shores of Lake Erie, lies the sleepy little town of Port Dover, a quaint seaside place with a sandy foreshore, ice cream parlours, and curiosity shops. Just to the left, as you enter its main street, you might notice a smart, new, two-storey grey house on a grassy slope facing the water. Beyond, you will sometimes see a red and white boat, a fifty-three-foot cutter bearing the Canadian Coast Guard insignia. This lifeboat station is staffed twenty-four hours a day from April until December. The Canadian Coast Guard has a big presence on this Great Lake because of the long history of carnage on its waters.

▬

"Three or four years ago, I was a guy carrying a suitcase," says Brian Riddell, coxswain at the lifeboat station in Amherstburg. "I went from base to base, relieving for the guys who were off on vacation or sick. I liked it at the time as I got to see some of the countryside. This one time, I got sent to fill in for the coxswain at Port Dover while he went off to get married. We're inside there with the TV on, tuned to an American station when we hear a news clip about a small Cessna plane that has disappeared from all air space—Toronto and Buffalo have lost it from their radar. It seems that an aircraft has just fallen out of the sky, or otherwise gone missing. Not long after, we get a call from our rescue coordination centre in Trenton: can we go looking for it?

"We gear up the boat to go out searching in one of the new Arun class cutters—brand new, a 53-foot boat called the *The Sora*. She's a beauty, and had just been delivered to Prescott from the shipyards in Sept Iles, Quebec, and I was trained on how to operate her on the journey down to Port Dover. It was late in the afternoon, and very rough on the water—so wild that out on the oil rig they couldn't get to change crews."

The job of Riddell and his crew is to search this large inland sea in severe weather conditions for the small plane that is lost, until the aircraft and its crew are found. With characteristic understatement, Riddell describes the conditions on the lake simply as "rough."

"It's cold now," says Riddell. "The seas whip across the decks, blown by the wind that whips at forty knots across the water. But in spite of this, the four-person crew remain out on the open decks to prevent themselves from getting sea sick—men who don't get sea sick."

Riddell marks out a search grid, and the cutter tosses violently as she goes from point to point. "I was concentrating very, very hard," he says. "It's tough, trying to keep on the search pattern, trying to keep from being sea sick, searching in the dark, hour after hour. We go on all through the night. After about twelve hours I lose some concentration, you know, the heavy seas pounding, and being forced to stay out on the deck."

Visibility is poor, and none of the crew is on the radar. Riddell happens to look up and sees a freighter coming toward them out of Port Colbourne, the vessel about one hour distant. He knows he will be in close quarters with the freighter in about thirty minutes—not really that close, he thinks, but made the more so because of the reduced visibility. Riddell concentrates on his search pattern, forgetting about the freighter. When he next looks up, the ship is looming at him out of the mist about one nautical mile distant. He figures contact will occur in three to

A vessel for every job: a new Arun-type lifeboat, an old 44-foot lifeboat and an inshore rescue boat.

five minutes if both vessels remain on their course.

"At one moment I'm in a search, a grid pattern, concentrating very hard because of the conditions, and within two minutes I'm on a collision course. I'm not watching the radar, and it's too rough to see anyway. Our cutter is being tossed about pretty bad, and we have to concentrate just so we don't get sick. I look up, and here we are about to tangle with a freighter. I'm a little uncomfortable when I see a big ship bearing down on me," he says laconically. He believes that the freighter will not have seen the Coast Guard cutter, as her radar will most likely pick up only the tops of the waves. And because the freighter is just leaving the canal, Riddell surmises that her radar will not have been turned on, or if it is, anti-clutter controls may not be turned up.

"But, because of the laws of relativity, the freighter is in command of the lane, and the Coast Guard cutter *Sora* has to get the hell out of the way," Riddell says. "I'm crossing him, on the wrong side, naturally, because I don't know he's coming. As soon as that happens, everything goes wrong.

"I perform a well-used nautical maneuver exercised by every seaman since the early days of sail," he says. "'Speed her up,' I yell to the engineer. 'Let's get our ass out of the way!'"

Objects in the boat start to fly—paddles, lifejackets, a host of other objects. The distance between the two vessels is closing quickly because of their speed, approximately twenty-three miles an hour. There are just minutes between them.

"We just miss the freighter by a few minutes. A close call. Quite a scare," says Riddell. "Once we get out of that, out of the path of the big ship, we just keep on going, searching the lake for the missing plane."

At about five in the morning, he directs his cutter to dock at Port Maitland, a small town about halfway between Port Dover and Port Colbourne. The engineer is not familiar with the new boat and not sure how long the fuel will last; the crew is in a state of exhaustion. All need food, rest from the pounding in the storm, and a break from the intense concentration required to search in the dark for parts of a small plane. The crew refuel, rest for two hours, and return to Lake Erie to comb the water. Once more they search until noon the next day, when they are relieved by the incoming crew.

Afterwards, they learn that they had come within eighty feet of part of the plane wreck, but couldn't see it because of the roughness of the water.

This effort, far beyond the call of any duty, was initially in the hope, perhaps, of finding someone alive, and then to find airplane parts and the body, or bodies, of its crew. Answers—and closure—are needed. Search and rescue workers understand this. They have been tasked to a mission that they do not consider complete until the lost persons and objects have been found. No thought is given to the danger, difficulty, or the seeming impossibility of the task, no consideration given to their own comfort or safety.

The Relentless Call of the Sea

Lake Huron, Ontario

I n 1975, Danny Coultis was a young married man living in an apartment with his wife, not far from the shores of Lake Huron, in Parry Sound, Ontario. One evening in late spring, as he stood at his kitchen sink washing dishes, he heard it: the shrill, yet mournful whistle of a ship in the harbour. He heard it through the closed windows of his apartment, a kilometre or more from the lake—a sound that would remain with him for the rest of his life. This whistle was a siren call to a job that would entwine his life with vessels that sailed the oceans and Canada's inland seas. Great ships and small, all types and sizes. They enthralled and enchanted him, just as they did two of his brothers. Kyle Coultis, the eldest, would choose the life of an engineer, but each of the three younger boys—Danny, John, and Mark—would stand one day on the bridge as the uniformed captain of a ship.

This night, Danny dropped his dishcloth and ran out into the evening, jumped in his car, and followed the sound, zigzagging the streets of the small town down to the port lands, where ships lay out on the waters. He stood on the shore and gazed at the freighters, tankers, and tugs being prepared for the upcoming season. From this moment on, he was to be haunted by ships and the sea.

After that, Danny slept with his window open—even in winter—so he could hear the ships on the inland seas, their whistles and foghorns calling across the water. The snow blew in, the wind howled through the opening, and a bone-chilling cold crept across the sill to the bed where he and his wife slept. But the window remained open.

—

A quarter century later, in 1999, Danny Coultis sits behind a large desk on the second floor of a grey slab building in Trenton's military naval base. He sits in the Coast Guard's Joint Rescue Coordination Centre as the superintendent of maritime search and rescue, central and Arctic regions. This dry and dusty office buried deep in the heart of the complex seems a long way from a small boy's dream when, at the age of four years, and later as a young man, he declared that one day he would be a ship's captain. What happened to this boy who became a sea captain but now sits behind a desk?

Danny Coultis and his brothers were born in a lighthouse, to a lighthouse keeper and his wife. Their maternal grandfather was a fisherman, the paternal *grand-père*, an engineer on steam tugboats that plied the waters around Manitoulin Island. Most family members, from distant memory, had worked in marine-related and outdoor jobs in the small Ontario town of Tobermory.

The lighthouse was the only home that Danny and his three brothers knew. It stood silhouetted against an ever-changing sky, a lonely tower thrust up on the rocks on the east side of Flowerpot Island. Their boyhood playground was a picturesque blip of grass, trees and rocks, washed on all sides by the waters of one of Canada's Great Lakes. It stood like a small sentry at the northern tip of the Bruce Peninsula, a narrow arm of land that extends into the waters of Lake Huron and points toward Fitzwilliam and Manitoulin Islands. Snake and Bear's Rump Islands guard its western flank. The lighthouse keeper and his family lived their lives on this speck of land, each one trained to be on constant vigil for signs of vessels and people in distress. This marked the boys with a particular philosophy of life: a readiness to help others in need and to put themselves in danger to save the lives of people in trouble.

For the brothers, in many ways, it was a dream childhood: an island for a playground in an inland sea as vast, as challenging, and as mighty as any of the world's oceans. But there was also isolation, sometimes a great loneliness, and the brothers felt different from the other kids in school. For Mark, it was a sense of inferiority stemming from the fact that he lived on an island. He had to go home every day and all summer to this island, and move every winter to the mainland. Only much later in life did he learn that the kids in his school envied him his island and lighthouse existence.

The brothers remember days and nights when storms raged and all they knew were the violent waters of the lake heaving themselves upon the rocky shores of their island home, days of

The light-
house and
fog alarm
building on
Flowerpot
Island,
Georgian
Bay.

vicious and blood-curdling cold before they moved to the mainland for the winter. And then there was the fog.

"I loved the sound of the foghorn," Danny says. "It meant
lifeblood for the ships, protecting them as they plied the waters
of the Great Lakes, telling their pilots they were close to land. But
it was also sort of scary. When it's really bad, you can't see anything. It's like you're living in the clouds. Nothing exists because
you can't see any contours of the land—in fact, you can't see
your hand in front of your face. The sky and the water are all
mixed up and heaving about together. Imagine the ships steaming straight for the giant rocks of this island and not even knowing it."

The four brothers learned to be sensitively attuned to weather
patterns, and particularly to the creeping in of fog. They were
taught to be alert for signs of the deadly blanket that could roll
in across the sky in a few moments, to fling itself across Georgian
Bay and Lake Huron, putting all vessels out there in jeopardy.
Danny learned that if visibility dropped below two miles, the
foghorn had to be pumped to life so that the ships would know
they were close to land, with help nearby if they should need it.

"We lived for summer vacation," Danny says. He tells of days
that were long and vigorous, the island in full green bloom, the
inland sea that washed the rocky shores of the Coultis boys' playground warming itself enough to test the brave or foolhardy who
ventured in. The water temperature would reach ten degrees
Celsius, not much more, but the boys did not feel the chill of this

ancient lake. They swam in it and rowed on it. Tourists came from great distance, or from local towns and cities, hiring a guide to take them to the dim forests for walks on lonely paths. They hired Danny and his boat to take them to where the fish swam, and for the pleasure of boating in the rippling waters. All the while, and for the whole summer long, the brothers would row and swim, and row some more. In their little boat they became small, skilled navigators among the myriad rocky inlets all about the island.

The legacy of this outdoor and isolated childhood was a dislike of crowds, a closeness among the brothers, and, for Danny, a contentment with his own company. Mark, the youngest of the four, lives today in Ottawa and works as commanding officer of the Port Dover lifeboat station of the same name on the shores of Lake Erie in southern Ontario. He dislikes crowds intensely and avoids downtown areas as fastidiously as he can.

"We grew up in a natural world of trees and grass and water. Big skies, big seas, and weather. We learned to look about and above us," he explains. "We searched the skies for changes in weather, for patterns. We listened to the natural world, the birds, clouds, things out there. In the city I still do it. I look up and outward, and I bump into everything: people, fire hydrants, hot dog stands. I can't bear to be in crowds. I make sure I don't look backwards to see the stream of them when there is a parade or something the family insists I take them to. People, they're like ants. They crawl along, hurrying to their work, not looking at anything except their feet and the elevator buttons. They do things without thinking or seeing. It sure is entertaining to watch the ants."

Audrey Coultis, the boys' father, was the lighthouse keeper. A navy war veteran, he found work that involved boats and islands on his return from active duty: caretaker of Cove Island and worker for the Transport Company in Owen Sound. Whenever possible, he worked on and about ships. In 1950 he was appointed lighthouse keeper of Flowerpot Island, the perfect job for a returned war vet. He could be his own boss and work largely in isolation, making responsible decisions without the bother of having other people around. He hired an assistant, and the two men worked six hours on and six hours off, from April to December.

The family lived in a small, cramped house until a better one was erected. The lighthouse keeper's assistant moved into the old one. Of the lighthouse itself, Danny remembers polished floorboards, wind rustling outside the windows or, howling like a mad animal hurling itself at the windowpanes. He loved the soft yellow glow of the oil lamps that warmed the cold stone floors and walls of the building, the smell of kerosene and the aroma of oil. At that time, there was no electricity on Flowerpot Island.

As a boy, Danny and his brothers had specific responsibilities for the running of the lighthouse. Each morning, the boys would fill the lamps with oil and polish the glass. They would trim the wick, then put up the shades in the house. In the afternoons they helped their father with gardening and general maintenance work on the grounds surrounding the lighthouse. Coultis was a hard taskmaster; he expected perfection and absolute obedience.

One late afternoon, Danny, still a child navigating his way among the rocky inlets on the west side of the island, watched the sun make its slow descent over the distant shores of Georgian Bay. The sun shone hot and burning after the fog had rolled away and now cast an amber glow in the sky. Suddenly he was arrested by something not quite right. He stared across the water to Bear's Rump Island, the pile of rocks and trees a short distance away. It must be fog. But how could it be, when it had burned off earlier in the day and the sky was mostly clear? It must be smoke. He stared for some moments, then paddled furiously back to shore to find his father.

Coultis was up in the tower of the lighthouse; he listened to his young son.

"Maybe fog, some of it is still hanging around," he said. "But maybe smoke signals. We'll get off and see what it's all about."

Indeed, the fog that had swathed the island from early morning was still hanging about in pockets. The air was still, the sky now overcast. Father and son trekked off to fire up the Coast Guard vessel anchored on the east side of the island and to scour Bear's Rump Island.

As they approached the small island, the bits of greyish haze became recognizable as smoke plumes that curled above the trees. The tall man and his son scrambled up the rocky shore where a strange sight met their eyes: a small aircraft lay with its propeller stuck among the brush and sandy scrub. Its pilot stood in the midst of the trees, busy stoking the flames of his fire to attract attention to his plight.

"Oh, thank God," he said when he saw his rescuers. The young pilot, who had departed from Gore Bay on Manitoulin Island, headed for Wiarton, explained how he had become disoriented in the fog and, unknowingly, had flown about in circles until he found himself out of fuel and was forced to make an emergency landing. He had chosen Bear's Rump as the most suitable emergency landing site, probably the only one, among the islands in the area.

The pilot was ferried off the island to buy replacement parts for his damaged plane. In his absence, Danny, his brothers, his father and the lighthouse assistant toiled on the island, cutting down old spruce and pine and springy saplings, digging up and unearthing roots and stumps, and removing old logs and scrub. Worst of all was the herculean task of moving giant boulders and rocks in order to level an area large enough for a makeshift runway. An entire week went by before the crude runway was ready. At the end of each day, there were bruised and bleeding hands, screaming muscles and aching joints.

The pilot eventually returned with the replacement parts for his airplane, including a prop and a wheel, and he worked to repair the damaged wing and get it ready to lift off. But there was still a problem: the home-made runway was much too short for him to rev up the engines and taxi sufficiently before take-off. What to do? Danny's father decided to attach the aircraft to a tree with a strong rope, so that when its engines revved, it would remain stationary. At a signal from the pilot, the rope was untied, and the aircraft ran the length of the small bumpy runway and lifted off into the air. Danny stood, a small boy on the rocky runway, staring after the plane until it became a speck in the sky. He felt proud, yet curiously deflated.

That summer's blaze faded slowly into autumn. A wicked night raged outside, the wind howling about the house, thundering on the rocks all about the island. Danny, half awake, heard the front door crash open. From the warmth of his small bedroom upstairs, he heard the voices of his father and—who was the other? It was the park's guide, John Deschardine, standing in the open doorway, the blackness of the night flooding in, the rain lashing him.

Danny tiptoed to the top of the stairs and peered through the railing. He had to know what the hurried voices were saying with urgency in the middle of the night. He crept down a few stairs to listen. At that moment, another voice came from the kitchen— his mother's. He ventured down another step. Mr. Deschardine stood dripping in the hallway with blood pouring from his hands. Wild bears, wolves, a madman with an axe, a fall down a cliff—Danny's imagination ran wild. He watched his mother run about with cloths, soap and bandages.

"How would you get your hands into such a state?" she asked.

"Rowing the little boat, ma'am. Eight, nine hours I've been out in that storm. I had to come up around Snake Island and head out into the wind to land on the east side of Flowerpot, where there's an area of flat rock." He told how he had come in on the east side because winds drove him off the near shore, and he could make no headway. Deschardine had left four people in the big boat, drifting. The group had been up in the Killarney area and were on their way back when the engine suddenly quit. A strong nor'wester was blowing. The guide got into the little boat and paddled toward the lighthouse, leaving his boat and its passengers drifting toward Half Moon Island.

Danny's father and John Deschardine went out into the night. Deschardine could not be persuaded to remain in Mrs. Coultis' care and let someone else go to the rescue. He insisted that he was responsible for the people in the boat. He knew where they might be drifting, so he must go.

The two men struggled on the twenty-five minute walk through the bush to the east side of the island, lashed by rain and carrying five gerry cans of fuel on their shoulders. They reached the lighthouse vessel—a wooden-hulled, twenty-two-foot boat with a four-cylinder inboard motor and small cabin—and loaded the gerry cans onto it. Coultis cranked it to life and steered it out into the heaving waters of the lake. As the seas washed over them and a strong, northwest wind screamed in their ears, John Deschardine stared grimly into the black night, straining his ears for sounds of his boat and the half dozen people on board. It had been six hours since he had left them to drift with only a sea anchor to drag the ship. The outlines of the rocky islands of Fitzwilliam and Half Moon loomed out of the stormy night as the boat drew close to the shores. Coultis located the tour boat in a small cove on the east side of Half Moon Island, twenty miles distant from where it had first begun to drift, its passengers none the worse for their mishap.

High school was over, and so was the life at the lighthouse on the island when Danny Coultis, a young man with energy to burn, took a job with the Upper Great Lakes Shipping Company. He was hired as deckhand, with two of his brothers, on a ship stationed at Goderich in 1966. These "Lakers," as they were known, mostly carried grain. Danny's misfortune—or so it seemed to him at the time—was to suffer a severe allergy to grain products. About nine months into his first work experience, and what may have been a career with the Upper Great Lakes shipping company, he had to call it quits.

What to do? He went after positions with the Coast Guard, with oil companies, and with Great Lakes commercial freighters, even though he was only qualified to work as a deckhand. The first to respond to his application was the Coast Guard. Danny accepted immediately, and began the long climb up through the ranks from the bottom deckhand, galley assistant, seaman, coxswain. He went to marine college in Owen Sound in pursuit of his third, second, and first mate's certificates, to return in the capacity of bosun and quartermaster, known at that time as wheelsman. Danny was a man who knew exactly what he wanted.

"I loved the work on the Coast Guard cutters that sailed up the lakes doing buoy tending," he says. "It was the best time of all, really. We got put adrift, as it were, on the barges from the mother ship, to check, clean, and repair the buoys and markers out in the lakes. We would be off all day on our own, laughing and singing and clowning around with each other, and getting all the work done. We were out in the sun and the rain and the wind, in smooth waters and choppy, sometimes with big swells, and we would look at the sky and think how we should get back to the ship before a big storm blew down on us. It was a great time: free and fun and outdoors and right on the water."

But always before him, like a shining beacon was the goal of achieving the position of commanding officer of a ship for the Coast Guard.

While Danny worked at his first job on commercial freighters, with the young Mark still at school and Kyle at university studying for a degree in engineering, John Coultis removed himself from a life that had everything to do with ships and sailing. As a newly qualified electrical engineer, he set out for Toronto and to his first job on shore as an engineer at a power station. But life on the land soon became a life without meaning, devoid of the markers he had always known. Slowly, almost imperceptibility, he became ill, and eventually he slid into a deep depression.

"It's not like I'd never been away from the island and the

water," he says. "I had done ordinary, land-based jobs. We all did. We worked in general stores and at the pumps, at the marina at Tobermory during and after high school. This was different. I was out of my element, like a fish stranded on a beach."

He couldn't tolerate Toronto, its noise and crowds and bustle. It was a place that seemed to him to be fast and rude and dirty. He struggled with a deepening depression until he found himself not able to function at all. After just eight months at his job, he was put off work on sick leave. He lost weight and became seriously ill. His brother Danny came to visit, lured him from his small apartment, and took him down to the water to look at the sailing vessels out on the lake, to watch the ships in port. Danny hoped that this might help cheer his brother up, help make him better. But John knew he would never get better living in the city and being away from ships and the water.

"I felt half dead," he says. "I gave up it all up and went back to Tobermory and to the ships." Tall, weatherbeaten, tanned, with a lithe, athletic body and an air of quiet self-confidence, John sits at his desk today by a window that opens on a view of the rippling waters of Lake Erie.

"I spent 28 years at sea," he says. "Then I took an office job on shore that involved monitoring environmental pollution. You might think that strange, having had that stint at a job on shore when I was young, when I couldn't hack being away from the sea. But there is another condition that search and rescue guys must have, and that's non-routine, which is just what this job's about. Each day comes and you never know what it will bring, because it's never the same. It's still all to do with water and ships and people on boats." John's job has an expanded scope, too, in that he deals with international issues—like cross-border water pollution and working with the United States Coast Guard.

"For me, working for the Coast Guard means something much more than any of the jobs on the tankers or freighters could ever have," Danny says. "They were good jobs, but work for the Coast Guard makes you feel that you're doing something important. It's your life, not just a job."

"There are people who work for the Coast Guard who treat it as just a job," adds John. "Like a nine-to-five thing, and then they go home and don't think about it. Except that it's not nine-to-five; it's shift work. But the majority do this work because it is the Coast Guard. They are the Coast Guard.

"In the Coast Guard there are many roles: teaching boating

safety to children, doing search and rescue work out in storms to try to save a small boat and the people on board. You could be on an icebreaker up near Alaska, no one to relieve you and no port in sight. You could be on a month or two-month-long buoy-tending mission that's long and dirty, but sometimes lots of fun. It's your life and you're committed to it. You couldn't imagine any other."

Coultis explains that when one spends so much time and shares such experiences with one's mates, a deep bonding takes place. He imagines the feelings and commitment are uncommon in other jobs.

"Some of the characteristics come from within the person and they bring it to the Coast Guard. It was there within them before they came, a personal thing, genetic makeup, call it what you like. Take us, three Coultis brothers. Is this all we knew? Is it in the blood? Is it socioeconomic?" John pauses and stares out the window, gets up and moves restlessly about his office. "We were all exposed to other experiences," he continues. "Danny worked on the commercial ships. I tried shore life as an engineer in a city. Mark worked on land during high school, and Kyle, well, he was the only one of us who took himself completely away from a mariner's type of life."

Coultis believes that many who make a career out of the Coast Guard don't mind the solitude. He believes that they simply cannot tolerate being around groups of people for any length of time. He describes them, in a social situation, as eventually slinking away to a dark corner. A few who do this work do it because it beats working in the coal mines or pulp and paper mills, he says. But times have changed. College graduates, many of whom are pursuing a career path enter the Coast Guard. But many become disillusioned: the work doesn't fit their glamorous image of being a commanding officer on a Coast Guard vessel and sailing the high seas. Some get seasick and never get over it. Others leave because of the effect the job has on their family life. Many leave and go to the commercial world for higher pay, where it is easier to get a promotion. Many Coast Guard workers lack qualifications such as certificates in engineering, or masters and mates certificates, and are therefore stuck working for the Coast Guard in low-paying jobs where there is little chance of promotion. And because of the competition for promotion, there is often disappointment. Despite this, many Coast Guard employees—like the Coultis brothers—do not see what they do as work. They can't believe they get paid for what they enjoy so much.

A Fisherman's Long Nightmare

Lake Huron and Georgian Bay

The day dawns like so many others, but as one who knows about the legendary November gales and storms in these parts, Francis Lavelley knows he is pushing his luck.

November 5, 1993. Lavelley's thoughts are of his home and family as he heads north toward Cape Hurd and Tobermory on the Bruce Peninsula. He's finished his summer and fall fishing, but once around the cape, he plans to fish the quieter waters on the eastern cape before heading for home. It is a hard life: he is away most of the season working twelve and fourteen-hour days, always on the look-out for rough weather, worrying about his catch, his income, and, sometimes, his own safety. He is a long way from his home at Cape Croker, the native reserve on the eastern edge of the long arm of land that juts up into Lake Huron to form the western boundary of Georgian Bay. This is his birthplace, a wild and lonely spot where old-growth cedars grow right to the waters' edge, and where long stretches of rock and pebble beach rim endless vistas of blue waters. He lives in the much the same manner as his father, his grandfather, and perhaps his great grandfather before him, a solitary life in a rugged landscape, described by the young man as a place full of rock faces, caves, boulders, and bears. It is also a place of sudden, violent storms that blow up out of nowhere.

A family reunited: Francis Lavelley with his wife and child.

Nothing much changes here. The giant trees stretch high above the settlements at their feet, as they have for a thousand and more years. Only Lavelley's plans and ambitions change. Earlier this year, at the age of thirty-one, he makes the decision of his lifetime; calculating his financial resources, taking stock of his skills, his knowledge and experience, risking all he has, he engages in the business of deep-water fishing. He invests heavily in the venture: fifty thousand dollars for a boat, a license, and thousands of dollars in gear and equipment. This includes fishing crates and a generator—a capital outlay that will be in perpetual jeopardy because of the nature of the business and the type of weather on the peninsula. The fish catch is unpredictable, the income always precarious, and the stormy weather always uncertain.

Driven by capricious winds, several seas might run simultaneously in the huge bodies of water surrounding the peninsula. The knowledge that he might lose his catch, that he might not return even, lurks always in dim corners of a fisherman's mind. The shoreline is a true sailor's nightmare—rocky outcrops lie barely submerged all along the coast, projecting outward from boulders at the foot of the cedar forests that crowd the water's edge. These outcrops extend in ragged formation deep into the lake, guarding the shores from encroachment by people and boats. Deep-sea fishing in these parts is not a venture to be undertaken without considerable thought, preparation and knowledge, and not something for the faint of heart.

Like most of his friends, Francis has been schooled in the arts of inshore fishing. But when, in 1993, the courts recognized the rights of native Indians to operate a local commercial fishery, he was one of only a handful of fisherman to take up the challenge of the big boats and deep sea fishing.

"It's a hard business," he says again. "I bought my boat—called the *Polygon*. She was my baby, old though she was, built in 1954, but I had her re-built and refitted. I worked hard—from about 4:30 in the morning until 6:00 or 7:00 at night."

The *Polygon* was indeed sleek by fishing boat standards. Her graceful lines now lie scattered on the floor of Lake Huron somewhere between Dorcas Bay and Cape Hurd at the tip of the peninsula.

Francis Lavelley's *Polygon*.

It is the last run of the day, one more flight down the ski slopes, one more time around the track; for Francis Lavelley, it is one more casting of the fishing line. But this is November and the end of the fishing season. The young man knows all too well about the November gales and how a person can be caught by surprise far out on the lake, at the mercy of wind and storm.

This day, the weather forecast is unremarkable. A storm rages northward but is not expected to travel south, and the reports call for diminishing winds. Lavelley does his boat check: oil and transmission fluid, radio, pump, hatches...the process takes him over an hour. One thing gives him pause: he would have preferred to take the trip with a first mate on board, but all the local fishermen are too busy to accompany him. Resigned to making this trip on his own, Lavelley plans it carefully. He will sail his diesel-powered boat around the peninsula in two stages. Early in the morning, he'll cruise to Tobermory, where a friend will pick him up in the evening and drive him to Cape Croker for the night. Lavelley will then return the next day for the final leg of the journey down the eastern shores of the peninsula.

"To get where I wanted to go isn't easy, and the hardest part is getting around the shoals in the west. It's a tricky passage, but I know it pretty well, figure I'll be okay if the weather holds."

Five hours into the trip, Lavelley hears warnings over his marine radio about gale-force winds, that have taken even the forecasters by surprise. But he doesn't need a forecaster to tell him what's coming: he's been out on these waters all his adult life and understands what the stiff breeze from the northwest means for him as he heads northward. The *Polygon* bucks the waves but Lavelley persists, certain he can make it to where he wants to be—with luck—and he pushes ahead, telling himself he will be okay.

All about him the sky darkens, and it is only mid-afternoon. It is not long before snow squalls hit and waves smack from every direction, sloshing across the bow and over the stern. The sea is quickly becoming an ugly and violent monster. The *Polygon*, like a plastic plaything is tossed mercilessly on the crests of waves.

On this bitter afternoon, Lavelley reminds himself that he knows these parts intimately and has been out in such weather before and survived. He must survive, he tells himself, or what will his family do? No insurance, no savings, nothing. He doesn't panic—until the noise of his engine dies. His propeller suddenly ceases and the fishing boat begins to wallow and flounder. He is now completely at the mercy of the storm. Lavelley gets on his marine radio and calls the Coast Guard through the Wiarton radio station. He is about four miles out on the lake and two miles away from Cape Hurd.

At the Coast Guard lifeboat station, coxswain Steve Cooper—along with leading seamen Jim MacDonald and Dave Huber—watches the storm whipping up, winds sweeping the water in heaving swells through the narrow entrance to Big Tug Harbour. The Coast Guard cutter swings against its moorings down below; the station is perched up on rocks above the narrow entrance to the harbour. Pines and maples bend in the wind across the channel. The crew knows that, sooner or later, they will be out in that storm to rescue hapless and helpless boaters. From their windows, they watch the lake waters raging ever higher down the channel. It is mid-afternoon when the Wiarton airport radios through to them.

"A fishing boat out there taking on water," says the operator's voice, and gives the location. "Failed transmission, no power. Owner panicking, says he's sinking."

The search and rescue workers are out the door in a flash and into their cutter, the *Tobermory*, revving her engines and preparing for the stormy passage in the direction of Cape Hurd. Cooper, well-seasoned and experienced in all types of weather, is unconcerned—just another job, he says. Nevertheless, he knows that these waters of the Great Lakes are considered the most disastrous in the world per square kilometre, if only because their weather patterns and sea conditions are underestimated.

"We call what we get here 'lumpy waves,'" says Lonny Adams, coxswain on the shift opposite Cooper. "They're formed by winds coming from the east, the north, and northwest. They shift and change abruptly, and blow all at once."

MacDonald and Huber, equally experienced, are also unfazed by any situation out on the lake. "We are a team," says MacDonald. "Each of us knows without speaking what the others will do in any situation out there. We trust each other to know what to do—we have to. It could mean our lives."

The passage down the west side of the peninsula is wild and stormy. The cutter heaves and tosses in swells that aren't really swells as much as ugly short waves that threaten bow, stern and portside all at once. The rain comes in sheets, then turns quickly to sudden snow squalls. Cooper, not yet concerned about the safety of his own vessel, has difficulty finding the fishing boat. MacDonald pulls his oilskin tighter about his spare frame. Halfway down the Cape Hurd channel, they are still unable to contact Lavelley by radio. The crew needs to get a radio direction finder to be able to home in on him.

Lavelley, out in the black madness of a wild afternoon, sees himself either sinking or being blown in toward the treacherous shore. His anxiety changes to horror when he goes down below to try to fix his transmission. He opens the hatch, hears the sloshing of water, and sees, by the dim beam of his flashlight, that his boat is taking on water. Two to three feet of it swirls about the cabin walls, and everything in his living quarters floats about—television, portable stereo, other personal items. The water seems to be pouring in through the water jacket that cools the motor, a device that uses the lake water as an engine cooler. He frantically attempts to start the pumps. They refuse to work. Lavelley guesses that an air leak is causing a block but this knowledge doesn't help him.

He leaps back up the companionway and radios the Coast Guard a second time. "I'm sinking, I'm sinking!" he shouts into it. "I'm in danger, I need help now."

"Hang on, and we'll get you off!" The Coast Guard crewman's voice booms over his radio in return. Now Lavelley can only wait and pray. Rain and snow lash at him and waves crash over his deck. Lavelley knows his boat; it will go down very quickly when it does. In spite of his careful maintenance, the *Polygon* is a very old vessel that has endured many years of thrashings by wind and wave.

Does Lavelley recall the famous shipwrecks of the past, vessels that came to grief in just these waters, and in conditions much like these? Do the names *Cascaden* and *Avalon Voyageur II* flit into his mind to haunt him? He has plenty of time to ponder their fate and his own, for it takes the Coast Guard three-and-a-half hours to locate and get close to his *Polygon*. They have difficulty picking up his signal and finding him in the savage darkness. They plough on through the storm to within three miles of the fishing boat before they detect its signal.

The swells reach twenty feet and the waves cap. The Coast Guard cutter faces the Three Sisters—rogue waves that come in threes, longer than the rest.

"The first one, you go over it," says Cooper. "The second, you know you'll have trouble, and the third will get you if you don't pay attention."

"They have a hard time getting a fix on me," Lavelley says. "The storm interferes—rain and hail and snow squalls everywhere and she's blowing pretty hard. I have no GPS system, and my Loran C—I have it on the boat but it's not working—never did get it going properly. The Coast Guard pilot manages to find me by using the Wiarton radio station to get the fix on me, because I can't tell exactly where I am on a global plotter, don't know my latitude and longitude. I tell you, it's the longest three hours of my life. And at this moment, I don't know if I'm going to have any more of my life until I hear the coxswain of the Coast Guard cutter on his radio. 'Hang on and we'll get you off!' he tells me. Best thing I ever heard. Now I know I'll be okay. By now, the water's up to my wet deck and I got little buoyancy left in my boat. I figure I got about fifteen to twenty minutes before I go down. The old boat, she has a bellyful of water."

But the nightmare is not over. Once they locate the fishing boat, the Coast Guard cutter cannot get closer to it than 150 feet. The unpredictable 20-foot waves thrust the cutter close—too close—only to toss her far away again. If the coxswain pulls in too close to the sinking vessel, he might find his own ship being sucked or smacked right into it.

The attempt to get close enough for Lavelley to jump ship is made over and over, and all the while the water creeps up inside the *Polygon* and she sinks further. The crew on the Coast Guard vessel is frustrated, while Lavelley grows increasingly desperate. The coxswain now decides to gamble on the small, rigid-hulled dinghy attached to the *Tobermory* as a lifeline for Lavelley, but his crew has difficulty unleashing and getting the small zodiac in the water because of the high winds and waves. Cooper becomes concerned for his crew. MacDonald and Huber, fingers stiff and frozen, hang onto the railing with one hand while trying to put the boat over with the other. Snow squalls strike their frozen faces as they release and lower the boat, while keeping it attached by towline to the cutter. Cooper takes his vessel upwind and tries to keep her to the stern of the fishing boat while his crew floats the dinghy downwind, close enough that Lavelley might be able to jump into it.

"My stern comes upwind and waves are washing right over it," Lavelley says. "I cling onto the railing, waiting for the Coast Guard boat to come up, and it does, but the waves force me back."

It is a tenuous lifeline for Lavelley. Exhausted, cold and soaked, he holds tightly to his deck rail, waits for the cutter to come up to his bow, steps onto the outside railing of his boat, leans far out and hooks the little zodiac with his leg, to hold it.

One leg on the *Polygon*, and the other on the small boat, he is momentarily suspended above a raging sea. He hesitates, then jumps, landing in the little life raft and clinging tightly to its sides. The crew in the Coast Guard cutter draw in the cable attached to the raft, pull it alongside their vessel, and draw the exhausted man to their deck.

Turning their cutter about, the rescue workers begin the interminable and still-dangerous journey back to the lifeboat station. Cooper opens up the throttle. The cutter bucks wildly and almost rolls, and the coxswain cuts back his speed. The evening labours on until the exhausted crew and their passenger finally arrive at Tobermory, where Lavelley's wife is waiting for him. The Coast Guard's job is done.

Lavelley is financially ruined, having lost his boat and all the equipment, and materials he needs to earn a living.

"But I have my life," he says.

Long afterwards, like a man on a mission, he searches for parts and equipment from his boat, for anything that might be floating on the water. It is a lonely and tragic mission for him. He rents boats and vainly searches the waters off the west side of the peninsula. He rents an airplane to search by air. But all he finds of his *Polygon*, of the investment that was to earn him a good living, are bits of debris and an oil slick on the water. It is time to start all over again.

"What else can I do?" he asks. "I've been fishing for my old man since I could pull an oar," and adds, laughing, "He paid me every time I put my feet under the table. Built myself punts and small tugs, but the fishing business never got big, not until after the Fairgraves Decision (the 1993 legislation that gave local Indians exclusive rights to fish the area) was made."

"It's a hard life by the yard, sure enough," Lavelley says. "I figure it's about the third most dangerous job in the world—after crab fishing and rescue work, you know, what the Coast Guard guys do."

Search and rescue work dangerous? Is Cooper ever afraid for himself, his crew, or his boat?

"None of us feel fear," he answers. "You haven't got time; you're concentrating on the job. I mean, this is what it's all about—to rescue people, save their lives. It's all you think about, really. You could say it's all in day's work."

What motivates this quiet, kindly, early middle-aged man to leave his family and their farm near Kingston to spend two weeks out of every four in Tobermory doing this sometimes boring, but often risky work?

"Well, when I look way back, I can tell you that I've loved the water from the time I was a child," he answers. "When I was young, I became an underwater diver and took some power squadron courses. At the same time I went to school to study civil engineering to become an engineering technologist. After I graduated, I worked for consultants, but I got laid off every winter. I went from job to job, was never home, and lived out of a suitcase. I worked twelve-hour days. It was hot, dirty work all summer but I stuck it out for ten years."

Finally, Cooper decided to look for something else. Home in Prescott, Ontario, meant a lake and harbour that saw vessels of all kinds coming and going. Freighters came in and sailed away; Coast Guard ice-breakers moored there for a time, left, and returned. Most of Cooper's high school friends had worked on the ships as deckhands for a time, some to stay, so it seemed natural to him to apply to the Coast Guard as deckhand for an interim job. Working aboard the Coast Guard ships *Simcoe* and *Griffon*, he found he liked the outdoor work, the freedom, the opportunity to travel and see other places. And, of course, he loved boats of all kinds, and the sea. He was hooked.

"My skills I'd learned through experience," says Cooper. "I painted lighthouses, built wooden boxes, spliced rope and steel wire rope. I would tear down booms and rigging and put them back together. I trudged up and down rock faces to get supplies to lighthouses, regardless of the weather. But I didn't care what I had to do, what I had to learn. This is work that other people don't do, and I liked it.

"I've worked for the Coast Guard since 1976, coxswain since 1982. I like everything about it—working with my mates who are a bunch of hard-working guys, being in the outdoors, on water, in boats, making split-second decisions, and helping people. My only regret is that I didn't get into it sooner, that I spent ten years working as an engineering technologist when I could have been working for the Coast Guard.

"You know, this one the *Polygon* was a good story—we saved someone's life. But often we find ourselves doing recovery work—finding dead and drowned people. We had a weird one a while ago, and we never did find out whether there was foul play involved or not—it was the case of a missing American, found face down in the shallows…"

Chaos at Crystal Bay

Amherstburg, Ontario

When Brian Riddell left high school in 1973, he needed a job. His home was in the Brockville area of Ontario, and even though he lived close to the water, boats and ships were far from his mind. He looked around, took a job in a linen mill as some place to start—and lasted six days.

"I was late every morning, and left early every day. I hated it," he says. "My friend and I talked. I said how I couldn't stand being indoors and doing the same thing over and over, no challenge, no responsibility. What was I going to do with my life?"

When Riddell mentioned this to his friend's father who worked down at the Iroquois Locks, he gave the young man the name of a shipping company in Port Colborne. With his letter of reference and a cheque from the linen mill in his pocket, Riddell took off, thinking to stay there and see about a job with this shipping company. His friend applied at the same time. Riddell figured he could afford a room for a night or two at the Duke's Hotel. He applied, and he waited. He walked the streets, up and down, hung about, walked up and down again. Then he got a call from the company's office; they said he was hired to work as a steward on a lake freighter, washing dishes and making beds.

Riddell's initiation into the sometimes strange and different patterns of life on a freighter was made easier because of his friend, a deckhand on the ship. But a month after Brian began his nautical career in this humble fashion, his friend quit the freighter to take up an offer of a job with the Canadian Coast Guard.

"One day, not long after he'd been gone, out of the blue, I got a call from the Coast Guard asking me to come in for an interview," he says. "I was out there in the middle of the lake. The captain called me to the bridge, said I had a shore-to-ship phone call. It happens it was from my aunt who told me I was to contact the Canadian Coast Guard. What the hell did I do wrong? I thought it was a joke. I'd never heard of the Coast Guard—well, heard of it of course, but didn't know there was a big Coast Guard base in Prescott, just ten miles from where I lived."

Brian Riddell got off his ship at the Iroquois Locks, hitchhiked to Prescott, and presented himself for the interview. Once it was over, he hitchhiked back home to Brockville where he found, to his astonishment, that he had been hired before he had even arrived.

The Coast Guard told him to pick up the ship on which he would be working, in Thunder Bay. "I guess they think that you can just drop everything and get in your car and drive to work, but I'm here on a freighter in the middle of lake," he says. He made two more trips with the freighter, from Thunder Bay to Toronto, a return trip to Duluth, and back once more to Toronto. He hitchhiked home, changed his clothes, and went to work for the Coast Guard. At that time, his qualifications included experience on ships, lead deckhand experience, and knot-tying. This was a time when the Coast Guard no longer hired people without qualifications. It was a fortuitous call, providing an opportunity for Brian Riddell to begin a career that has become a way of life for him, lasting for twenty-five years, and to this day.

"I never really tried a desk job, even though I won competitions to get one," he says. "When it came down to it, I couldn't quite see myself behind a desk."

The small town of Amherstburg, where Riddell works as coxswain at the Coast Guard's lifeboat station, lies a short distance from the banks of the northwestern reaches of Lake Erie. This Great Lake sweeps into the mouth of the Detroit River to join the St. Clair, eventually flowing into the lake of the same name. This lake connects with Lake Huron and Georgian Bay, allowing passage to Lake Superior and the Lakehead. A sleepy little border and river town with considerable history, it is the site of an old British Fort known as Malden, built during the war of 1812.

Not far beyond the town on Highway 20, a gravel road wanders south toward a group of low-slung grey buildings inside a high wire fence. Two warehouses sit at the edge of the riverbank housing equipment for pollution clean-up and materials for buoy tending and lighthouse supply. At the far end of an oblong stretch of asphalt, a small trailer sits unobtrusively a few yards from the river. This is the Coast Guard's lifeboat station, positioned here where the lake runs into the river, for two compelling reasons. First, a huge boating population lies at the doorstep of this small town. Second, the lake and the river form a shipping lane, a high marine traffic corridor where deep-sea commercial freighters, lakers, and large private cruisers pass back and forth between Canada and the United States along the lakes and waterways, and out to the east coast.

The Coast Guard cutter from Amherstburg comes to the rescue of a sailing boat on the north shore of Lake Erie.

The lakes and rivers offer a big summer attraction for the large population scattered about both sides of the border. But Lake Erie is an infamous body of water, elongated and shallow. The winds shift about abruptly, storms blow up without warning, fog can suddenly obliterate the landscape, and sheltered ports are few and far between. Boaters cruising along the northern shores toward the forbidding reach of Long Point are sailing a watery highway that has witnessed untold numbers of ships lured to destruction.

The abandoned lifeboat stations of Port Burwell and Port Stanley stand as silent witnesses to the ships and men destroyed in these waters in the earlier years of Canada's history. In the late nineteenth century, the Canadian Coast Guard placed additional lifeboat stations at Port Pelee and Long Point in an effort to halt some of the carnage on this lake.

Today, the focus has shifted: the patterns of traffic have altered over the years, there are fewer commercial ships plying the shipping channels, and recreational boating has dramatically increased. Freighters and lakers now have sophisticated navigational systems. As a consequence of this shift, the Coast Guard has relocated its two lifeboat stations on Lake Erie to Port Dover and Amherstburg, where the greatest number of marine incidents occur.

To further protect mariners in this area, the government, in

Congested waterways like Crystal Bay on the Detroit River keep the Coast Guard busy. Long weekends are especially hectic.

the 1920s, built a dyke—known as the Amherstburg channel—down the middle of the Detroit River to facilitate the passage of the ships. In the 1950s another dyke—the Livingston channel—was built to help slow the river current and to further improve navigation in the narrow shipping lanes. This most recent channel carries all marine traffic down river, while the former carries it upstream.

The crew at Amherstburg's lifeboat station, one of the busiest in Canada, receive up to 137 calls in a boating season. Holiday weekends are hectic, and during one recent Labour Day weekend, the base received over seventeen calls in two-and-a-half days. Brian Riddell explains why, in this part of the country, recreational boating accidents occur so much more frequently than elsewhere.

"It's the most congested waterway in North America for pleasure crafters," he says. "The population around here in the Detroit-Toledo-Sarnia area is five and half million; the waterways are not huge, so there's not a lot of room. In the summer, a lot of people don't think about anything—they see water and get out on it, think it's safe. They just get in their boats and go. They're out there on the water and they run out of gas, get lost, get themselves grounded. Getting stuck is very common. They drive their boats up on rocks, run aground on shoals, sandbanks, bars—it's amazing. Here's a guy with a two-million-dollar cruiser; he gets it in the water, and, next thing, its way up on the rocks—right out of the water. Some of them, if they have charts, they don't even look at them."

"You wouldn't believe what these guys do," says Jeff Faucher, the Rescue Specialist with this crew. "At night, out at Crystal Bay, they have a barbecue on board and the next thing there's a fire, they get drunk and fall overboard. Some of them may go out twice a year in their boats, and so aren't used to it. They're out on the water, they take a drink, lots of drinks...they do a lot of stupid things. We, the Coast Guard, go out and rescue them, we look out for them."

Up river, beyond the huge hunk of rock known as Grosse Ile, which straddles the river, lies a sheltered area called Crystal Bay, a place considered either famous, or notorious, according to one's point of view. Thousands of boaters on both sides of the border converge there all summer, particularly on the long weekends. The large expanse of sheltered water poses a big headache for the search and rescue workers at the station who call in a second crew as back-up for these periods. One crew takes care of day-to-day matters while the other patrols and responds to distress calls. Without the second crew, staff would get little sleep, and would have difficulty responding to every call.

Constant radio chatter crackles into the Coast Guard lifeboat station. The crew sits about the trailer, exhausted and edgy after the evening before. The parties will be cranking up again at Crystal Bay. Radio chatter fills the room. What's important? What's not? Is this call a prank?

At seven in the evening, the little Coast Guard cutter, the *Sora* noses its way through the thousands of boats scattered about the bay as dusk settles over the water. Many of the boats are rafted together to form what looks like a boardwalk.

"Two guys are in a fight," says Dan Charette. "Not surprising as there's lots of alcohol about. They're firing flares at each other at close range. It seems that the fight started when one man tried to raft up to the other, then the other guy didn't want him there. He fires a flare that just misses the boater trying to raft up. This guy gets up close, jumps on board, and chases the first guy down into his cabin and fires a flare back at him. It just misses. Lucky, because it could have killed him had it struck him."

Jeff describes parties out in the bay that go on all night, people who get drunk, have fights, fall overboard, jet skiers who collide with each other and hit rocks.

One time, says Brian, the Coast Guard is called out to Crystal Bay by a man who says his wife is acting strangely. He asks if the crew will come out and check her over. Resigned to the idea of spending another evening in Crystal Bay, Brian Riddell and Jeff Faucher (the crew's rescue specialist) gear up the cutter and speed off into the night, toward the bay. Lights twinkle across the water from the many thousands of vessels. Loud music and laughter carry across the water. The crew know the location by the number of boats rafted together and the people crowding the decks.

"A lot of very drunk people here, and fires from flares and barbecues." Jeff jumps aboard the end vessel. The husband is waiting for him and takes him into a cabin below, to a woman who lies prone on a bed. She drifts in and out of consciousness. Those who crowd around say they know nothing about what she has been drinking or smoking. Something is definitely wrong, and Jeff is not happy. All the training he has done to qualify as a rescue specialist—the first-aid and paramedic studies—does not tell him what is wrong with this woman. He and Brian have her lifted on to the *Sora* and take her back to the lifeboat station. They radio an ambulance to pick her up from the shore, and she is taken to the local hospital. There, it is found that she has been given a drug, one commonly used in date rape.

"We get so many calls, that after a while, you learn to pick up on what's a hoax, but you still have to do something about it," says Brian. "Sometimes we ask a vessel of opportunity—whoever is out there—to go check something out, or to help out, if we can't go ourselves."

Tornado Alley:Lake Erie at the Detroit River

T he area where Lake Erie approaches the Detroit River is sometimes called "tornado alley" because of the ferocity of the storms that frequently lash. Residents along the shores, and all mariners, are warned of an approaching tornado or waterspout by an alarm placed on Grosse Isle. One Saturday late in spring, the siren wails its dour warning at about the same moment the thunderstorm hits. The Coast Guard crew at the lifeboat station receive three simultaneous calls for help. They race the *Sora* into the mouth of the river near the islands, a river strewn with logs, tree branches and a mass of other floating debris.

"Three missing persons," comes one call to the station. The second is for the rescue of a boat blown onto the rocks at Point Bloise, and the third is a Mayday call from an American boater reporting that he can see a small aluminum boat being tossed about like a rubber cork.

Brian Riddell asks this boater why he himself does not go the aid of the small boat. The boater admits he is afraid to do so. Brian tells him politely that if he does not, he can be liable under

Boat aground—a not uncommon sight on waters, like those of the Great Lakes, frequented by pleasure boaters.

the law of the sea, which requires that one boater go to the aid of another. The boater refuses to speak further to the Coast Guard crew, refuses even to give the location of the small boat. The crew go out and begin methodically searching the river and its shores, having to guess at the possible spots which the small boat might have been blown to.

"It helps us that the lightning lights up the lake and the river, makes it like daylight," says Brian. "The thunder is very close, and hailstones are as big as ping pong balls, an altogether nasty storm. We find the small boat and its owner blown onto the shore further upstream. We take him back to where he started, and then we search for the three missing persons. We find one, but we never hear about the other two. We don't know what's going on but figure they may not have been lost at all. Some people call to tell us that they're lost, or they know someone who is lost, but they often forget to tell us they are okay, that they've been found, and so we go on searching." The Coast Guard crew finds the boat that was blown onto the rocks at Point Bloise and pulls it off.

At about four in the morning, another storm front approaches as the crew are returning to the base, the throttle of the *Sora* wide open. Each feels anxious to be back at the station to get some sleep. Suddenly, for no reason he can identify, Brian pulls back on the throttle, stops, and lights a cigarette.

"What's that?" asks Jeff into the sudden silence. Directly in front of the cutter floats a huge wooden dock constructed out of expensive, pressure-treated wood.

"What made you stop?" asks Jeff.

"I dunno," comes the laconic answer.

"What would you have done had you hit it?"

"I would have been through the windshield and eaten the stairs," answers Brian. "It would not have been pretty."

The Coast Guard crew tow the dock with its railing and stairs back to the shore so no other boater will hit it.

Back at the lifeboat station, the crew sit around, exhausted after fourteen straight hours of search and rescue. A half hour passes and the radio crackles to life. It's the local police, asking if the Coast Guard will take them out in the cutter to a disturbance in Crystal Bay. Occasionally the local police request transport on the lake and river to break up fights and impose order. The crew know well the territory in Crystal Bay and can help direct police, but they are reluctant to act as water transportation for them.

They have learned that if they become associated with the police some people will not call them for help. The consequence could be a loss of life.

Brian Riddell remains today as coxswain of the lifeboat station at Amherstburg, although he has had other options. He recently found himself having to make a difficult decision: to remain at the lifeboat station and on a boat, or to take up a position as operations officer in the regional office in Sarnia, a position he won through competitions. He was attracted to the desk job and had enjoyed the two months he tried during the winter. What to do? The desk job meant a move to Sarnia and his feet beneath a desk. It also meant a significant hike in salary, and a job that was exciting in its own way. Riddell imagined a life indoors, behind a desk; he knew he would sorely miss his mates, the boats, the water, the direct involvement in search and rescue missions. After much soul-searching, he eventually chose to remain at the lifeboat station, feeling that is where he belongs.

A Sheepish Affair

The Welland Canal, Ontario

T he Welland Canal is a modern-day marvel of engineering that began with a river, a man, and his dream—the dream of a waterway for shipping from the mighty Atlantic ocean, through Montreal, to the head of the Great Lakes. The deep sliver of water that became the first Welland Canal opened in 1829. Along this narrow channel, the world's great ships of commerce sailed and steamed, along with pleasure boats of all sizes. They traversed the St. Lawrence Seaway and River to the Great Lakes and into the heart of the North American continent. The guardians of this canal and lock system today are the search and rescue workers of the Canadian Coast Guard, men and women who assist the passage of vessels through the canal and rescue any in distress.

The workers operate out of a low-slung, grey wooden house built in 1931 near the site of an old lighthouse on the west side of the canal. It is a beautifully landscaped arm of land that juts out in to the waters of Lake Ontario. The station as it is now did not exist when Wade Buell was a young man. In 1978, he slept beside the waters of the canal in a rough trailer on its opposite bank, together with two strangers, not far from Port Weller in St. Catharines.

Inshore rescue boats participating in a training exercise.

"It was my third day on the job with the Canadian Coast Guard," says Buell. "I was the new recruit who didn't know anything, didn't have a clue what to do. I'd been hired to work on the Coast Guard cutter *Griffin*—to be a deckhand—but the ship was in refit in Thunder Bay, not yet ready to sail. So I got sent for three days to this station, which was just being started up on the east side of the Welland Canal."

Young Buell sleeps his first night uneasily on a hard, narrow bed in makeshift accommodation. At two in the morning, the radio phone shrills its summons into the trailer, startling him so that he almost falls out of bed. A voice booms into the darkness, "There's a lifejacket floating up river, nobody in it. No body, nothing else around—need you to go check it out." The three Coast Guard rescue workers jump out of bed, into their clothes, and are out the trailer door in what seems to Buell like mere moments. Before his eyes are half-open, he is aboard the 41-foot Coast Guard cutter and speeding at fifty knots up river. The powerful beam of a searchlight illuminate the water ahead. A helicopter flies overhead. In the murky darkness, the new recruit clutches the sides of the boat tightly. The wind whistles and the choppy waters of the river wash right over the sides of the boat.

"I felt a great rush of adrenaline," says Buell. "The wind, the speed of the boat, the helicopter flying overhead. We're here on the river looking to save someone's life, to rescue a drowning person. I think of the poor guy in the water...I tell myself at this moment that this is the kind of thing I want to do for the rest of my life. I'm like a new-born duckling being imprinted by its mother to a certain type of life. Imprinted to this job, to this life." Buell stares out the window over the choppy grey seas of Lake Ontario and falls silent for a moment.

"What about the lifejacket?"

"We picked it up," he says. "But we never found a boat, a body—alive or dead—or anything else. My very first experience with the Coast Guard ended up being nothing more than picking up a lifejacket out of the river," he muses. "And my first real rescue operation was saving the life, not of a man, a woman or a child, but of a prize-winning goat from the Welland Canal." Buell laughs as he recalls the experience.

"The Coast Guard will rescue anything that's living and breathing," he says. "People call us for the most unimaginable things. They know we'll do everything in the world, whatever the situation, that there's no limit to what we'll do. And we do it because that's the nature of our job—and because we want to."

"There's a goat drowning in the canal up at the locks," says the radio operator. "The owners want to know if you can help get it out."

"A goat! My God, they want us to rescue a goat!" says one of the crew. And the summons draws the rescue workers out of bed at two in the morning. In a few minutes, Reg Clark, Bob Whiteside, and Wade Buell, the new recruit, are on the cutter speeding up river to the lock system on the canal. The lights on the seaway cast yellow beams across the water, on the stream of cars lined up to cross the bridge—stuck there because the bridge is raised for a ship to pass through— and on their occupants who hang over the lock's railings. A truck is silhouetted above the line of car roofs. This is the truck that carries a load of prize-winning goats.

The bleating truckload was jammed among the cars lined up waiting for the bridge to open when something startled the animals, and three of them jumped off the vehicle. The truck owner and driver, joined by people loitering about the canal, chased after them, . Car horns blared, and people laughed until someone shouted, "There's a goat in the water. A goat's fallen into the lock!"

"Like a circus it was, when we arrived," says Buell. "We beamed our searchlight over the docks, the locks, the ships, the cars, and all the people—it was surprising the numbers out and about at this time of the night."

The truck owners had captured two of the runaway goats, but the little one, cornered, had panicked, climbed up the railing and leapt into the lock itself, thirty feet below.

"We steam our ship into the lock and catch sight of the little fellow in the beam of our searchlight," says Buell. "It swims around, and all we can see is this little head sticking out above the water. It swims to the port side of our boat, and then seems to go underneath it. We worry about him, then, that he won't have the strength to last much longer because he's been in the water a long time. And we really want to save him. Suddenly he appears over the starboard side of the bow, but we can't lean over the sides of our boat and try to grab him because there's too much free board. The people above are shouting and laughing, and we're all feeling a bit embarrassed."

Clark takes a mooring line, makes a lasso out of it, and tries to throw it over the goat's head. The little goat seems to swim right into it. The crew tighten the rope, and on the count of three, give it a quick hoist. The little goat flies out of the water and lands right on the deck of the boat. It's done with speed and skill so the lasso won't strangle the little creature. The crowd cheers.

"I'm standing by the rail on the starboard side," says Buell. "The goat has no sooner landed, looking half drowned, a skinny little thing with his hair plastered to its sides, than he scrambles to his feet and prepares to butt anyone or anything in front of him. I'm within his line of vision and within range of him, and he goes for me. He butts me in the side of the leg and I suffer the worst charleyhorse I've ever had in my life."

The Coast Guard crew, to the cheers and the shouts of the crowd, tie the goat to the deck, turn up the boat's engines and return to their base. They tie the goat to a tree near the trailer to keep him safe until the grateful owners come to claim him. He is a prize-winning goat, they say, a costly little fellow. Of their entire truckload of prize winners, he's the best of them all.

"A sheepish affair altogether," says Buell. "We got laughed at by the others for a long time after, and I could hardly walk for a week."

The Boat That Vanished

T he search and rescue crew members look at each other, then beyond the windowpane, to watch the storm blowing up across the lake. Small craft warnings have been broadcast from Radio Prescott, and before the day is over, the crew knows they will be out in that tempest on their way to a rescue before the day is over.

Thunder cracks directly overhead and the mid-afternoon gloom is scorched with sheet lightning. Coxswain Wade Buell wonders about Bosun, his dog and his best pal. Bosun is terrified of thunder; he will hide under his bed and whimper for his friend. There are just the two of them, and they mean everything to each other. Does his dog understand that his master isn't like other people who come home regularly every night, that he must finish this work at the lifeboat station?

As a boy, Buell and his family had lived in Germany. He and a friend, sons of Canadian Airforce personnel, had found their way into one of the remaining World War One bunkers on the famous Seigfreid Line. The young Buell could almost see the grey-coated soldiers in their high jackboots standing rigid in these trenches, waiting for the enemy to rush over the hills in a barrage of gunfire. The experience touched the sensitive boy deeply.

"Even though I was so young, I felt like my life was whizzing by before my eyes," Buell says. "I knew from that moment I must dedicate my life to the saving of lives, preventing more death, needless death. It was like I personally witnessed massive destruction so that I had an overwhelming urge not ever to take life, but to protect and preserve it all costs, at any cost to myself."

Mark Mailloux, deckhand on this crew, wonders what his kids are doing, smiles when he thinks of them—Mandy Marie, seventeen, grown so tall; Marie Lynn, thirteen; Marc Raymond, nine; and Amber Anne, just four years old. He knows they won't worry about him being at the lifeboat station even when the winds roar, when thunder and lightning rend the heavens and the lake takes on monstrous shapes, so pervasive are the stories they've heard about their dad and his work.

Mailloux has some regrets—not for any of the things he has done, but that they take him away from his family, sometimes for months at a time. That's how it is in the navy, and one of the reasons why he left. There were other reasons, too: into the navy straight out of high school, Mailloux learned that you had to wait for someone else to retire or die before you moved up. He had trained as a combat diver and mine disposal expert, a role that required him to dive beneath ships to ensure they are clear of mines.

Not content with courting danger and achieving the near-impossible in these positions, Mailloux became a surface swimmer, rescue coxswain, a Master Seaman of the Watch, and took upon himself the responsibility for everything at sea—stores and ammunition, deck evolution, replenishment. He raced and dove, stretching himself to his limits against the sea, prizing the adrenaline rush, the sheer exhilaration of a life lived where all the senses are engaged to the fullest. This is what he knew: a marvellous sense of achievement at the end of a venture and nothing dull or repetitive. None of it confined him. But he had reached a plateau; the navy could not offer him anything more. Mailloux considered his wife and family, the three acres of land in Brockville where he raised turkeys and hogs, and considered alternatives to the navy. Eventually, he and the Coast Guard found each other.

"The Coast Guard is about the sea, the sky, the elements, and racing off to the rescue of people in danger," he says. "And, unlike the navy, it's not about seniority. You have to compete for a position, and the best person gets it." He pauses and looks at his mates. "It's also about working with people you know and trust. When you're out on a rescue, you have to know the other man you're working with inside-out. You have to live and work with him, never second-guess him. Wade and Gerry are the best I've ever worked with. We're out there on the water and see distress and panic in peoples' eyes, see their boat foundering. Although the three of us know what's going to happen because we've done these rescues hundreds of times, each mission is still different. As we get near a scene, tension rises and the adrenaline mounts. Gerry will bring everything to a climax because he's an excitable fellow; you hear the levity in his voice, watch the interaction, and you can tell what's going to happen. Oh, he might ask permission for what he wants to do, but you already know how it's going to be. Wade, when we go out with him as coxswain, no matter what the conditions, we know we'll be coming back."

The shriek of the wind outside the lifeboat station increases. Mailloux watches crewman Gerry Brown-Thierren stride back and forth before the window that opens onto Portsmouth Olympic Harbour, his eyes straining to look for vessels still out on the tossing waters. A slim and intense young man, he has a touch of the carefree wanderer. As a young man, Brown-Therrien attempted to get into the army, wanting to work with his hands and to travel, but he found himself on board a navy ship where he worked for six years. He, like his mate, Mark, left the navy to work for the Coast Guard, on contract.

"I have to be free," he says. "Free to travel from one place to another to meet different people, see other places. I don't want to be in one place with the same crew for ten, fifteen, twenty years." Perhaps Brown-Therrien's penchant for a gypsy life lies in the circumstances of his birth. Given away at birth by his mother, he was raised by a succession of strangers in foster homes, and eventually adopted by a monk in a seminary. As a young man just out of the navy, he travelled about Quebec and Ontario picking fruit and working on farms.

"I have a jeep. I just get in it and drive. It's a nomadic life and I love it," he says. "I consider I'm a lucky guy because I do things other people just dream about. But then I decided I wanted to work on boats and on the water, so here I am with the Coast Guard. I feel lucky to have this job. I could not bear to work in an office and every day go to the same place, work with the same people, have the same routines in a confined space. Now this work, it's like a drug."

Wade Buell sits at the desk in the little office in the unassuming Coast Guard building perched at the breakwater of Portsmouth Harbour. The historic city of Kingston slopes up and beyond, to spread itself above the shores of the mighty St. Lawrence River where it meets Lake Ontario. At this juncture the river is at its widest in its eight hundred-mile foray into Canada's hinterland. A good place to build a city, Buell thinks, irrelevantly, spot where it can brood over the mighty river that widens into the lake here, and all the ships that sail her.

He watches the trees outside bend in the gale-force wind, and Lake Ontario thrash itself in fury against the retaining walls. He listens as the Prescott weather office warns of two storm fronts approaching. He thinks over the many years of his service with the Coast Guard, how he has sat at this desk, staring out over the famous stretch of water at the foot of the old city where sailboats race. He knows he is likely to be out in the storm before the day is over.

George and Jeannine Booth and their dogs Molly and ChinChin are cruising the lakes and waterways of central Canada. Their luxury floating home is a 1995 Bayliner 4587 motor yacht with twin diesel engines. Including the anchor pulpit and swim platform, the ship is fifty feet long. The Booths have named her *Second Mates*, because each is the other's second mate and this luxury floating home is their second landing.

Through the oval windows in the master bedroom, the couple awakens each morning to an ever-changing expanse of water—a glinting blue, a sullen grey, or gentle, flecked green swells. One flick of a switch sets the coffee percolator brewing; another turns on the radio on the mahogany bedside table. Many years have been spent dreaming and planning for these extended boating forays from their summer home on Lake Erie in Huron, Ohio. Their floating home includes a television room and lounge, and stainless steel "his and hers" bathrooms. The cruiser has been designed with a thirty-foot sleek bow and a three-tiered navigational bridge, equipped with every sophisticated navigational and communication system available. George has had a bow thruster, fuel FloScan, Walker air separators and a new rub rail installed during the winter, the bilge pumps upgraded, and the generator relocated from the cockpit bilge to the engine room.

In the summer of 1998, the husband-and-wife team, together with their two dogs, cruise along the eastern seaboard of the United States up the Hudson River to Troy, New York. They continue on, up the St. Lawrence River to Montreal, to the Thousand Islands, and on to Cape Vincent. Although one can tour the Cape Vincent in about an hour, the Booths spend four days here because the weather is not fit for further travel; eight- to ten-foot waves are breaking on Lake Ontario.

George Booth signals the Coast Guard when his boat, *Second Mates*, begins taking on water as it tries to navigate twelve-foot swells.

On June 8, NOAA weather channels three and four announce that small craft warnings have been lifted and the forecast is for waves three to four feet out of the west, subsiding to two to three feet in the afternoon. The skies are clear. At 1:30 in the afternoon, after consulting with a pilot who has just crossed the lake, George and Jeannine leave the marina with the agreement that they will return if the lake is rough.

"I rationalized that, with the wind and the waves out of the west, we, being at the east end of the lake, should encounter the biggest waves as we enter it," George explains. Their destination is Rochester, New York, seventy-five nautical miles west.

"We cruised at sixteen knots, and our ETA was 6:30 in the evening," he says. "But the waves continued to get bigger, and at ten nautical miles, they'd increased to four feet. I shut off the auto-pilot and Jeannine and I got into our lifejackets. It got worse: at thirty nautical miles, the waves were towering up to six feet and a rogue wave hit our bow, lifted our boat out of the water and slammed it hard."

George cuts back his speed to six knots. A short while later he notices that the mid-ship lower bilge pump indicator light has come on, and remains on. George asks Jeannine to take the helm so he can go below and inspect. She looks unhappy at this request and confesses that she doesn't feel that she can control the boat, so George asks her to go below, lift the salon floor hatch and describe what is happening. He figures there is either a broken water hose or a hull leak. The boat tosses wildly as Jeannine stumbles down the three steps to open the sliding salon door. George hears a shriek.

"George! The galley has about six inches of water in it," she cries. George is shocked because the galley floor is about two feet above the engine room floor.

"The television is lying face down on the floor and everything's a mess," she says, upset. She sits down on the cockpit step and clutches the two dogs to her.

George looks at the dark clouds behind him from the east, thinks hard for a moment, and makes his decision. He hails the Coast Guard on channel sixteen, tells them his way points, says he is taking on water and that he and his wife are facing waves that are about ten feet high and erratic, making the boat difficult to handle.

Above the noisy fury of the storm, the crew at the lifeboat station hear a voice on the phone from the Joint Rescue Coordination Centre (JRCC) in Trenton, tasking them to go to the rescue of the *Second Mates*, a fifty-foot cabin cruiser that is taking on water. An elderly American couple and their dogs are on board.

"It's what is known as a pan pan call," Buell explains. "Help is needed, but it's not an emergency. They give us the approximate position of the sinking boat, somewhere southwest of False Duck Islands and twenty-seven miles out from shore. We're told that a United States Coast Guard vessel is also on its way out to the boat in distress."

Buell and his crew, without words, load extra supplies and equipment they think they might need into the Coast Guard cutter *Bittern*, and Buell, as commanding officer, roars the vessel into life. He tells the JRCC they are on their way.

"We thump and crash the cutter from one swell to another, making a top speed of twenty-three knots," says Buell. "We reach the crest of a wave, and then slam into the bottom of a trough with a thump, like a giant slab of concrete dropping on concrete. Ours is a small boat for these conditions, but there's no question, we have to get to these people, do our best to rescue them, and with luck, their boat. I plough the *Bittern* as fast as I dare into the waves. She thumps so hard that things start to come loose, like all the fire extinguishers fall out of their holdings. I have to slow her down a bit then. I can tell you, there's lots of adrenaline pumping among the three of us."

—

Back on *Second Mates*, George takes a quick look down the carpeted stairs into the salon below. The water that swirls through the galley and the main bedroom is half way up the cupboard doors, and is warm; flotsam floats and swirls about all the lower decks. George is horrified. This is a sailor's nightmare: a boat taking on water in a violent storm, in an unfamiliar area where the places of shelter are unknown to him except as markings on a map. *Second Mates*'s internal engines are filling the boat with water instead of pumping it out. He slows his sinking boat to four knots and tries to keep it quartered to the waves coming over the upper helm. Suddenly the forward hatch comes off, and water begins pouring into the forward stateroom.

"I've been radioing our way points every ten minutes because I don't know when the batteries will be under water and the radio will die," George says. "The Coast Guard notifies me that a cutter and its crew is on its way and will reach me in less than ninety minutes. I don't know if I can hold out that long, and that's what I tell them. They say for me to inflate our lifeboat. We manage to do it, but it's an exhausting ordeal. And then, an hour later, we lose the starboard engine. The water is up to the portholes and I calculate that the Coast Guard is still about thirty minutes away. I put out a Mayday call on channel sixteen. We're approximately twenty miles north of Oswego, New York, and about twelve miles south of False Duck Island in Ontario, by this time."

The response to the Mayday call from the Trenton JRCC is immediate. Ten minutes after George Booth issues a Mayday call, a large aircraft—a Canadian Armed Forces C130 Hercules—roars toward them to hover scarcely a hundred feet above the water. The pilot radios that he has seen the Booth's boat and that he is dropping a gasoline pump with a five-hundred-foot line attached. A moment later, a red container parachutes into the water. The pilot asks George if he can see the line. George says no, but that he can see the pump and will try to retrieve it, but in the conditions, with only one engine, he is concerned about the line fouling his propeller.

A tremendous noise begins to drown out his voice and the twelve-foot seas are suddenly reduced to a two-foot chop. The Booths look skyward to see a huge Labrador helicopter hovering overhead, and a new voice comes over the radio.

"We'll get the pump for you," says this voice as the downdraft from the two propellers creates a hundred-foot circle of calm water.

The Coast Guard's helicopter pilot radios the search and rescue workers on the *Bittern* to give them the location of the sinking boat. Buell heads the cutter into the wind to make for the area, twelve nautical miles the other side of False Duck Island, and twenty-seven miles from the lifeboat station in Kingston. The coxswain listens as the JRCC controller explains that a United States Coast Guard vessel is also approaching.

"The conditions are poor," the Controller then says. "A second storm front is approaching and an SAR tech in the helicopter is at the scene. You can return to base."

"You *can*, not you *must*," says Buell. "What did they think? That we would turn around and go home, leave an old couple and their dogs out there? Sure, the U. S. Coast Guard will get there. Sure, the SAR tech is there, but we're the guys who've been around a long time, had lots of experience, know what to do. We're the ones who know about the seas, not an SAR tech." He pauses. "Our cutter, like the American one, is rated for a six-foot following sea and we're out in twelve-foot swells. We know there is a cell approaching from the east, and that worries us a bit. But this is what we do, we go out to rescue people—it's what we know how to do, and we can handle it."

Determined, he pushes the *Bittern* to its limits through sleet, grey seas and blinding rain. Thunder growls overhead and sudden bolts of lightning sear the gloom. Twelve- and fifteen-foot waves tower above the ship and water rushes across the decks of the cutter to drench them. They bounce from crest to trough like a bobbing rubber ball. It is, as Buell knows, a small boat for the conditions, but he doggedly persists. As they draw close, they hear the droning of the helicopter, and see outlines of a vessel rising on the crests of a wave, only to plunge immediately out of sight. The *Bittern* rides the giant swells to within a few yards of the stricken boat.

Jeannine Booth sits shivering on the galley step, clutching her dogs. George, cold and anxious, watches as the SAR tech, in a wet suit with helmet and fins, is lowered by cable about twenty feet above the water, then free-falls the rest of the way. The SAR tech swims to the red object containing the pump, a small blob rising and falling with the crests and troughs of the waves. He makes it to *Second Mates* and climbs on board their boat as a second SAR technician is lowered onto the deck. Buell and his crew on the little Canadian Coast Guard cutter now arrive, and a loud cheer goes up. The Canadian Coast Guard cutter has beaten the American cutter by just a few minutes, or twenty-five to forty feet.

"That's when I realize that all these people here are Canadians," says George.

The SAR tech examines Jeannine and turns to George. "I'm taking Mrs. Booth off the boat. She's in shock and should be evacuated immediately."

"Of course," says George. The SAR tech tells Jeannine to put down the dogs so he can get her harnessed. She says flatly that the dogs are going with her.

A Coast Guard ship and a helicopter on a training exercise at sea.

"Impossible," says the SAR tech. "How can it be done?"

"Wait," she says, and scrambles around to find two knit shopping bags hanging on the aft-deck wet bar. She places a dog in each bag, slips her arms through the handles, and says she's ready. The SAR tech hooks the cable above Jeannine's head, wraps his legs around her waist, and signals they are ready to be lifted. At this point, something happens: the winch backs off, or the helicopter dips, or the boat is raised up. In any case, both fall back into the open cockpit, twice. The third attempt is successful, and Jeannine Booth is up in the helicopter. Once there, she realizes, to her great dismay, that ChinChin is missing.

On the seas below, Buell and his crew are attempting the maneuver that will bring them close enough to the rolling and pitching vessel to throw a tow line, close enough perhaps for one of them to jump on board. Brown-Therrien, his fear locked away until the rescue is over, has dozens of thoughts flitting through his head. In his mind he has saved the couple, their dogs, and the boat many times over before they have even come close to the scene: "This is how I'm going to tie the knot, this where her bow will go…"

"We'll make this approach, and if it doesn't work, we'll try another, like, take the cutter upwind," Mailloux shouts above the roar of waves. Buell struggles to control his vessel, to time the rise and fall of the waves as he's riding through them. He must pass the other vessel at the split second that she breaches on the *Bittern* so that they can make contact with her. The plan is for one crew member to board the *Second Mates*, pump the water out of the sinking boat, and tow it to shore.

Brown-Therrien has attached the defenders and thrown them over the sides of the cutter; Mailloux has been struggling with the towline when suddenly, miraculously, the hook-up is made: he has a kicker line attached to *Second Mates*. Buell immediately turns the *Bittern* into the wind while Brown-Therrien pays out the towline and makes it fast. Buell steps the cutter, timing it between each wave so that the line never comes out of the water.

"We know we can tow their boat," Mailloux explains. "But it will be tough. What can happen is that one boat might be climbing a wave while the other falls back, dropping and sliding and putting undue stress on the line, risking it breaking. Then all your efforts are in vain. You pay out the line, you watch like a hawk, you step the vessel—it's intense concentration." Buell explains how the crew will watch the cruiser come up on a plane to see if she's exceeded her safe towing speed, knowing she has twenty tons of water in her and that she'll fall back a little and send all the water to the rear.

After the hook-up, a line is left attached while the cutter is maneuvered so that one of the crew can board *Second Mates*. Mailloux will try to make the jump from one vessel to the other.

Before this perilous move is made, George Booth is on the radio, talking to the *Bittern*. He tells them that his wife and a dog have been evacuated into the helicopter, and he's being advised to get off his boat as well.

"The SAR tech says my wife is in shock and needs immediate medical treatment. They're down to twenty minutes of fuel and have to leave. He advises I go with them." Booth asks what his options are—if he stays with his boat, how long will he be on it? About five hours, he's told.

Booth considers his options. He knows that the Coast Guard has a towline attached to his boat. He tells the SAR tech that he will be okay. The SAR tech confers with him again. At this moment, the commanding officer of the Hercules aircraft, who is in charge of the rescue, comes on the radio and tells Booth that it's time for him to get off his boat.

"In the end, I decide to go; I tell him that I want to be with my wife," says Booth.

A two-person lift is arranged, and the SAR technician radios the JRCC to say they are abandoning the boat.

"I need to get some things," Booth says. He is told to hurry. He collects ChinChin, and his vessel's logbook, and puts them both into a canvas bag. The SAR tech returns for them; safe in the helicopter, George opens the bag and is dismayed not to see ChinChin.

"My dog's jumped out!"

"Sorry," says the SAR tech, "we have to leave."

"I can live without ChinChin," George says, "but Jeannine will have a very tough time." He pleads with him until the SAR tech says that he will radio the Coast Guard to see if they can board the sinking boat and retrieve the dog.

Before they receive this request, the crew members aboard the Coast Guard cutter have the same idea.

"Hey, while we're here, we might as well do a few maneuvers, do some training," Buell says; "Heck, we've got twelve to fifteen foot swells...great opportunity for an exercise. Let's cross the T a few times, come alongside the boat..."

"I'll jump on board," Mailloux says. "Set their anchor for them."

"No problem," says the coxswain.

The three workers stand within earshot of each other in the foam and spray. Thunder claps above them, and a sudden bolt of lightning rends the clouds. The outline of the sinking vessel rises ten feet above them, then falls ten feet below, barely visible to the crew who strain their eyes through the gloom. The momentary calm caused by the hovering helicopter provides the opportunity for the jump to be made, and Buell attempts to bring the lunging cutter's bow at right angles to the cruiser. He times his vessel's rise up the crest of a wave while the cruiser rushes down into the trough. For one fraction of a second, the ships are level. Mailloux grabs the railing with one hand while he aims a cross T tow line and, with consummate skill, manages to hook the kicker line to the bow of the cruiser to jump aboard it. He might easily find himself swallowed up in the foaming waters or crushed between the two boats, but Mark Mailloux is an old hand at this game against the sea. He's doing what he likes to do: taking bold and even reckless chances, trying to beat the odds.

"If you're a second too slow, or too fast, you'll cause a catastrophe; it has to be timed perfectly," he says. "Once we've got a tow on it, we can do anything with it."

Buell has brought the cutter alongside the other vessel, but at an angle so that he will not smash into it. The rise and fall of the waves are timed once more. Mailloux prepares himself, and Brown-Therrien counts him off. Mailloux jumps. He lands with a thump on the deck of the *Second Mates* and slithers across it to crash into the railing on the starboard side. Thumbs up! He picks himself up, finds the kicker line, and tosses it across the water to Brown-Therrien. The American Coast Guard cutter hovers at a distance, but close enough for her crew to witness the daring maneuvers of Mark Mailloux.

Fork lightning continues to illuminate the gloom, rain lashes, and thunder rolls across the sky as the luxury cruiser slowly buries herself in the heaving waters of the lake. Mailloux examines the cruiser; he finds that the pumps have not been primed, and that the water in the boat is warm. This suggests that the sea suction pump is loose, or its valve malfunctioning, so that water pumped in to cool the engines was not being pumped out but into the interior of the boat instead. He uses his handset radio to call across to Buell in the *Bittern* to explain what he's found. With this news, Buell and Brown-Therrien are astonished that the owner of the boat has been advised to abandon his vessel.

"Maybe the guy panicked," Buell says of the SAR tech. "I have tremendous respect for him and what he does, but he's not used to being rocked about in twelve- to fifteen-foot seas. What he did, by removing the people from their boat, was to abandon it. Once the owners are taken off a vessel, it's considered abandoned, and we, the Coast Guard, can't touch it. It becomes the business of the salvage companies." After a pause, he adds, "Of course, I don't know who said and decided what. The guys from the Department of National Defense up in the Hercules aircraft are the ones in charge, and they would be getting information from JRCC in Trenton, and from the radio station in Prescott about the two storm fronts. From their point of view, it must have seemed the most reasonable thing to get the Booths off, up into the helicopter, and to hell with their vessel."

Gerry Brown-Therrien has his own theory about the fate of the cruiser. "The boat didn't collide with anything, and had not run aground. I think the maintenance work that had been done on it did not hold up. A pipe or hose came loose and could have easily been fixed," he says.

Mark Mailloux, on board the cruiser, gets to work to activate the pump on *Second Mates*, thinking that he can save the boat. As he works, the radio crackles with the voices of the United States Coast Guard.

"Get off!" they order their Canadian counterparts. "You are to leave the boat." And the JRCC in Trenton warns them again of the storm fronts rapidly approaching and not yet at the height of their fury.

"Cut the towline," orders the JRCC voice. "Leave the boat and get yourselves back to base."

"I know they were concerned about our safety," says Buell. "It must have seemed suicidal to them that we're out in this storm and on board the sinking boat. And, of course, there are rules about abandoned boats—but we know we can save it!" Buell shakes his head, sorrow in his eyes. "Such a waste. We don't feel we've properly completed a rescue unless we save the boat as well as the people. You feel you're taking a part of their lives away when you don't save the boat."

He skillfully maneuvers the *Bittern* into a position to enable Mailloux to make the jump back on board. After many attempts, he has angled it into a position where Mailloux can jump. As they begin the long journey back to the lifeboat station, they get the message from the helicopter pilot that one of the dogs is still on *Second Mates*. Is there any chance they can get him?

"We keep thinking about that dog and how he obviously means so much to the couple, more than his boat," says Buell. "We do it all again—the timing of the crests and troughs of the waves, getting close but not too close to crash into it, Mailloux making the leap on board. The wind has shifted, and this time we have to come up from the stern, face into the wind. The bow of the Booth's boat is much deeper in the water now, but we believe we can still save it by pumping it."

Mailloux finds a shivering and terrified little charcoal-grey poodle crouched on a settee, with flotsam strewn about. He picks up the distraught animal and takes him to the aft deck. He watches the *Bittern* rise and fall with the waves. Buell is timing it, talking to Brown-Therrien and using all kinds of throttle just to keep his cutter off the cruiser.

The crew is tired; it's been a long and exhausting day and

night. But the coxswain and his second mate, with scarcely a need for words, time the rise and fall of the swells. Mailloux shouts that he's about to throw the small animal; Brown-Therrien yells, "one, two, *three!*" and Mailloux pitches the little dog high in the air. The ball of fur flies through the storm until Brown-Therrien catches him in mid-air by his front legs. A cheer from all three goes up. Brown-Therioux lets the little dog run about the deck for a few minutes before stowing the small, shivering creature in the wheelhouse for safety. "Does anyone want any chocolate-coated nuts?" he asks on his return. ChinChin has left his droppings all over the wheelhouse and on the bridge.

Buell maneuvers the boat so that Mailloux can leap across. But before he attempts it, Mailloux lets out all three hundred feet of *Second Mates*'s anchor line, hoping that the boat will cease taking on water and drag. Next, he severs the rigid-hulled inflatable raft attached to the Coast Guard cutter, allows it to half fill it with water, and leaves it to drag alongside *Second Mates*. The small boat will be useful as a marker, assisting the salvage company to locate *Second Mates* when conditions improve.

Buell turns his cutter about and once again heads back for port. The seas are still huge, the rain turned to hail and thrown in their faces by a savage wind. As the cutter enters the harbour, the hail is turning to freezing rain.

George and Jeannine Booth have been admitted to the Kingston General Hospital for evaluation. That night, from his hospital bed, George phones a salvage company about his boat. He is told by the company owner that it is futile to go out on the lake in such weather, that waterspouts, tornadoes that occur over water, have been reported. He says he will contact an airplane pilot and have him search for the boat at daybreak.

The Booths leave the hospital in the small hours of the morning. They book themselves into a nearby Holiday Inn wearing green hospital scrubs and paper shoes because their clothes and shoes are still soaking wet. It is an embarrassing ordeal: Kingston has five penitentiaries, two of which are psychiatric. As the couple pass through the lobby, George hears people laughing, "...they must be escapees."

The crew at the lifeboat station cannot sleep. Outside, the night continues to rage black and violent. A branch of the giant oak overhanging the building makes intermittent thumps on the roof and rain lashes the windows.

Mailloux thinks of his wife tucked up in the big bed in their house in Brockville.

The young Brown-Therrien conducts his post-mortem of the rescue operation, and the fear that had no part of his thoughts at sea now floods him—"What if? If we had done this, if we had done that...?" Buell too, hunched in the worn armchair by the bay window, thinks about what he has just done. He knows that the deep physical and mental exhaustion he feels and the ache in all his muscles will not last, but he hopes it dissipates before another rescue requires him to do it all again. He thinks back over the years to the fellows he once knew when he worked in a factory that manufactured dog food, how they would think him crazy for doing this kind of work, especially now as he approaches his fifties. But Buell knows he cannot do otherwise.

"I'm from a long line of lobster fishermen and occasional farmers on Prince Edward Island," he explains. Like his immediate and distant forebears, Buell has a Conradian taste for restless wanderings to lonely outposts, learning early about the joys of moving about. His father, in both the army and navy, took his family with him to remote northern Labrador—where his sons learned to cope with severe cold and twenty-foot snowdrifts—then to Germany, where they learned to play every sort of sport, and where Buell experienced his life's defining moment deep in the old World War One trenches.

"Most people have their feet stuck in concrete," he says. "But mine are always moving. When we got back to Canada, my parents settled in Trenton, and I went to work in a factory because I needed a job. I hated it; I quit, and went on to become a driver at the nearby military complex. But I was restless, driven to the water, to be near it, work beside and on it. It was always my primary passion, still is. It doesn't matter whether it's the ocean, lakes, or waterways; I love boats, anything that sails. I can't imagine doing anything else, punching a time clock, watching it to see if it's time for a coffee break. Can't imagine getting up every morning and driving to the office, knowing every day what I'm going to do. I like to be physical and have physical challenges, to move around. To do something for the good of others makes my mind and body work, makes me feel good about myself, gives meaning to my life."

A thunderclap bursts overhead and startles the crew out of

their personal reveries. Buell hears a banging on the front door. He opens it to find a strange figure on the step. The crew stares. It's George Booth standing before them in a pair of hospital pyjamas, intravenous tubing still tucked inside his hospital gown.

"I got a taxi here to see if you have my dog," he says apologetically. "They told me you got him off my boat?" At the sound of his voice, ChinChin came rushing out of the corner with a loud welcome for his master. Mr. Booth's gratitude, and his respect for the rescue workers, is unbounded. He apologetically mentions that he also had a briefcase on board that's pretty important to him. He had not liked to ask if they could find it, for they were risking their lives being out there....

"No, no," Buell says. "Too bad you didn't mention it. If you'd told us about it, we would have found it. But we did save this for you," and he handed George Booth the lifering from his boat, its name engraved on it. "We're very sorry about your boat; we would have saved it for you, had we been allowed."

The *Second Mates* has never been found. When the storm fronts subsided and the salvage companies went searching for it, all they found was the Coast Guard's inflatable raft. *Second Mates* had vanished.

"It's very frustrating, " says Buell. "We'd come all the way out in twelve-foot seas to do a job. We get there, and we're not allowed to do it. We all felt we could have saved the boat. Mr. Booth was worried about the briefcase; we could have got it for him. Hell, we could have stayed and had a picnic on that boat! But we're ordered off it. But we'd left a towline—kicker line—on the boat, and so we thought we'd get it back. I mean, there's thirty feet of it, why waste it? And so we did; we got it. It sure bothered us that we couldn't save the boat."

After this rescue operation, the crew of the American Coast Guard cutter expressed admiration at how easily their Canadian counterparts seemed to get on and off the sinking cruiser and how they managed to get a towline attached.

"When they say this, I think: what are they talking about?" Buell says. "We do this all the time. Their problem is that because they are part of a military organization, they get moved around to different positions and don't gain the experience in doing these things. But you know, the Canadian and the American Coast Guard get along really well. We respect them, and there's a lot of camaraderie and cooperation."

George Booth phones the lifeboat station in Kingston, and the

Joint Rescue Coordination Centre in Trenton on every anniversary of his rescue, to thank them.

"The Great Lakes boaters are very fortunate to have services such as the Canadian Armed Forces and the U.S. and Canadian Coast Guards standing by to help in time of trouble. Jeannine and I will be forever grateful to them for their dedication and professional skills," he says.

Wade Buell remains today as coxswain of the Coast Guard cutter, the *Bittern*, in charge of his own little world at the Kingston lifeboat station. He supervises the crew and takes responsibility for all the calls the station receives, all operations, and the general upkeep and maintenance of the station. Mark Mailloux was seriously injured some time after this rescue operation while working on a Coast Guard buoy-tending ship. He stays at home, unable to work. Gerry Brown-Therrien now works on contract as deckhand for the Coast Guard, doing what he likes best: moving from one location to another. But he remains in close contact with Buell and Mailloux, who are like brothers to him.

"I have my mates alongside me," says Buell. "The camaraderie—when it works, there's nothing like it. It's a heady mixture when you work together with your mates to save people's lives. With the right crew, you feel you can do anything. When you trust your team absolutely you get energy from them.

"We all feel a sense of pride, of achievement, like we're the only ones who can do this, the only ones who can help. Machismo, I suppose you might call it. But it's a big high to know you've made a difference, especially after a difficult rescue. And I have my mates alongside me—for some of the time anyway—mates for whom I have a profound respect, and can trust with my life."

A Navigator's Nightmare

The St. Lawrence River and the Thousand Islands

The small grey house of the Kingston lifeboat station stares out at a mighty river, a thousand islands and their labyrinthine channels. Here, the upper reaches of the St Lawrence River meet the eastern sweep of Lake Ontario. The search and rescue patrol area extends outward from the old city of Kingston in a radius of 125 miles, encompassing most of the Thousand Islands.

The large, bulky mass of Wolfe Island rises up in the middle of a river dotted with the smaller islands of Simcoe and Garden to the north and east. Duck Islands brood from the mouth of the harbour across to the hill where Old Fort Henry, its gun emplacements still in the ready position, stares over the lake. The cutter *Bittern* cruises the southern shore of the west end of Kingston, up the north channel to Picton, Prince Edward Point, and the Upper Gap where Lake Ontario meets Amherst Island. Eventually, the ship steams into a rising sea created by the southwest winds that dominate eastern Lake Ontario. False Duck Island and Timber

CCGC *Point Race* at sea.

Island now come into view. The southern reaches of the *Bittern*'s patrol take crew to a well-known area: Schoolhouse Bay on Main Duck Island, infamous for shipwrecks and the drowning of hapless people, in the past and today.

The crew thinks that the danger may lie in sailors' proximity to the mainland—they relax their vigil, believing that once they are anchored in Schoolhouse Bay they are in a safe harbour and need concern themselves no further about the elements. In doing so, they underestimate the danger of the lake's winds, which can change abruptly and frequently. Feeling secure at anchor in Schoolhouse Bay, the sailors go to bed. In the middle of the night, winds shift from northwest to southeast, and the bay is rocked by the full fury of the wind blowing right onto shore. The vessels drag anchor towards the rocky shoreline. The owners panic, and start issuing Mayday calls.

Fire on the Water

Kingston, Ontario

(Adapted from Dana T. Bowen's *Shipwrecks of the Great Lakes* "The Ocean Wave," with permission of Freshwater Press, Cleveland, Ohio.)

In April of 1853, the *Ocean Wave* called into the port of Kingston to load passengers and freight, as well as cordwood for her boiler fuel. She was a fine passenger steamer of the mid-eighteenth century, built in Montreal to trade between New York and Hamilton, Ontario. Her passage was slow as she made stops at most of the ports along the way. Steamships, at this time, used fat fuel under the boilers and carried logs full of flammable sap piled up on deck. This gave quick and plentiful heat that maintained the steam pressure required by the ship's engines, but that, together with any freshly-painted wooden surfaces, presented a considerable fire hazard on board.

The vessel was loaded and sailed before midnight. By one o'clock in the morning she was twenty-three miles from Kingston, and close to two miles off the Duck Islands, when the purser was told of a fire. Flames were already leaping up from the boiler room. Fanned by northwest winds, the flames spread with abandon. The heat was intense, fire spreading so rapidly that the crew could not launch their lifeboats. Crew and passengers tried desperately to reach for the water buckets, but the cabin walls on which the fire buckets hung had already been devoured by fire.

Within twenty minutes, the ship's cabins were a flaming furnace that lit up the sky for many miles around; those living on the nearby Duck Islands claimed that they were able to read by the light from the burning ship.

Two schooners, the *Emblem* and the *Georgina*, steaming near Duck Islands about this time, were drawn to the steamer's terrible plight by the brilliance of the sky lit up all around them. The schooner captains thrust their engines into full steam and headed toward the flaming ship.

The daring runs made by the sailors from the two schooners toward the blazing *Ocean Wave* have become legendary: sailors repeatedly risked their lives in their attempts to take people off the burning ship. In the end, twenty-one people survived and twenty-eight died. The *Ocean Wave* sank, as did her cargo of three thousand barrels of flour, several hundred bags of seed grain, three hundred kegs of butter, sixty barrels of potash, a large number of hams, as well as some general package freight. A tremendous loss in both lives and property, the tragedy presented a staggering blow to the Lake Ontario marine shipping interests of those days. But it did nothing to pave the way for safer navigation in the following years. No changes were made to the marine conditions that helped cause the fire.

▬

In Canada, prior to 1882, the government did little to enhance safety on its seas and waterways, so the young country suffered tremendous loss of life, ships, and property, the *Ocean Wave* but one among untold numbers. Consider the loss of life in the early 1880s: 226 in 1882, 157 in 1883, and 160 in 1884. That changed when A. W. McClellan, minister of Marines and Fisheries, and William Smith, his deputy minister, organized the nucleus of a rescue system under the authority of the government. Several stations were established, including one on Main Duck Island.

By 1897, Canada had 184 light stations, 235 lights, 17 keepers, 3 lightships, 2 fog whistles, 11 fog horns, 5 bell buoys, and 2 gas buoys. Most were positioned on the Great Lakes, considered to be one of the world's finest but most difficult navigable waterways in the world.

Poor charting was the first serious problem in the early years, but the greatest difficulty was the lack of sea room. When ships ran for shelter in artificial harbours, they often missed and struck rocks, sand banks and piers. They encountered sudden gales that swept anchored vessels fore and aft and forced the crew into the rigging, where they clung until they perished in cold seas that swept over them or until they were rescued, often against all odds. Feverish government activity took place up until 1897, when lighthouses increased from 227 to 783.

In 1887, a lighthouse established at Main and False Duck islands on Lake Ontario was built to help sailors and to prevent vessels from grounding on the many rocky shoals along the shore. At times, the islands also housed an occasional family or an idle visitor—witnesses, too, to a Great Lakes freighter destroyed by fire, or dashed on the rocky shores, lost in the channels and the fog. The lighthouse station was run by a keeper who was required to be fit, a master of boat craft, skilled in the art of surfing and in wreck operations; the keeper selected his own crew.

In 2000, the *Bittern's* coxswain and his crew are on their search and rescue patrol among the Thousand Islands. If they know the early history of this area, they must be grateful that the work they do takes place in this century and not a century earlier. Back then, a wreck was not usually discovered until morning, perhaps many hours after the ship had been struck. On its discovery, a courier on horseback might be dispatched to a local station—if one existed at the time—a telegram might be sent, or a train taken to the site of the shipwreck. Horses may have been hitched to draw the boat wagon with its boat and a crew down to the shore, close to where the ship had foundered. They would launch their boat into huge inland seas, straining at the oars. Seas might overwhelm the little lifeboat and put the oarsmen in danger, or the lifeboat might capsize. If it did, the men would try to cling to it while it shuddered over rocks and shoals as it ground itself upon the shore.

Today, the lighthouse on Main Duck Island is abandoned, the meandering path leading up to it now overgrown. The lighthouse has been replaced by detailed navigational charts and sophisticated navigational aids: radar, depth sounders, global positioning systems, Loran C, and VHF radio.

What meets the eyes of the crew patrolling in the modern Coast Guard cutter today is a different universe from the one that met the eye of the early French explorer. At the discovery of the Thousand Islands in 1650, the governor of New France is reputed to have said: "a melancholy abode, nothing agreeable about them other than their multitude…an infinity of little islands of such number and variety that the most experienced Iroquois pilots sometimes lose themselves…" [1]

Navigation along the river proved so difficult that the French planted a particular type of poplar along a channel that hugged the north shore of Lake Ontario, much like Hansel and Gretel leaving a trail of bread crumbs behind them so they would not get lost in the woods. Tragic shipwrecks of old have entered the lore and psyche of the local people here, and of sailors everywhere. A hundred, several hundred years later, the desperate tales are not forgotten.

Brockville, witness to some of these terrible wrecks, is built on the riverbanks opposite many of the Thousand Islands. It began as a series of little creeks and marshland; by 1785, its few inhabitants had a tree-lined path for wagons that stretched before and beyond it, skirting the edge of the swamps. *Bateaux* and large and small scows crowded a river that jumped with black bass. In 1816, following the War of 1812, the river was surveyed and a zigzag line drawn through the middle of both river and lake that, for six months of every year, provided a marine highway to the west. 1820 saw steamboats such as the *Frontenac* plying the river, allowing freedom of travel without dependency on the weather. This was a time of steam whistles, and large, gaily-coloured crowds gathered on docks and wharves.

Islands often create images of escape and seclusion, of romantic idylls and hideaway places. But two hundred years ago, these islands were stripped of their forests, and reduced to bare rock, cliffs and brush cover. They were inhabited by people that the Indians considered squatters: fishermen, wood cutters, and boatmen.

However, the exhilarating majesty of the area did not go unrecognized. Hotel and guesthouses were built, navigational lights and lighthouses were created and positioned, and channels explored, although the smaller ones long remained unknown. This was the beginning of a boom in a tourist industry that flourishes to this day. In these early years, hunting, fishing, and beautiful scenery attracted wealthy tourists to the Thousand Islands. Father would be out hunting in the woods, the children playing on the riverbanks, and Mother sitting on the hotel verandah, gazing at the largely vacant islands. Perhaps she wanted to own one; the building of island homes and castles, of stone walls, gardens, and orchards soon bloomed in the middle of the river. Shipbuilders designed craft ideal for river transportation, the ubiquitous "skiff" being the most popular. Constructed of oak and pine, it was approximately twenty-one feet long, had pointed ends, a sail, and a retractable folding centreboard; there was no rudder.

The early popularity of the Thousand Islands was not sustained. The fires of 1911 and 1912 demolished many of the grand houses and hotels, and the islands were closed when World War One was declared.

However, this area of the St. Lawrence River is still famous for its pleasure boating. The islands provide much of the attraction because of their abandoned homes and castles, places of historical curiosity, peace, and beauty. Houseboat rentals have soared, but not without frequent mishap. Among their other responsibilities, Coast Guard rescue workers find themselves coming to the aid of those who get lost, run out of fuel, or get stuck, sometimes because they think driving a houseboat is as easy as driving a car.

The CCGC *Point Race* responding to a pleasure craft on fire.

Generations later, people still get lost or stranded among the watery labyrinths formed by the islands. Today, most of those caught by the river are pleasure boaters without adequate navigational tools or boating experience, caught in sudden, severe storms. They keep the lifeboat station crews at Cobourg, Kingston, Prescott, and Goderich busy.

[1] Don Ross, *St. Lawrence Islands National Park.*

A Boat is
Not a Bus

The St. Lawrence River and the Thousand Islands

(This incident is true, but Bob and Connie Jones are pseudonyms.)

"If I can drive a bus down city streets, I can drive this thing," Bob Jones spat as he glared at his wife, one hand on the wheel of the rented houseboat, the other holding a beer can.

"You can't drive nothin," Connie Jones shouted back. "See, you can't even get this thing halfway close to the dock, and how many times have you tried, eh? Drive a bus, drive a boat—same thing, you say? I don't think so. Let's see just how good you are at driving." She shot a look at her husband, then wandered across the wide deck and into the galley to pour herself another drink.

"It's only a damn houseboat. Nothing to it, I can drive it!" These were Jones's famous last words before a sudden, violent jolt sent objects flying about in the forty-foot houseboat and over its railings into the river. A loud splintering sound burst the air: Jones had driven his unwieldy craft not alongside the dock in the outer harbour at the historic city of Kingston, Ontario, but straight onto the gravelly beach about twenty yards distant from it. The boat groaned, shuddered, buried its bow into the sand and stuck fast. Connie Jones flew out from the galley.

"Now you've gone and done it. I told you that you couldn't drive a boat. Now what are you gonna do?"

Bob Jones swore. Roughly he thrust the boat's engines into reverse and roared them. But the houseboat would not budge. He revved again and again. He wandered up the side railings to the wide-open front deck and stared at the sand and pebble beach that embedded his bow. The roaring of the engines had drawn a small crowd of curious bystanders. Seeing that his boat was stuck fast, Jones went inside and got himself another beer. The crowd of amused onlookers increased on the dock and walkways above them.

Connie Jones retreated into the galley and remained hidden

inside. Bob Jones, reappearing, beer in hand, cursed as he wandered back and forth over the deck staring at the damage, and, in futile gestures, continued to rev his engines.

Someone in the crowd left the scene to phone the Coast Guard.

Dave Hubert, coxswain at the Coast Guard's lifeboat station in Portsmouth Harbour, responded to the request for help. With his crew, he negotiated the *Bittern* upstream along the St. Lawrence River, toward the hospital near the Holiday Inn and the docks. The day was overcast and the river "sloppy," a word used to describe short, choppy waves about three feet in height.

Hubert's crew—Steve Cooper and Wade Buell—tossed a coin to decide who should board the houseboat and meet the couple who had driven it smack onto the shore. Buell lost. He climbed aboard and came face-to-face with its driver.

"Aiming for the dock, or for the beach?" he asked amiably. "You missed one, but it looks like you got a little close to the other."

"Well now, I guess I didn't judge it quite right, but look here, these damn big flat beasts don't go where you point 'em, can't get them around easy, that's a fact." A flush crept up Bob Jones's cheek as he stared out over the river. "Can you pull her off?"

"Yeah, we can do it, shouldn't be a problem," said Buell.

"Like a drink?" asked his suddenly hospitable host. Buell saw that the man had been drinking heavily and declined, explaining that he could not drink while working, but added that a can of pop would be fine.

Jones turned toward the galley and shouted, "Hey, Conn, how about a drink for the young fella." A moment later, a can of pop flew through the galley door like a missile, missed its human target and landed with a smack against the railing on the opposite side. A string of curses about having a dumb, stupid husband followed it.

After explaining what he could do to free the houseboat, Buell hastily moved himself out of range of flying projectiles and returned to the Coast Guard ship. Grinning at his mates, he told them how they had missed out on a fine conversation. He and Cooper got to work and attached a towline to the houseboat and secured it to the cutter. The *Bittern*'s engines roared into reverse, and slowly the houseboat's bow was drawn back from its pebbly cradle, and out into the water. The Coast Guard towed it slowly a short distance down river, maneuvered it alongside a dock, and fastened the boat securely. Buell went back on board to get the details of exactly what had happened, as he was required to do for his reporting procedures. He arrived in time to witness Bob Jones leaning over the side and vomiting into the water, immediately below the diners on the outdoor patio of the Holiday Inn.

"It's them gasoline fumes from your ship that's making me sick," he feebly explained.

"The Coast Guard cutter only uses diesel fuel," Buell said under his breath. He took notes for his report, and said good bye and good luck to the couple. The search and rescue team cruised back to their base and quickly moved on to the next task. They were reminded of it four days later when the local police called to ask questions about Mr. and Mrs. Jones.

The men recounted the help they had given the couple and asked if there was a problem. The police wanted to know about the couple's relationship, as they were investigating a bizarre incident that had taken place a day or two after the rescue. Apparently, the Joneses had cruised their houseboat downstream toward the islands that dotted the river. They had managed to dock, but, in the process, had struck the wooden jetty with such force that Mrs. Jones had fallen overboard.

Mr. Jones insisted that he'd tried again and again to pull his wife out of the water, but finding he couldn't do it on his own, had gone for help. Before Jones ambled off to get help, he had taken a line of rope, tied it around his wife who was clinging to the stern, and fastened it to the boat railing, the police said.

The crew grinned at each other, imagining the strings of curses that must have accompanied this procedure. Jones had then said he wandered to the Legion Hall and went in to ask for someone to help him pull his wife out of the water. He decided to stay and have a drink, and unfortunately, forgot about his wife.

"How long was she in the water?" asked Buell, still grinning.

"About an hour or so," the police told them. "She yelled and screamed so hard that passers-by phoned the police station.

"A strange tale, you could say," comments Buell, "but not to us."

Just Like
the Movies

Schoolhouse Bay, Ontario

*(The name of the vessel in this story has been changed
so that the owners may remain anonymous.)*

They go there for picnics, to lie on the small, sandy beach at the foot of the cliffs, or simply to escape for the weekend. Schoolhouse Bay on Main Duck Island in the St. Lawrence River is also a place of shelter, a refuge from storms that blow in from the west and southwest. But on this lazy weekend in early August, the dozen or more small boats that have enjoyed a weekend in the bay are busy pulling up anchor. Winds have shifted during the course of the day and now, in the late evening, they blow with increasing ferocity from the northeast directly into the bay. Finding themselves being blown in toward the beach and the cliffs, the small boats scurry out, to head toward Portsmouth Harbour in Kingston.

As these sailors fight their way in increasingly boisterous seas, they notice that the long, sleek, sailing boat *Leisure* stays where she is, roughly bouncing about just outside the bay. Surprised that she does not move and find some place to shelter, they watch her as they buck their way across the gulf. The *Leisure* remains where she is, alone except for two small sailboats anchored right up near the beach, at the far end of the bay.

In Portsmouth Olympic Harbour at the foot of the historic city of Kingston, the winds howl around the small lifeboat station at the water's edge. Search and rescue workers are preparing for bed when they hear the Mayday call radioed from the Joint Rescue Coordination Centre in Trenton: "sixty-five-foot sailboat lost her anchor in Schoolhouse Bay, her engines have quit, and she fears she is in danger of being washed onto the cliffs. You are tasked to go out to her."

Brain Riddell looks at his watch: 11:00 PM. He reckons that it will take a couple of hours or more to go the seventeen miles to

Schoolhouse Bay, against the direction of the prevailing winds. He and his crew get up, get dressed, and prepare the *Bittern* with emergency supplies, and are soon bucking their way across the lake toward Main Duck Island in the Gulf of St. Lawrence. As coxswain of the *Bittern*, Riddell is on the radio to connect with the couple on board the *Leisure*, a husband and wife in their early fifties.

"Hey, can you guys get us out of here? My bow anchor seems to be stuck on something, and my wife's going crazy," the husband says. "I tried to free it by letting all the chain out and backing off—engine's an eighty-five horsepower diesel—but the damn chain stuck. I marked the anchor, swung the boat around to head toward Kingston, and then the engines quit."

"Got your stern anchor out?"

"Yes. But I dropped it over the stern instead of the bow, unfortunately, and the seas are washing over. The line's only five-eighths inches thick, and a bit frayed. I'm afraid it won't hold, and my boat won't turn herself into the wind."

While he speaks, in the background, the *Bittern*'s crew hears the wailing of the wife crying a tirade of abuse and lament at near-hysterical pitch. They learn that the two sailboats at anchor inside Schoolhouse Bay have tried to help the large sailboat; they attempted to get out to her in a little Zodiac to bring them another anchor, but were driven back by wind and waves. About fifty to sixty people stand like wind-blown sentinels on the cliff tops, watching, and some on the shores of the bay. They have tried repeatedly to throw a line out, but the wind each time has caught it and blown it right back at them.

"The winds are howling, oh, just howling something fierce," Brian Riddell says. "We're being whopped while we're getting out there. I'm worried. Worried about the panic in the guy's voice, and about the wife, what she might do. I'm not surprised that she's pretty upset because it's a serious situation they're in. I mean, their boat could be dashed to pieces against the nearby cliffs. We do the best we can to get out there as fast as possible, but, boy it's hard going. We take a real pounding, and I have to keep revising my estimated time of arrival. And all the time I hear the guy's wife screaming in the background: 'Get me out of here! Get me out of here!' We got to do something to calm her down, I think, or else I don't know what will happen. If I keep radioing them, and talking to them, maybe that will help take their minds off their danger. My heart is sinking for the poor guy.

I ask him questions, like, 'Tell me about your stern anchor. What else is broken?' Then, after a while, suddenly I say to him, 'I'm going to be sending a guy out to you in a small rubber boat. He's bringing another anchor and a tow line.'"

'"You can't be doing that," says the husband. I ignore that. "His name is Kenny," I say. "He's going to be giving you a hand. Now, listen carefully: I want you to prepare for this man. Do you have a refrigerator?"

"Yeah." Now a note of incredulity creeps into the husband's voice.

"I want you to haul out all the stuff inside it, and stack it away somewhere on deck."

"Yeah, yeah, yeah."

"Do you have a chain?"

"Yeah..."

'"Wrap it around that fridge. Kenny, this guy who's coming over, he's hungry. He'll eat you out of house and home.' The guy laughs a little and it calms him down for about a half hour or so."

The Coast Guard crew in their cutter arrive at about one-thirty on a bleak and blustery morning to the spot where the *Leisure* swings precariously near the cliffs. A helicopter sent out by the rescue coordination centre circles overhead, helpless to do anything in the conditions. Below, the sailboat tosses wildly back and forth, one of her sails flapping furiously. It is impossible for the pilot to land one of his crew on the *Leisure* because her masts pitch and roll with the vessel; he can only circle overhead and watch the efforts of the crew in the Coast Guard cutter, ready to go to their aid if necessary.

Riddell, with his considerable skill and all of his effort, at first can get the *Bittern* no closer than a few hundred feet of the big sailing boat. Above the roar of the wind and the storm, he talks now to his crew, asks if anyone is willing to go out in the cutter's little ten-foot zodiac to try and get to the *Leisure*. He himself would go, but he is coxswain, and it is his responsibility to keep the cutter upright. But he does not, and never has, asked anyone to do what he himself is not prepared to do. Kenny Beckman volunteers immediately. Riddell is at the helm of the tossing cutter. Richard Beaudoin and Donny Strong, the two deckhands, prepare to launch the zodiac over the side, holding it while Kenny tries to get himself in it.

"We have to just throw him off in the end," Riddell says. "By this time, there are fourteen-foot seas like green-eyed monsters curling all about the cutter. We're putting Kenny out in it. I feel bad, worried; all three of us do. But Kenny just throws himself in. We wait for the crest of a wave, and then push him off. Whoops! And away he goes."

One man in a tiny boat swallowed up by giant swells: it is an extremely perilous journey for the rescue worker in a boat that is only ten feet long, with a small engine, and no self-righting capabilities. The remaining three on the deck of the Coast Guard cutter are filled with foreboding; Kenny Beckman is in very real danger of being swamped and turned over, swung against the sailing boat as he approaches it, or dashed onto the cliffs that guard Main Duck Island.

The tiny boat bobs like a child's rubber toy in the watery tempest while the two remaining deckhands rapidly pay out the zodiac's towline. Beckman has taken an anchor with him, but not a towline. If he makes it to the sailboat, he will have to return for the line so the sailboat can be attached to the cutter and towed to safety. Then he will once again brave the seas to carry that line back to the *Leisure*—three journeys between the cutter and the sailboat. Each time he has to get his own line attached to the *Leisure* and get himself aboard.

All the while, Riddell struggles to keep the cutter as close as possible to the sailboat. They are, at this moment, about 150 feet apart. Beckman, in his little boat, has managed to come up alongside the *Leisure*; he times the rise and fall of the waves, waits for the crest of a wave, and gets a line attached to the big vessel. He waits for another chance and, at the height of a wave, makes a leap, anchor in hand, onto the sailboat.

"I scare the hell out of the two of them on board," he says. "I walk across the deck. The husband is in the doorway of the cabin, wet and pretty unhappy looking, like, this is a real big strain on him."

"'Hi everybody!' I shout. He just stares at me. The wife is somewhere in the cabin. "Hey, isn't there anything to eat around here? I'm a pretty hungry guy," I say. A small grin comes over the man's face.

Kenny attaches the anchor to the sailboat and throws it over the bow.

"Okay, I'm going off again, but I'll be back," he says to the stunned couple. He waits his opportunity to get back in his small boat, which swings wildly at the side of the sailboat. Soon a tiny speck that rises and falls like a rubber cork in a big sea is struggling to get back to the *Bittern*. Kenny works heroically to stay upright, and to keep from being dashed against the cutter as he comes close, his motor chugging furiously. Donny Strong throws him the towline that will be attached to the *Leisure*, and, once more, Kenny takes his boat back to the sailboat. Again he manages to tie off the zodiac to the *Leisure*. He times the rise and fall of the giant swells, and climbs back onto the sailboat. Riddell instructs Kenny to stay there with the couple. It will be a comfort to them, and it is too dangerous for him to make yet another trip back in the zodiac to the cutter.

With the towline attached from the cutter to the sailboat, Riddell, slowly pulls the *Bittern* away. Sixty-five feet of sailboat and the length of anchor line pass before the strain is felt on the towline, and the tow is underway. Only then does Kenny cut the *Leisure*'s stern anchor line.

"You have to be sure that the towline holds and the tow is going to work before you cut the only thing that's holding the boat."

Once they are underway, Kenny hears a violent flapping and creaking. He looks up. "What the hell is that?" He sees that the jib sail is not tied down properly and is flapping furiously in the wind. Suddenly the sail breaks loose, hits one of the stanchions and smashes it, and a railing with about eight feet of cable connecting it to the next stanchion. The jib whips violently back and forth, and Kenny tells the owner of the boat that he's going to crawl up to the bow and tie it off. The husband argues. It's his boat, he says, and his responsibility, so he should do it. Kenny is unhappy about this, but feels he has no choice but to let him try. The wind shrieks and the waves wash over the decks. Kenny suggests that the husband crawl on his hands and knees, and, unknown to the man, he himself crawls after him. If the guy goes overboard, Kenny will be in trouble.

The boat owner does not know that Kenny is following behind him, so intense is his concentration to hold on. A rogue wave suddenly washes over the deck and the man in front is thrown backwards. Kenny, a foot against one of the stanchions, catches him.

"Hey! This is just like in the movies," he jokes. There is no argument now about Kenny crawling up to the bow to tie down the jib.

The helicopter, tasked by the Joint Rescue Coordination Centre to help, has been flying overhead all this time, not willing to return to base while the sailboat, and possibly the cutter, is still in trouble. The pilot remains flies low over the two vessels until he is almost out of fuel.

"It's a nasty tow home to Portsmouth," Riddell says of the interminable pounding journey back to the harbour. "We get the *Leisure* safely tied up, and by this time it's dawn. We're all hungry and exhausted and want to go to bed and get some sleep. But as soon as we get in to the station, there's a pan pan call to Main Duck Islands, the place we've just left. It's a boat called the *Jade*, stuck right up on the beach in Schoolhouse Bay. The only other boat in the bay is attempting to pull her off but can't do it. The *Bittern*'s crew is tasked to go out once more and pull her out to safety.

For this pleasure boater, striking a rocky patch will mean a call to the Coast Guard for a tow.

"Before we have anything to eat or have any rest, we're out there again, pounding in the storm to Main Duck Island," says the coxswain.

Brian Riddell put Ken Beckman's name up for an award as acknowledgment for his courage and out-standing work in saving the *Leisure* from disaster. Today, on a wall in the living area of the lifeboat station, hangs an award in recognition not only of Ken Beckman but of the entire crew of the *Bittern*. A few months after the heroic rescue, the lifeboat station received a letter from the owner of the *Leisure*:

"This is to express my deep appreciation of both my wife and I relative to the rescue effected at Main Duck Island on the night of August fourth and fifth, of both ourselves and our vessel, the Leisure. This was, of course, the most traumatic experience in my twenty years of sailing. If it were not for the professionalism and competence of the staff Cardinal Coast Guard Radio, the crew of the Bittern and the crew of the Canadian Forces helicopter, we would most certainly have lost our vessel and quite possibly have been seriously injured or drowned in attempting to abandon the vessel in the huge swells along the cliffs of Main Duck Island occurring during the night.

During the rescue we met Ken, a crewman from the *Bittern*, who brought the towline aboard and stayed aboard our vessel during the tow to Kingston, and the *Bittern*'s skipper. It is most gratifying to know the Canadian Coast Guard is composed of people of this calibre. I also understand that the rescue helicopter remained overhead in very bad conditions until just a few minutes of fuel remained. Please accept our compliments and appreciation."

Brian Riddell currently works as the coxswain at the Amherstburg lifeboat station, Kenny Beckman and Richard Beaudoin remain as deckhands on the *Bittern* in Kingston, and Donny Strong has retired.

Turbulent Tobermory

Twenty-seven ships lie scattered on the bottom of Lake Huron and Georgian Bay around the little town of Tobermory, silent testimony to the topography and weather patterns in these parts of the Bruce Peninsula. The sheer numbers of ship's skeletons in these parts prompted the Canadian government to build lighthouses at Flowerpot Island, Cove Island, and Big Tub Harbour in the second half of the nineteenth century. This was a time when the lake bustled with vessels of all kinds, carrying people, goods, and supplies to the towns and hamlets dotting the shores of the Great Lake.

Today, the people of Tobermory—many descendants of early settlers who witnessed the death of some of the nation's great ships—act as guardians of these wrecks. Glass-bottomed tour boats glide above shipwrecks that litter the lakebed, and scuba divers come from near and far.

"The Bruce," as it is popularly called, is a beautiful arm of land that juts up into Lake Huron to form the spectacular western shores of Georgian Bay, a place popular with boaters and holiday-makers. A lonely ribbon of land, it blooms with dense concentrations of maples and the oldest white cedars on the North

Coast Guard Base at Tobermory, Lake Huron.

American continent. Farmers' fields, punctuated with rocks and rough boulders, lie scattered among hardwood forests. Small towns and villages dot the landscape here and there, including the native reserve at Cape Croker.

The small town of Tobermory is perched at the northern-most tip of the Bruce. Town life revolves around its two harbours, Big and Little Tub, both busy with maritime activity. Each each harbour offers refuge for canoe, mackinaw boat, schooner, steamer, and yacht; an ideal base for fleets of fishing tugs, the Manitoulin ferries, national park guide boats, and tour boats.

From left to right, Steve Cooper, Herb Thompson and Jim MacDonald of the Tobermory Coast Guard Base. The fraternity among SAR workers is unparalleled.

Due to the Niagara Escarpment, a ridge of rock that runs through southern Ontario, submerging and reappearing thirty-two kilometres north of Manitoulin Island the waters of Lake Huron have the unenviable reputation of being treacherous. In between, the rock re-emerges in the form of islands and shoals, all obstacles to ships sailing between Lake Huron and Georgian Bay. Three channels near Tobermory offer passage: Main Channel between Cove and Lucas Islands, seven kilometres wide; Devil Island Channel between Cove and Russell Islands, three hundred metres wide in parts; and Cape Hurd Channel, between Russel Island and the mainland, the most treacherous of the three, and less than 275 metres wide. The latter two are channels bordered by large areas of shoal that rise quickly out of the depths to within a few metres of the water's surface.

Weather patterns add to the difficult passage for boating traffic, which remains unfailingly brisk. Ships of commerce ply the channels from the United States and other parts of Canada. Deep sea and local fishermen, together with pleasure-boaters and tour boats, crowd about the indented coasts and islands all around the peninsula. Pilots of commercial freighters and most of the deep-sea and local fishermen are familiar with the unpredictable weather patterns. They know the extent of the barely-submerged rocks and shoals, sharp as shrapnel, that dot the shoreline and extend far out into the lake waters. However, many casual boaters, fishermen, and visitors are not familiar with these hazards, and many get into trouble. Even seasoned freighter pilots sometimes experience difficulties.

Because of the frequency of maritime disasters and near-disasters, the Coast Guard, in 1978, built a lifeboat station at the tip of Tobermory and staffed it with two crews of three who work opposite shifts around the clock from early April until mid-December. While fulfilling other responsibilities, they go to the aid of boaters in trouble, and search for lost and missing persons on the water or among the islands. They live at the station for half their working life, venturing out to rescue the missing, the foolhardy, and the unfortunate.

As for the foolhardy, there are many. Crew members, even on a calm, sunny day when the blue waters of Georgian Bay barely ripple, know they will be out in their cutter searching for lost boaters who use a road map to navigate from Sarnia to Ottawa, or a restaurant placemat to get from one body of water to another.

LAKE WINNIPEG

Manitoba

Lake Winnipeg

Winnipeg •

Ontario

Thunder Bay

Premonitions and the Grampa Woo

Thunder Bay and Lake Winnipeg, Manitoba

The wind howled outside the Coast Guard's small search and rescue base on Lake Winnipeg. Inga Thorsteinson looked at her crewmates, shrugged, and said she might as well get ready for bed. Devil's night coming up, she thought to herself, feeling restless. She crawled into her small cramped bed in the station before she remembered: this Halloween night was the anniversary of the rescue of the cruise ship *Grampa Woo*. The search for the ship, and its subsequent rescue, had been one of the defining events in Inga's life, a rescue operation that had demanded all her faculties—her strength, courage, and endurance—to the very edge of death. For this, she and all the Coast Guard crew involved had received a medal for bravery.

On that Halloween night, Lake Superior, a cold, hard lake that often turns treacherous, had grabbed the 110-foot cruise ship *Grampa Woo* to toss her about like a child's plaything. The American freighter the *Walter J. McCarthy*, loaded with coal and passing close by at the time, managed to get her under tow to haul her to shelter in Thunder Bay. At the same time, the Coast

Just getting to the scene is often half the battle. *The Westfort* (in foreground) faced 18-foot waves trying to reach the *Grampa Woo*.

Guard crew geared themselves up to go out into the bitter night. The events that followed are seared in Inga's memory: eighteen- to twenty-foot waves, blowing snow and freezing spray, vicious crosswinds, the night black but for pinpricks of light on the shore. Snow bombarded the forty-four-foot, twenty-five-ton Coast Guard vessel *Westfort*, tossing it like a pingpong ball in the tempest, almost blinding her crew.

"My feet left the deck, the motion was so violent," Inga wrote later, in a letter to her parents. "The guy at the wheel and throttles tired quickly...Willie and I switched positions whenever one of us was played out. At all times, one of us was on the wheel and the other was on the radar keeping track of the positions of the [other] three vessels out there, the coxswain in command. The *Ogleby Norton* was out there, a ship in transit, as well as our cutter, and a harbour tugboat, the *Glenada*, hired by the captain of the *Grampa Woo* to come out to the rescue—he got hold of him on his cell phone."

The tow between the *Grampa Woo* and the *Walter J. McCarthy* broke, and the *Grampa Woo* drifted helplessly on the lake; the *Walter J. McCarthy* took herself off to find shelter. The survival of the crew aboard the *Grampa Woo* was now dependent on the efforts of the tugboat, the *Glenada*, and the crew aboard the Coast Guard cutter.

"We both chased the sinking boat in conditions that were terrible," Inga says. Indeed, the Coast Guard cutter was slow in moving through the snow and the build-up of ice, taking on water in the buoyancy chamber. Even to its crew, their rescue mission seemed insane.

"Both of us chased that ship, to try and get close enough to get a tow attached. Our *Westfort* is powerful for her size, but handling a tow the size of the *Grampa Woo* may have been too much for us," Inga says. "It was wild out there, and if we had lost our instruments, or an engine, we probably would have lost our boat."

The crew aboard the *Glenada* were also having a very hard time. The engineer was sick from the diesel fumes, smoke, noise, and action. The crew up on deck stood in enough water to "float their legs." Captain Dawson, at one point, believed his deckhand had gone overboard, knew his engineer had been rendered helpless, and believed himself to be alone.

The Coast Guard crew continued to struggle—at one point, their vessel almost capsized. Repeated attempts were made to get close enough to the wallowing *Grampa Woo* to throw a towline. But the conditions were too fierce to make a hook-up and tow, and it was not long before the crew of the *Grampa Woo* were forced to abandon ship.

Out in the stormy waters, the captain of the tugboat got close enough to snatch the men as they were leaving their foundering ship, hauling them on board his tug. But both tug and cutter knew they could not make it into Thunder Bay to anchor there, because of the sheer strength of the wind that gusted around the Sleeping Giant. They headed instead for the relative shelter of Tee Harbour, where captain Gary Dawson deliberately ran the *Glenada* hard aground on some old dock cribbing, and the smaller Coast Guard vessel rafted alongside. Both the *Glenada's* 15,000 horsepower engine and the *Westfort's* 280 horsepower engine ran all night to keep their vessels fastened on the crib.

"None of us slept that first night in Tee Harbour," Inga writes. "We were all too physically pumped up, the adrenaline flowing...I was physically sick from the ordeal for a few hours after."

The following day dawned very cold, and storms still raged over the lake and its shores. As engine-room watch keeper, Inga kept a close eye on the fuel supply. She compromised between keeping the crew warm, keeping the batteries charged, and saving fuel by running the engines for half an hour every two hours. The three crews remained imprisoned in their makeshift shelter from the storm for 38 hours until the weather allowed them to travel the sixteen miles back to Thunder Bay. This trip, too, was rough, Inga recalls, with seas washing over the entire deck and the little cutter ploughing through ten-foot waves.

"But it was daylight," says Inga, "and we weren't making ice! We all whooped it up and cheered for joy."

Tonight, Inga is on Lake Winnipeg in Manitoba, having exchanged her Coast Guard position in Thunder Bay for a season here, the home of her childhood summers.

"This is what's great about the Coast Guard," Inga explains. "You can move around to other bases if you can find anyone to do an exchange with. Freedom, you know, to make your own choices, see other places."

The lure of childhood summers spent on the shores of her beloved Lake Winnipeg proved a powerful one for Inga. Visions of endless vistas of sparkling silica sands, so clean that one's feet squeaked when walking on them, of limestone shores and of the granite of the Canadian Shield on the lake's northern reaches— these had never dimmed in her memory.

"It was a good season," says Inga, "the one after the episode of the *Grampa Woo*. It was the time of the Manitoba floods and here I was on Lake Winnipeg, really busy. It was great to go back to the place where I'd grown up, see my family and friends, come home to a place that I love.

"On search and rescue missions, things don't always happen in the orderly way that they do during drills and training sessions," she says. "You have to think on your feet and adapt to the situation. The Coast Guard trusts you to make good judgements because you're the only ones who really know what it's like out there. Our training and protocols help us to make the best decisions under the circumstances.

"There was the fisherman who got in trouble up north on the lake," she says by way of explanation. "We didn't just get in the cutter and steam up there, but took the truck and drove it along the roads that ran around the lake. We pulled our boat behind us down the lonely roads, through the bush, and onto the beach to launch it from there."

Inga explains that it was much faster to drive as close as possible to the location on the lake where they were to search, find a ramp from which to launch the boat, and begin their search from there. They have become very proficient at getting the zodiac up on the trailer, towing it, and then re-launching it with a speed and efficiency born of long practice.

In 1997, Inga works as a search and rescue worker on the *Waubuno*, a small Coast Guard cutter that patrols the northwest areas of Lake Winnipeg. The vistas of bush surrounded by vast lake waters take her back to the lonely setting she had so loved as a child and as a teenager.

Lake Winnipeg is not one of the renowned Great Lakes, and yet at 9,400 square miles, it is more than 2,000 square miles larger than Lake Ontario. Because of its northerly latitude, its season is brief, running from early May to late October, but the number of calls to its one Coast Guard lifeboat station almost equals those received at other bases where crews work extended seasons or all year round.

"We had fifty-seven calls that season," says Inga. "We lived at the station right down at the harbour, a bit small and cramped, but I enjoyed being there. We get support and respect from the community. It is a good feeling to know we're doing something really useful."

The night wind howls through the trees and washes the lake waters right over the breakwall and into the harbour, blowing out of the northwest with a force that raises the water levels six to eight feet. Waves surge right up the beach and push the boulders up the sand. The town's old people drive down to the harbour in their trucks to take a look at a lake whose dramatic moods are well-known to them.

"Never seen anything like this," they say, "not for many years."

The Coast Guard crew huddle inside their trailer but keep watch over the harbour waters, trying to keep track of how many boats are out there, hoping none will still be out on the lake. Tonight is the anniversary of the big storm in Thunder Bay, and the rescue of the *Grampa Woo* lurks in the back of Inga's mind. The wind moans and rocks the trailer, and rain lashes its windows.

The crew go to bed, their sleep made restless by the storm. As she sleeps, Inga dreams she is busy conducting a shoreline search for the body of a man; she is wearing her dry suit. The search proves difficult because of the dark and the cold. The snowdrifts and the debris at the edge of the water make it nearly impossible to traverse. The coxswain calls her on the radio, asking her what her position is.

"Five miles northeast of the Canadian Tire store," she tells him, and he is stunned because the response makes no sense. The dream continues; Inga is stumbling along the shore, when suddenly she looks down to find that her feet are bare, and that she's wiggling her toes inside the rib cage of a dead man. The horror of the image awakens her. She lies in her narrow bed, listening to the wind howling outside with a sense of foreboding, as if the dream is a premonition. Then, still tired and restless, she gets up and goes into the living room. It is two o'clock in the morning, and one of the crew is still up watching a movie.

"Geez, Gordie, I just had this awful dream," she says, and tells him about it. Restless, disturbed, and driven by a strange compulsion, she goes to the bathroom to wash her feet.

The storm is still raging at eight o'clock the next morning, and there are fresh snowdrifts blotting out the familiar contours of the land. The crew thump about outside, checking storm damage. The phone rings at eleven; it is the RCMP, asking for assistance to search the lake's shoreline for a man who might still be alive. "It is the Coast Guard's responsibility to search for missing persons in trouble, and it's the province of the RCMP to conduct the search to recover a body," the crew explains. "But when the RCMP requests our help, we always go out for them."

The crew get into their dry suits. The coxswain drives the truck along the road that hugs the shore, dropping off his two crewmembers at separate locations along the shoreline. Each is to walk toward the other, searching the shore and the adjacent scrub and bush as they go, eventually meeting up to walk together up through the bush back to the road. The coxswain will try to figure out where they will be, pick them up, and repeat the procedure.

"It's a big snowstorm and it goes on all day and all the next night. It's awful," says Inga. "I know the others are thinking about my dream, and we're all worried about where we're putting our feet. I keep looking down unconsciously, to make sure I've still got my shoes on. The coxswain keeps radioing me, saying, 'Come on Inga, where's this body? Can't you remember what was around you, what you were looking at? Where you were walking on the shore...?' It's all a wretched business; we're really miserable and just want it to be over. I feel haunted by the dream of my feet inside a dead body. Part of me doesn't want to find him."

The search by the cold, exhausted, and spooked crew continues until late at night on October 30—'Devil's night,' as it is known. The coxswain receives a call from the regional controller at the Joint Rescue Coordination Centre in Trenton, Ontario.

"Look, you can stand down this job," he says. "You can go home." He explains that the search has been downgraded to a recovery because there is no hope of finding the missing man alive—that it is past time to close down the base for the season. Fall fishing is finished and the lake has begun to freeze over.

As a teenager in the guidance counsellor's office, Inga was asked what she planned to do after high school.

"I want to join the Coast Guard," she'd said.

"Girls don't do that kind of thing." The counsellor was abrupt and dismissive. Later Inga took a summer job on the passenger ship *Selkirk II* to earn the money to pay her university fees. Her mother wanted her to go to university, get a graduate degree, then attend the fresh water institute at the University of Manitoba, after which she might land a job with the Department of Fisheries.

A hefty vessel—1,500 tons gross, stretching 175 feet in length—the *Selkirk II* carried 130 passengers on tours of Lake Winnipeg. It also carried general cargo north to communities around the lake, and transported freshwater fish south to the markets in Selkirk and Winnipeg. Young Inga was one of a thirty-five-member crew. The position of stewardess—serving tables and cleaning cabins down below—was not a position she'd wanted, but being a woman, it was the only one she could get.

Regardless of her lowly position, she loved being on the ship. Spending time on the deck, she learned what the seamen did. She longed to be up there too, where the action was. She hung around the wheel and the bridge, bugging the captain to let her get a job up on top, a deckhand's job.

"Oh, come on now," the captain said when she approached him. "You'll get dirty fingernails," and he brushed her off.

She persisted. "No, " she was told repeatedly. "That's not a job for a woman."

The dishwasher was complaining about his job, and threatening to quit. Inga heard the chief steward trying to placate him, and an officer promised that if he would stay, he would give the fellow a job as deckhand.

Inga was furious. She raged around the dining room, outraged that the job she had begged for for more than a month should be offered to a man who had just come on board as a dishwasher.

Eventually the captain said, "Calm down, calm down! Look, I'll let you try the job for a week or two, show you what it's like." His tone told her, "you'll find out you don't like it; then you'll shut up and go away back to your job below."

This is how Inga got up on deck, and cast off the stewardess's position to become a wheelsman. The responsibilities were not all new to her because of her previous experience on the riverboats. And she saw herself again as the way she'd been on the banks of the Red River that flowed through Winnipeg: a child who ran around in rubber boots with a boat hook in her hand, who leaned out her bedroom window to watch the river flowing by and all the boats and ships that sailed it.

She was the slight, blond-headed girl at the edge of the river, who, seeing the wreck of an old wooden rowing boat floating by, chased it down river through all the neighbours' backyards until she hooked it with a pike pole, pulled it to shore, and dragged it home. She worked to restore it so she could race it alongside the excursion boats that plied the river. How she'd loved those lit-up boats going up and down: the lights in the evening, the live band music floating across the water, the people dancing and laughing. Absorbed and fascinated by this life on the water, she worked feverishly to get her own boat fixed up so she could sail it.

Later, Inga would laugh at the memory of her young self racing the riverboats—the captain throwing her cans of pop and packets of potato chips, the passengers leaning over the sides of the ship, cheering her on. She remembers one unforgettable day when the captain invited her on board and allowed her to steer the boat, and how moved she was by the magnificent, traditional six-foot brass bound mahogany wheel that she controlled with her small hands.

"You'll grow out of it," her parents said to their youngest daughter when she announced she intended to become a ship's captain on Lake Winnipeg, perhaps on one of the excursion riverboats. But perhaps they overlooked the influence of her inheritance. Her passion for boats and ships and the water came from her father, the man who purchased the family home on a riverbank, who built boats in the backyard and took his family to a cabin on the shores of Lake Winnipeg for long summer vacations.

During all the summers at the lake, Inga had absorbed the activity that had taken place: barges plying the waters carrying salt, pulpwood and silica sand; freighters or cargo boats hauling fresh and frozen fish—pickerel, golden eye, and whitefish—to the markets. At the time, there was no road going all the way around the lake, so much of the transportation was by barge, boat and freighter. The waters of the lake were very busy.

"That's all I wanted to do—be on the boats," Inga said, and she struggled to make sure it happened.

Years ago, idly flipping through a magazine in the public library in her native Winnipeg, Inga noticed an advertisement for crew to work on an old Baltic trading vessel in Virginia. Inga envisioned the old vessel, a three-masted topsail schooner, sails billowing as it ploughed the seas. Inspired, she fired off a resumé; she was accepted one month later, and took to work as deckhand on the schooner *Alexandria*, which sailed up the east coast between Virginia and Canada.

Inga's mother knew that when her daughter flew south to assume this position she would never be returning to university, most likely never get a 'real' job. For Inga, her work in the square rigger would be an unforgettable experience of going back in time: crew accommodations were up in the foc'sle, while the officers were at the back, aft. Wood was stored under all the bunks, and everything was done by hand. Inga was the only Canadian on board with the otherwise all-American crew—who supposed she could speak French and would communicate for them while they were in Quebec. Inga spoke no French, but she had a particular usefulness to the crew as they sailed up the St. Lawrence River and Seaway: her experience was largely on rivers, while theirs was on oceans.

Inga felt privileged to be able to sail the historic ship. She sailed up the St. Lawrence River with the crew to help celebrate Cartier's arrival in Quebec City two hundred years earlier.

"Sailing ships such as these are used to train ship's officers," Inga says. "The crew develops knowledge and skills that they don't learn on a ship where instruments and sophisticated technology are available. One of the most valuable things for us was learning an intimate knowledge of the weather. On a square rigger, you have to stay completely tuned into wind and sea conditions and how they affect the ship. It was a valuable training method; I got really good at it, and have never forgotten it."

"The weather became dirty as we headed in the Strait of Canso and anchored in Port Hawkesbury," Inga wrote in a letter to her parents. "So here we sit...gale warnings out, having a quiet day inside. Once per hour we row the *Bobby-Jean Hopper* ashore for those who want to stretch their legs. If we can get fuel, we will light the fire to get the dampness out...all of us planned our day of easy watches and time ashore."

Inga watched the passengers and most of the crew depart for shore—all except a deckhand, the mate, and herself. The schooner was anchored off Port Hawkesbury on the south coast of Cape Breton Island, a pretty little coastal town that hugs the rugged shores. The captain left the ship to pick up mail, the cook to get supplies, and the passengers to enjoy themselves ashore. The off-duty crew could stroll about and stretch their legs. At the time they disembarked, the day was beautiful: the trees were in their first burst of fall colour; the ocean glinted blue in the sunlight, and there was not a breath of wind. Inga was writing letters.

Now it was her turn to board the small boat and row ashore for time on land. Most of the crew were still strolling about the small town. Just as she was about to step into the yawl, the first breeze whipped across the water, enough to create some difficulty in managing the small boat. Inga never did make it to land. Not long after the captain had departed the schooner, and with most of the crew on the shore, Inga, always acutely aware of the slightest change in the weather, felt a breeze nudge the ship, and saw the rigging suddenly tighten. Then, with unbelievable suddenness, a violent wind blew out of nowhere, increasing until it was of gale-force strength. "Its noise was uncomfortably loud in the rigging," Inga says. "And whitecaps formed on the bay." A gale had blown up on the sea while most of the crew remained stranded on the dock.

Inga and her fellow deckhand watched with dismay as the ship inched backwards towards the break wall and the shore. In the distance she saw the crew and a gathering crowd of spectators standing helplessly on the dock as the schooner began dragging anchor toward sailing ships anchored directly behind. She let out more cable, and watched. The ship continued shuddering backwards, so they dropped the second anchor. The remaining few crewmembers fired up the engines.

Amid her struggles, Inga glimpsed the captain and his crew on the end of the pier, running back and forth, straining through binoculars to see what was happening on the schooner. The wind was still too fierce for the pilot boat to ferry them across the stretch of water. Inga saw cars and trucks driving down the hill, could see their lights on, and knew they were coming because they understood a ship was in trouble. But there was nothing they could do.

"While the mate, Bert, and Laurie tried various strategies with the anchors and balky windlasses, I wrestled with the wheel and the throttle," she says. "I tried to keep the ship headed into the wind, but it was gusting now between fifty and sixty-seven knots and blowing spray in sheets across the decks."

She stood on an open quarterdeck, lashed by the rain while the seas swept over the decks. Cold and fearful, she searched her mind for some way to keep the ship out of trouble. If the thought, 'how did I get into this?' surfaced, it was only momentary. Inga stood, a small figure with blond hair blowing in the wind, struggling at the wheel of the schooner.

A giant wave broke over the decks. She struggled as the ship continued to lurch toward the break wall. Suddenly the engines quit; the shaft bearings had seized up. The winds were increasing to hurricane force. Inga had seldom encountered weather so brutal and an atmosphere so tense. She had no steerage with engines down. All that held the old vessel was one anchor and a thirty-five-foot launch that was valiantly attempting to hold the ship out from the break wall and from collision with the sailing vessels anchored beyond her. Inga couldn't allow, even for a moment, the ship to fall away from the wind; only full port rudder, full power and the small, stabilizing effect from the launch would eventually bring her nose up.

An eternity passed—at least it seemed so to Inga and the two other crew members on board the schooner. The windlass was slow; the chain, cold and wet, kept slipping off the broken wildcat. Normally, two crewmembers would be stationed at the chain locker to physically stow the chain so it would run clear when the anchor was let go, but they were all busy on deck and nobody could be spared to go below. The chain spilled out onto the foc's'le deck. A call had gone out to the Coast Guard for help, and close to two hours afterward the *Thomas Carlton* arrived to assist.

"Finally, after one aborted attempt, we berthed alongside the Baltic schooner the *Elinor* and the German drill rig supply vessel the *Kaubstrom*," says Inga. "The crew of this vessel was very kind, offering hot showers and freshly-cooked lobster. We slept like the dead that night; we had struggled for seven and a half hours in that storm."

Inga was not deterred by this exhausting ordeal on board the *Alexandria*. She took to a life on the water and loved it, saying simply that it just felt right. She became a leading wheelsman, and the next season was promoted to boatswain on a deck crew of six. After that she advanced rapidly, never returning to university. Her mother was disappointed, but to Inga, life had no meaning unless it was lived aboard ships; this is what she passionately wanted, and it was the life she pursued.

In 1984, the only sailing ship available for Inga to work on in Canada was Nova Scotia's *Bluenose II*, and its captain refused to hire women. "Girls don't do that," Inga was told once again.

While she was working on the *River Rouge* and the *Lady Winnipeg* on the Red River in the summer of 1988, the relief mate on board told her about his regular job with the Coast Guard.

Inga liked what she heard about it—work that involved rescuing vessels and saving lives, two weeks on and two off. Inga had been experiencing some disenchantment with life as a ship's officer: the hours were exacting, and she was tired of working the entire season with rarely a day off.

"I had always known about the Coast Guard because it had a big presence on Lake Winnipeg," she said. "Then I saw a Coast Guard rescue mission on the Rice River, a narrow, rocky little river where boats often got into trouble. It was shallow and filled with shoals, a navigator's nightmare, but a good place for fishing and hunting. You really had to have good local knowledge of it to be safe. I was on the excursion boat the MS *Lord Selkirk II* when I heard a Mayday call go out for Rice River. A yacht had taken some people in around Rice River and had hit a rock. He radioed that he was taking on water.

"You could hear the people in the background, those passengers who had remained on board, talking. Then they were screaming, yelling and crying...Then suddenly the radio cut out," Inga says. "A naval reserve ship happened to be tied up there, as was the CCGS *Namao*. I watched them galvanize into action, jump into their fast rescue boat, and tear off to the sinking ship. It seemed very impressive to me at the time and I said that's what I wanted to do—to rescue people, just like that.

"I inquired about working for them, and, in 1989, I was accepted."

While Inga Thorsteinson had been told all her life that ships do not take women, she had always been driven to work on them, to be on the water, regardless of the fact that it was a male-dominated world.

Following the season on the *Alexandria*, Inga had gone to marine school in Winnipeg to get her commercial ships officer license. It was the very last class, and she was the first woman in Manitoba to graduate as a master minor waters. Afterwards, she was recruited onto the *MS Lord Selkirk II* as second officer, to find herself alongside the captain who had thrown her pop and potato chips as she had raced her old rowing boat alongside his river tour boat as a child.

"So, it's come to this, eh?" said the old man.

Today Inga is the one female member among a crew of five

The only Coast Guard base on Lake Superior, at Thunder Bay.

permanent employees at the only lifeboat station on Lake Superior, located in Thunder Bay.

"How women are treated varies," Inga says. "It depends on the guys you're working with. With some crew, you feel you have to walk a fine line, but not with others. Some accept you completely and you mesh right in, you're just one of the guys. But among others you feel you are not quite part of the rest of them. You're very conscious that you have to meet the demands of the job, no slip-ups, and that you must always pull your weight. If you throw a heaving line to a casualty and you miss, it's because you're a woman and you don't have the strength in your throwing arm. If a man misses, it's just that he missed. What it's really about, is that this is a skill that some are better at than are others. And it doesn't matter whether you are a man or a woman, you have to pull your weight."

PACIFIC

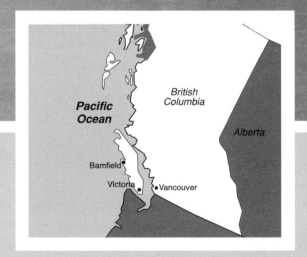

Pacific
Ocean

British
Columbia

Alberta

Bamfield

Victoria   • Vancouver

Terror Inside
A Lifeboat

Vancouver, British Columbia

O n the morning of November 9, 1998, beneath the frowning, half-shrouded mountains that tower above Cates Park in North Vancouver, nine men plunge into the frigid waters of Vancouver Harbour from their capsized lifeboat. Six fall free and thrash about beside it, but three are trapped in the upside-down boat that has all but disappeared below the surface. Because of the water temperature, the men have approximately forty minutes before they will succumb to hypothermia, if they have not already drowned.

The Coast Guard's hovercraft vessel with its crew of rescue specialists and divers from the Sea Island base in Richmond are currently fighting a bush fire at Wreck Beach near Point Grey. Above the noise of the blaze that engulfs the trees and burns deep into the beach itself, the black-sooted crew hears the message that crackles over the marine radio. Someone turns up the volume.

"An overturned lifeboat, with two, possibly three people trapped inside," they hear. "Divers will be needed." James Garrett stands out on deck and looks over at John Merrett: they will dive together and each will be the other's lifeline. They have worked together before, and now few words are needed.

The lowering of the lifeboat is a routine training exercise for the men who work aboard the *Iolcos Grace*, a Panamanian registered commercial freighter carrying shipments of grain and lumber. Sailors all, the crew comes from southern Russia, the Philippines, and Greece. Most have travelled widely, but rarely do they view vistas as awesome as this one of mountain and sea. When the mists clear and the clouds scud across the November sky, snow-capped mountains rise above them; the sea sweeps the rocky shores of myriad islands along the pine-forested coast.

After the ship's cargo is unloaded, the sailors must participate in a training exercise that may save the lives of all aboard in the event of an emergency at sea. The mountains disappear once more into the mist as the exercise begins.

Each man takes his place in the bright orange, forty-five-foot lifeboat. As the boat is released from its davits, it creaks and swings slowly out from the deck of the freighter. The lifeboat must descend slowly and evenly, so that it does not lurch and tilt, forward or aft. Halfway down the side of the mother ship, one of the davits comes loose; the boat lurches forward, breaks from its cable, and is poised for one terrifying moment in mid-air. Then, with a rush, it hurtles upside-down into the sea.

Shouts, screams, a confusion of bodies in the water—of the nine men who had climbed into the boat, seven are thrown free. The other two are believed to be trapped inside the vessel that almost immediately loses most of its buoyancy and sinks; all but a few feet of its hull disappear beneath the water. The men who are thrown free thrash about in the sea, while crew on boats anchored in the harbour race to the scene. Big and small craft churn up the water. People crowd the decks of fishing boats and tugs, searching for those in the water.

At Point Grey, John McGrath, commanding officer of the *Sea Island* hovercraft, turns his vessel toward Burrard Inlet and Vancouver's outer harbour, speeding past the deep-sea freighters anchored along the shore. The hovercraft seems to skim across the surface of the water, under bridges, past the forested Spanish Banks as McGrath pushes it to its limit of forty-five knots. The sky is clear, but there is a brisk wind and a choppy sea. As the Coast Guard crew come within sight of the freighter, they see many vessels dotting the harbour, those that have rushed to the rescue. The scene is chaotic.

John Merrett's adrenaline is flowing: he loves adventure, drama, and danger. He waited a long time to get a position in the Coast Guard—as a dive rescue specialist—to do just this kind of work. Had he not come into work this morning to make up hours for the week, Garrett would not have had a back-up, and so would not have been able to dive. Merrett is pumped and primed the moment he hears the call.

James Garrett, dive rescue specialist for the Sea Island base, lets the news sink in as McGrath pushes the hovercraft for its race upriver to the outer harbour, a race to rescue two trapped men while there is still a chance they are alive. Garrett's cool, analytical mind is also racing. Train for the worst, hope for the best; he and other members of the dive team have trained patiently and repeatedly, diving into a deliberately-capsized boat sunk near the dock at the foot of their Coast Guard base. They have learned how to get in and out of a small, sunken boat being whipped about by river currents. They have learned how to avoid getting entangled in a dark cave with zero visibility where flying debris can strike like missiles. They have suffered this traumatic experience over and over until it has become routine. But here is the test of that training.

The two divers don their dry suits and check their equipment, trying to visualize what they might have to do, what they might find at the bottom of the ocean. With the hovercraft only ten minutes from the disaster scene, Garrett feels the urgency .

"It makes it hard to prepare analytically for what you have to do when there is pressure to just get into the water and go," he says. "It makes the whole situation less stable. Prevention and preparedness: that's what a good rescue is all about. I remember all the training I've done, keep telling myself that I know what to do, that I've done it all before. I try to prepare myself mentally, and to listen in to the radio chatter at the same time to learn about what's happened."

What Garrett hears tells him this is not a good situation: the sailors are trapped in a boat that has largely sunk beneath the surface, and it is unlikely they are still alive. At least five people—maybe more—have already been pulled from the water. No one is exactly sure about the numbers because the tugs and some fishing boats have rescued one here and another there. There is no official communication yet among the boats.

As they get closer to the area known as Anchorage K, the divers strain their eyes to see the freighter and any part of the lifeboat that might protrude above the water. It's difficult to see anything at first as boats crowd about the freighter. In a high traffic area, the movement of other craft can change the position of the lifeboat, jeopardize what the rescue workers plan to do, and even endanger them. This is a scene that Garrett does not like because it is inherently unstable.

He is comforted to learn, hoevver, that a back-up dive team from the navy is on its way; and that the Coast Guard search and rescue crew from the Kitsilano lifeboat station in Vancouver has already arrived in their cutter, the *Manyberries*, and begun to manage the scene. This SAR crew, early to the scene, first attempted to take account of all the sailors who had been pulled from the water by local craft, then tried to locate the missing sailors—which vessel they were aboard and their condition. They tried to determine whether any sailors remained in the upside-down life raft. Knowing the hovercraft, with the dive team aboard, was on its way, they made efforts to provide a safe dive area by controlling harbour traffic.

The divers aboard the hovercraft briefly discuss what each will do. They are still doing their body checks as they pull close to the freighter *Iolcos Grace*.

"Actually, I had one train of thought while preparing," Garrett says. "What can go wrong? Once I'm right there in the situation, I focus on a risk-benefit analysis: Does the good outweigh the bad? Is there more potential for saving a life, or losing more? This is a touchy, subjective situation to be in. Because of my training, I always think I can separate myself from it. I keep asking myself questions—How many people are inside the boat? Where are the entrances? Are the people alive or dead? Can we get inside? Is the boat going to be disturbed and sink because it's unstable, as soon as we start doing anything?"

The Coast Guard's hovercraft has come to a controlled stop alongside the *Iolcos Grace*. The divers can now see a towline attached to a small, bright orange protrusion, the hull of the lifeboat. Crews on surrounding boats are thanked for their help but are asked to clear the area so the Coast Guard can deploy its divers.

First officer Al Taylor ties off the hovercraft to the lifeboat as Garrett and Merrett prepare themselves. Dave Cook, a student who is an extra on board, readies the communication lines, while Taylor performs the final buddy checks with the divers who have donned their fins and plugged in the communication lines. The plan is for Garrett to enter the upturned boat.

"A rescue diver doesn't want to send another into a situation to do what he himself does not want to do," says Garrett. "When you're into this kind of work, you're putting yourself into the most risk possible. And each of us knows that either one of us can call [terminate] the dive at any time if we aren't comfortable with the situation we're in."

The two divers look at each other through their full-face masks, then hit the water.

"Things go quiet once we're down under there," Merrett says. "All we can hear is each other. It's what we see that worries us." They swim quickly around and under the lifeboat, examining its exterior for breaches. It's badly damaged and torn apart on its port side. A hatch has broken and hangs by its seal, leaving an opening about two feet by three, with jagged, fibreglass edges protruding. Garrett knows this will be his entrance into the boat.

"It's better than pushing a hatchway door as you never know what might be behind it," he explains. "You might dislodge something and cause the boat to roll, to take on more water, even to sink. You might breach an air pocket that's keeping someone alive."

Merrett sticks his head through the hole. Just inside and to the left of the breach lie two of the raft's batteries, both broken open with their contents bubbling up. The opening is partially blocked by oars and debris. Merrett puts his head in further and is stunned by what he sees: a man, over to the far side, who seems to be vertical and kicking his legs.

Merrett tries to snap off some of the jagged, fibreglass edges that obstruct the opening so Garrett can wriggle through. Garrett examines the small breach at the boat's stern and figures that he can get in and out of it. Anxious that precious time is passing, he twists and wriggles his way into the murky depths of the sunken lifeboat. Merrett stays at the opening to make sure Garrett's communication line does not snag, and continues to break off the jagged fibreglass around the hole.

Garrett strains to see into the hull at the far end of the boat, the only part that remains above the water line. He, too, is stunned to see a man, frantically kicking his legs, wearing nothing but a pair of underpants—apparently treading water. There must be a small air pocket up there! Garrett catches sight of another figure, over to the side, fully clothed and also standing in the water. He approaches this man, cautiously touching him on the shoulder. The body —without head or limbs—floats away; Garrett has found an empty pair of coveralls.

"I was momentarily stunned, then relieved," he says. "I let the crew on board the hovercraft know that I've found one man alive," he says. "Then I swim over to the near-naked fellow amidships who frantically kicks his legs to keep his head above the water in the small air pocket above. I feel a terrible urgency to get him out while he's still alive, but I'm afraid for him, and for myself. How can I get us both out of here? It's a dark space filled with diesel fuel and objects that can injure or imprison both of us. The fellow up there must be fast running out of air. I know I have to be cautious, because I can imagine what it might seem like to this poor fellow, half crazed with cold and fear, suddenly to come face-to-face with a sub-aquatic creature rising up out of the depths."

The diver swims up into the air pocket and reaches out for one of the man's hands, hoping to instill comfort, but the dying man is beyond comfort: he's hypothermic and in shock. Garrett speaks slowly and quietly, telling him how he will be rescued, that he has to put on the spare regulator and mask, and swim underwater and through a small hole in the side of the boat.

"I realize, with a sinking feeling, that he doesn't speak English, that he's panic-stricken, and absolutely terrified of me," says Garrett. Debris flies about everywhere, most of it buoyant and overhead. Heavy objects, like the broken batteries, are below his feet on the inverted deck head of the lifeboat. Acid bubbles up from the batteries, and carbon dioxide is fast replacing oxygen in the air pocket. "I can tell that the crewman is losing strength," he says. "Time is running out."

Garrett grabs his octopus (a spare regulator on a two-metre line) and holds it up for the crewman to see. The bewildered man has no idea what it is, and Garrett can't explain. He tries several times, unsuccessfully, to put it in the other man's mouth. He turns him around and firmly cradles the crewman's head, holding the regulator on the man's mouth with one hand, putting the spare mask on his face with the other. He encourages the man to go down with him under the water by giving him a little tug. Garrett manages to get the man's head halfway under the water when the man torpedoes, panic-stricken, straight back up into the air pocket, the regulator falling out of sight.

"I tried, again and again," says Garrett. "Time's running out and I'm despairing. I try a different angle: I notify the crew on the surface that I'll attempt to put my full-face Aga face mask on him and take the octopus up myself—a riskier move, but the best hope for a rescue, I think. The moment I remove my mask and we're face-to-face, he looks at me with an expression of discovery, of clarity, that I haven't seen before, and now I know he's ready to go. I put the Aga back on my own face, hold his hand against his own regulator, wrap my arm around his back, and swim with him below into the darkness."

The two of them drop to the ceiling of the upturned boat and swim to the opening where Garrett can glimpse his dive partner. Merrett has ripped the hatch free, letting it sink one hundred and twenty feet to the seabed, and has struggled to break free other parts to make the opening bigger. He works the crewman's bare legs through the small hole in the boat while Garrett maneuvers the trunk through. Merrett then boosts the man quickly to the surface, the octopus falling away at the last moment as the two-metre line reaches its end, and they swim to the waiting hovercraft.

Garrett goes back inside the boat, looking for the second crewman. His own time is limited because the first man needs urgent medical attention; he and Merrett will have to surface and disconnect their communication lines so the hovercraft can speed the rescued crewman to the ambulance waiting on shore. The divers swim quickly around the lifeboat but find no sign of the second crewman. They surface together and swim to a nearby boat while the hovercraft roars off to shore. The divers climb aboard the vessel, which happens to carry commercial divers from the Pacific Marine Training Campus who have suited up and are prepared to assist if needed. Garrett and Merrett are removing their dive gear when they hear the roar of the crew aboard the deck of the freighter.

"One more! One more!" Garrett asks the commercial divers if they have a tendering line and if they are familiar with line signals; when this is confirmed, the two divers re-enter the water. Garrett is attached by a quick-release shackle that acts as his lifeline. Merrett, without a lifeline, stays within sight of his dive partner as Garrett dives under the lifeboat to see if the missing man is pinned there by his own buoyancy. Nothing.

He re-enters the lifeboat and searches among the floating debris, moving aside blankets, oars, pieces of clothing. He manages to get his head up into the bow, and it is then that he sees the missing man, pinned between the ribs of the hull and the buoyancy tanks. Only his head is exposed, and, although he is completely out of the water, he's unresponsive. He has died sometime earlier.

Garrett tries hard to free the body, but nothing budges. He and Merrett surface to relate their findings to the crew aboard the recently returned hovercraft. They say that there is no way the man can be freed until the buoyancy tanks are moved, as the upward force of the water is holding the tanks in place; the lifeboat will need to be lifted. There is a chance that the crewman could come free during this process, so the divers re-enter the water to secure him.

Coast Guard divers come to the rescue of a training exercise turned deadly.

"More life jackets, oars, paddles, and clothes are cleared away to allow one of us to poke our head through the hole," Merrett says. "Even with both of us pushing on the tanks, we can't budge them. In the end, I tie the dead man's wrist to a deck ring, and we come up."

Two tugs attempt to lift the sunken lifeboat. The pilots move toward the capsized craft, attempting to take her across their sterns. The currents are swift and the tugs lose the lifeboat, and, instead of lifting her, she is flipped hull-to. She floats alongside the tugs, and is tied to them. A paramedic immediately enters the lifeboat and formally pronounces the crewman dead. The lifeboat is towed to Cates Park where a coroner and the RCMP are waiting. The Coast Guard crew, in their customary manner, collect all the debris, thank all those who assisted, take a few polaroid photos, and return to their base.

Diver Jim Garrett, together with the crew, receives a debriefing of this rescue operation following the return to the base. He cleans and readies his dive gear and writes notes for a report. At 6:00 in the evening, he leaves through the high wire gates that seclude and secure the Coast Guard compound, driving along the edge of the river toward his home in Coquitlam. For Garrett, the episode is not over. Asleep and awake, he relives it: the terror of the dark cave with its missiles and entrapments, the body-blow of finding the dead man, the sense of hopelessness while trying to find a way to rescue the man clinging to life in an air pocket. He relives the rush and the urgency, the anxiety he'd felt about his own safety and that of his dive partner, the dread of the unexpected. There is also that indefinable sense of loss that the operation is over, that perhaps he could have done something differently, or better. But he is exhilarated too that he has saved a life, restored a man to his family. As for tomorrow, he must be ready for another rescue or recovery...or for long days without incident.

Jim Garrett's young dreams were of medicine, of restoring people to health, perhaps to life. He entered university, graduating with a degree in genetics as a pre-med student. During his years in pre-med, he leaned toward becoming an eye specialist. Then one day, Jim Garrett changed his mind, and his parents watched as he threw away all his studies and left university in search of work with the Canadian Coast Guard. In 1987, after training with the Coast Guard, Jim assumed the position of crew member of the Sea Island hovercraft base as a rescue specialist and rescue diver.

Garrett uses his analytical mind to assess and solve problems. But he shares with his dive partner, John Merrett, a passion for the physical use of his body, especially in situations that are challenging because they are always changing. To be in the outdoors, to get up in the morning and not know what the day will bring, or what he will be doing, is, for him, the perfect job. His choice of work allows him the privilege of rescuing people. To save a life about to be cut off through freak accident or mishap is a different kind of problem from diagnosing and operating on someone's eyes; as rescue specialist at the Coast Guard, there are tremendous physical demands that go along with science and analysis.

Mrs. Merrett is not surprised to see her son John's face shining out at her from the television screen because he has participated in some daredevil rescue operation. She remembers well how as a little boy he seemed to court danger, to defy gravity, flying through the air when he played. A little older and stronger, he streaked across mountain slopes and disappeared beneath the ocean. She remembers the 5:00 morning rituals—dragging him, rubbing the sleep from his eyes, to rugby fields, the running track, mountain resorts, ski fields, rowing and scuba-diving clubs. She knows how he exalts in the use of his body, and the use he makes of it now, as a rescue specialist for the Coast Guard.

John Merrett describes his search for a full-time, paying job in a career involving the physical world and outdoor activity. He looked into the possibility of being a provincial park guide, he says, but saw it as "hand holding," baggage carrying, babysitting. His investigation into search and rescue work meant considering three organizations: land, air, or water-based rescue. Air-based search and rescue would mean working for the 442 military squadron for six to seven years as a sort of apprentice; only after this could he apply for a position as an SAR Tech, and even then he may not be accepted. Land-based SAR did not interest him particularly, so he looked at water-based SAR—the Coast Guard. Having decided on this organization, he looked for the busiest station, and selected the hovercraft base.

He drove down to Richmond to apply for a position, asked what was required and, what kind of attitude he needed, to become accepted as an SAR. He was informed that he had all the qualifications but to come back in two months—there was no position for him at the time, .

He kept returning for eight months, in the meantime pursuing additional certificates, telling them, "Here's who I am. Look what I've become." Even with more qualifications, there was still no position open. "They told me they weren't looking for anyone at that time. This was not good enough for me. I wanted in, now." He updated his resume and went back—again. Three to four hours after that visit, Merrett got a call from the scheduling officer, asking him to come in for familiarization and training. "That was it!" Merrett exalts. He immediately quit his job on the ski hills and went off to the Coast Guard.

He began working on a contract basis in Richmond; wanting full time work, he entered into the competitions to secure a job on the ships. Merrett scored well and went to sea, finding it interesting but not really what he wanted. At sea for a month at a time on twelve-hour days on a search and rescue ship, and then only on standby because work was sporadic, he trained and performed maintenance work while waiting for SAR calls. Buoy tending was part of the job, as was medevacs—taking ill and injured persons from remote places and from aboard ships to the shore and waiting ambulances. He worked on ski hills between Coast Guard jobs. A part-timer at the Kitsilano base until 1996, he was finally awarded a full-time position at the Sea Island hovercraft base in Richmond. But why would Merrett choose underwater diving as part of his contract with the Coast Guard, work that poses the greatest danger of all rescue and recovery?

"That's what this is about—risk and danger," he says. "But it's a controlled risk. When you know what you're doing, it's not a big risk. It's complacency that kills. When you do a thing many times, are totally familiar with it, when it becomes routine, you get so you're not double-checking everything. Complacency in most jobs can be got away with. But not with this: it will kill you. Take diving, for example. You've dived hundreds of times. You're with a group, or another person. You're all talking. You all dive into the water, still talking. But as you sink below the surface, you realize your air isn't turned on—one of twenty or more things you are supposed to check with someone—a buddy—but you're all talking. It happens in life, but here, the consequences are death."

Does he ever experience a sense of fear?

"Fear is good," he says. "It makes you alert, on top of things. You have to be in the now; you can't think of other things. You have to concentrate on the fear. Harness it. Harness the alertness. But it's bad if fear takes you over, if you doubt yourself and what you do. You have to live in your body—enjoy it. Your mind cannot leave your body—that's dangerous. You must live in the now."

Would he be a rescue specialist for the Coast Guard, and an underwater diver, if he could choose all over again?

"Yes," he says without hesitation. "Absolutely! I really like the people, the shift work; I like the overall picture. It's not perfect; there are things that could be done differently, like in any organization. But there's a lot of individual initiative in the people in the Coast Guard—pride in the work, the base. We're proud to be working for the Coast Guard. We pull heavy loads, but there's no one telling you what exactly your load is. You have to figure it out yourself.

"I'm not there because of the security, the pay, the pension, the benefits. I'm there because the things I enjoy are very, very important and there's lots in the Coast Guard to enjoy—the rescues, the people, the camaraderie. I need challenges; most of us do. I guess you could say we're adrenaline junkies."

A Diver and
a Sunken Car

O
n a warm afternoon in early summer, Tim MacFarlane swung his van through the high wire gates that separated the Coast Guard base from Vancouver airport's south terminal, and into his parking spot beside the hovercraft base. Fitful sun and cloud shifted overhead, and a stiff breeze chopped up the waters of the Fraser River that flowed swiftly beneath the decks of the base. It was June 1992, and Tim was early for his night shift; today there was a visit from the commissioner or some other dignitary, and he felt he should be around personally to be on hand if needed. MacFarlane was striding down the corridors at the very moment the Mayday crackled through on the marine radio.

"Mayday Relay, Mayday Relay, Mayday Relay. Car submerged in Fraser River, foot of #2 & Dyke Roads, people trapped inside. Anyone able to assist, please proceed and advise Vancouver Coast Guard radio."

MacFarlane stopped in his tracks. He was a diver. In fact, he was the only one on the dayshift, as well as on the upcoming night shift. All his senses quickened. Had he not come in early, he would have missed the call, but now he was going out there to dive. He might get into trouble for doing this—hell, he might be sacked—because diving wasn't sanctioned, not yet; it might even be illegal. In 1992, the Coast Guard had no dive team; the federal government had made the decision that, for fiscal reasons, money could not be spent to maintain a highly-trained dive team. The ratio of lives saved to dollars spent was not acceptable. But MacFarlane carried his own diving gear with him, everywhere, all the time. It was in his van at this moment.

Brian Wootton, first officer on duty, filled the doorway of his office as MacFarlane appeared. "Oh, so you're here, MacFarlane." He spoke rapidly. "Who else is on—Garrett? Oh, and Jane Patrick. McGuigan, where's McGuigan? Everything ready? Let's go!" Urgency etched itself across Wootton's taut face. The engines of the hovercraft roared on the tarmac outside as First Officer Tommy McGuigan sprinted down the corridor and a young woman in navy overalls raced down the stairs from the conference room above. Jane Patrick, rescue specialist, had two hours of her day shift remaining.

MacFarlane climbed aboard with his bag of dive gear, although he was not officially on duty. The hovercraft's powerful jet engines picked up speed; it could skim the surface of the water at forty knots. They pushed the vessel to its limits.

"Our hearts were thumping, two hundred beats or more," Wootton later describes. "We were yelling over the intercom and shouting at each other. I shot the hovercraft across the marsh and up river while Jane Patrick got into her wet suit and MacFarlane ripped open his underwater dive bag, checked his equipment, and began a mad scramble into his gear."

The accident occurred at a spot on the riverbank in Richmond, not far down river from where the Coast Guard base was located. The spot was not difficult to find since ambulances, several fire trucks, a police car, and people all crowded the water's edge.

Wootton roared the hovercraft close to shore, and forced it into a controlled "crash stop." The vessel buried its nose in the water, its exhaust stacks belching. He maneuvered it along the riverbank as best he could, about twenty-five yards off shore, knowing he had to keep its engines running because of strong currents and a stiff breeze that blew from the north.

MacFarlane, dressed in his diving gear, positioned himself at the front of the craft. His lines and tank were checked. To him, the world seemed suddenly to have slowed down. He looked first at Jane, then at Brian Wootton; his expression said, "Look, I've got my diver's gear on. You can't stop me diving. There are people trapped in a car down there and you wouldn't try to stop me going down to see if I can rescue them. You're not going to stop me—you're going to let me dive." Wootton knew what MacFarlane was capable of.

"I have to say, this was an extremely difficult moment for me," Wooton explains, "perhaps not my finest hour. I was caught up in the passion of the moment, under incredible pressure. There were the crowds on the shore, the police, the firemen, ambulance people, the press. There were people drowning in the water below us. We are the Coast Guard. People expect us to dive. They'd say to us, 'you're the Coast Guard, you're divers, aren't you?' Well, we weren't really supposed to—there was no officially sanctioned dive team. Add to that, we had no specific backup diver, and the RCMP dive team wasn't right on hand to stand by for MacFarlane. The river water was cold, like treacle, no visibility whatsoever. The currents were very strong, and I had to keep the hovercraft's engines running to keep ourselves aligned to where the car had gone down—a danger in itself to the diver."

The man whose family was in the sunken car danced crazily back and forth across the beach in a grey wool blanket. He was screaming and yelling and no one could restrain him. Wootton absorbed all this and yelled to MacFarlane, "just go, *go, go!*" Jane Patrick was already in the water, poking about with a pipe pole where she thought the car might be.

"This was one of the most difficult moments of my life," Wootton repeated. "In terms of trying to save lives, it was the right thing to do. In terms of the choices a captain might make...you might well ask me 'where were your clinical and rational thoughts and judgements? Did you not see that the risks to the diver were very high?' My answer would be that at the time I was not a diver. I therefore accepted risks that today I might not."

By now, MacFarlane had dived beneath the surface. Down and down he swam into the murky depths. He knew this river: it flowed from high up in the Rocky Mountains, coursing into Georgia Strait, a thousand miles out toward the sea. The clinging layers of silt lay thick on its bed, lined its banks, and coursed through its waters. Once in it you were completely blind; you couldn't see your hand in front of your face. The silt clung, wrapped itself around you and weighted you down. MacFarlane could imagine the faces of the people trapped in the car, the gasping breaths, the frantic thumping on the windows and doors. He imagined the horror of it, the terror in their eyes, their screams. He had to find them and get them out.

MacFarlane's feet slid into deep, soft mud. He began the fireman's crawl, flinging his arms and legs in all directions, hoping that some part of his body might bump against the metal of the car. The mud sucked at him. His arms grew heavy, his legs pained, and his head began to throb. His hands fastened on a soft, yielding lump—could it be a body? His heart thumped harder. But it was only a hillock of mud and grass. He kept going. How long had he been here, flailing about? It seemed an eternity.

"I got kind of numb all over," MacFarlane says later. "Exhaustion, you know, and feeling really desperate to find the car and the people in it. I imagined I could even hear their gasps for air. I thrust my arms forward once more into the mud, and that's when my right hand struck metal." He ran his hands over the hump of metal: a trunk, windows, the axle, tires. He desperately wanted to hear thumping and banging on its windows from within.

"They could still have been alive," he says. "Back then—1992—we believed about the air pockets, that there would be some air trapped inside the car, and they would have enough oxygen to last them some time. Now we know it's not like that; there are no air pockets. But at that moment I believed the people might be alive. I was in a desperate hurry—every second might make a difference.

"I stood there with my feet in the mud for a moment and just listened," he said. "Listened for sounds that would mean there was someone alive in that car. I threw my body up against it but heard nothing. I could see nothing. I only knew the car was there because I felt it. It was a hopeless sort of feeling then because there was no good way to get the people out of it except by lifting it to the surface. I couldn't yank open a door and get one of them out, and if I could, I could only take one at a time. And once up on the surface, how would I ever get back down and find the car again? It was a miracle the first time."

MacFarlane felt an urgency to get to the surface. The car must come up. He hooked his feet under its front axle to prevent himself from being swept away by river currents, then struggled to free himself from his lifeline so he could attach it to the car. Once back on the surface he would easily be able to locate the car again. He reached with his right arm over his shoulder to grasp the hook on the oxygen tank that attached him to the line. After several attempts, he freed himself and clipped the lifeline to the axle of the car. He hung on to the line as he re-surfaced.

"He took his lifeline off!" Wootton says. "It was the only means we'd have had to pull him to the surface and get him out of the water if he'd been in trouble. He had no means to communicate with us or we with him, unlike today where he could have talked to us the whole time he was down there."

"I got to the surface and pulled off my mask," says MacFarlane. "I shouted that I'd found the car, that I had my line attached to it, but that I couldn't get the people out. 'Get it towed up,' I yelled. I could see the crowds on the shore, the police cars, and now the fire trucks and an ambulance."

A wrecker from a tow truck had a tow line. MacFarlane swam to shore, crawled up the rocks and grabbed it, then swam back to the hovercraft. He dove back down to the river bottom, following his lifeline to the car. He got the towline hooked onto the rear axle. As he began the climb back up the line, a foot struck him in the face. Then a leg, then arms. There was another body down there!

"I nearly freaked," he says. "Where on earth did it come from? I thought of dead bodies floating about me, crashing into me, and that it might be one of the people somehow ejected from the sunken car. Its legs were crashing into my face, and the body was almost in my arms in the slimy water." But the body coming down the lifeline was actually a scuba diver, a fireman sent to check that the towline had been well attached.

"We had no clue who each other was, because we couldn't see each other, but I realized it wasn't a dead body. He continued down to the bottom, and I went up. I got to the surface and pushed off my facemask while I treaded water."

"Go back down and get the fireman!" they shouted at him. MacFarlane didn't know whether the orders came from the hovercraft or the shore, but back he went once again, down into the thick brown slime. He felt around for the car, knowing the fireman would be there somewhere. Suddenly his leg became snared and was held by something. He jerked it, but couldn't free it. He yanked it again and felt around with his hands. It was a goddamn fishing line! He was snared at the bottom of the river by a fishing line! And where was the fireman? His hands clawed frantically at the slippery cords that held his leg. Where the hell had it come from? He thrashed about to free himself in a blind fury, but the line wrapped itself more completely around him. He was stuck fast.

"I lay there, stuck on the bottom of a muddy river," MacFarlane said. "I saw myself dying down there, slowly running out of oxygen. I got a pain in my chest, and in my head. Would I run out of oxygen first, or die of a heart attack? I couldn't believe it. The mud seemed to close over me and I felt like I couldn't breathe, even inside my mask.

"I remembered, as I lay there, all the dreams I'd had when I was a kid in high school. I saw myself as the big anti-terrorist commando who crashed through doors and gunned down the enemy, snatched the baby from him as he fell and put it into the arms of its mother. I saw myself dropping out of helicopters into huge raging seas to rescue people in a sinking ship. I wanted to do wild and desperate things, feel myself alive and know what was important in life. I wanted to be physical, keep challenging myself, help people, and show compassion.

"You know how they say when you're about to pass on into the next world—cross over to the other side—that your life flashes in front of your eyes? I saw my wife Robyn. She would be playing right now with our little girl Alexandria in our bungalow in Abbotsford. Robyn, she's beautiful. She pulls her hair from her face and ties it up. She has fine porcelain skin and big, cornflower-blue eyes, and she's so, sort of remote, elegant. The way she walks into a room—when I first saw her crossing the floor of the bar, I told myself that this woman would be my wife. Here was my wife, my baby, my house—my other life when I wasn't saving people in death-defying rescue missions. Life was going be beautiful."

"I'm going to die here," he thought, "and I'm not going to get out of it. Robyn will be a widow and my baby will grow up without a father." MacFarlane got cold, his muscles all sore and tight, his head about to burst. He lay for a moment, perfectly still in that few feet of mud at the bottom of a cold and dirty river beside a sunken car with dead people trapped inside. Who would have thought he would come to this end? His teachers? No. They thought he was invincible. So did Robyn. She didn't worry too much when he was away, or was late, because she thought he could do anything. His parents—well he'd scared them a few times.

"I realized I had to ditch my gear," MacFarlane explains. "That was the only possible way to get out of this. I ripped at everything, pulled my regulator out of my mouth, ripping and ripping to get my stuff off. I wrenched my foot again and again, yanked violently, and suddenly I was free! I got up to the surface. The fireman diver was already up there. Weird. I never bumped into him at the bottom." He signalled to them to bring the car up. The tow-truck engines roared and MacFarlane swam to get out of the way when he heard the sucking sounds of the water churning. The car was lifted to the surface about fifty yards from shore, mud streaming from its body. But it came up too fast. The explosion sounded like a bomb going off as windows smashed. Glass flew everywhere. But not just glass: MacFarlane, standing waist high in the water, found himself with a missile in his arms. It was a woman's body, forcefully ejected from the car, mud-splattered and covered in broken glass. A woman, her hair and skirt streaming behind her. She'd been ejected through the smashed window and had flown straight into his arms. And clinging to her was the limp body of a small child, its mother's skirts still clenched in its tiny hands. He struggled to the shore with them, hampered with all his diving gear, and they were passed along the human chain that extended from the shore to the waiting ambulances. Two lifeless bodies passed up the human chain.

"There was a pregnant pause above the sound of the hovercraft's engines." Wootton continues the story. "I heard shouting and screaming, but didn't know where it came from."

There was still a third person somewhere in the car, which now lay half-submerged and on its side. MacFarlane searched the vehicle, and there, half wedged under the back seat on the driver's side, lay the wet and slippery body of a very small child. He cradled her in his arms as he carried her to the shore. He was swimming back to the hovercraft when he saw the people on the shore waving their arms and holding up four fingers.

Treading water, he held up three fingers to indicate he'd recovered all the people trapped inside the car. They kept waving their arms and holding up four. He kept shaking his head and holding up three fingers. The pantomime was repeated. "Another one, another one," they kept shouting, but he couldn't hear.

"Then it dawned on me that everyone was trying to tell me there were four people, so I swam back to the car," MacFarlane said. "I felt sick. Perhaps the other person was still alive and taking a last gasp of air." He ripped open the door to the car, swept everywhere inside with his hands, under the roof, under the seats, but found nothing.

"It was like watching something in slow motion," Wootton said. "I saw MacFarlane searching and searching, twisting himself in and out of the car, finding nothing."

"Screw this!" MacFarlane said to himself in frustration, and dove down into the muddy depths yet again. In a few moments, he found a baby not far from the door seal near the bottom of the river. A tiny, lifeless body, arms and legs hanging limply, eyes wide open and an expression of terror frozen on her small face. He hooked her under one arm and carried her to the surface and to the shore.

"You expect you're going to find young adult males when you

go on rescue missions," MacFarlane said. "They're the ones most likely to be out boating and fishing, getting into trouble. It's a hard thing to find mothers with their children who've been picnicking in the sun. I kept hoping that the children would be alive, or able to be resuscitated, because they usually survive better than adults in the water. You keep hoping…that baby girl, she had a heartbeat when we got her to the shore, but she died in hospital later the same night."

The four-finger gesture was to haunt MacFarlane for a long time after his attempted rescue and recovery operation. Sometimes, unconscious that he was doing so, he was seen holding up four fingers, , a symbol of the trauma he experienced during this "failed" rescue and recovery.

After climbing back on board the hovercraft in the waning hours of the evening, the Coast Guard rescue workers sped back to the base, arriving there between ten and eleven at night.

"You don't hang around after an operation," MacFarlane says. "You go in, do the job, rescue the people—or recover their bodies—and get out, go back to the base. Whatever happens afterwards, you don't know about it, or maybe you read about it."

But the night was not yet over. Another Mayday call came for a rescue: The *Teacup*, a large private sailboat, was in trouble and sinking in the Georgia Straits. Midnight saw MacFarlane and his fellow workers speeding in the hovercraft to rescue the sailor on board. The crew performed a "medevac"—transporting an ill or injured person to shore and to a waiting ambulance—then returned to the base in the early hours of the morning to clean up the hovercraft and write up their reports. There were only two hours until the end of the shift.

The thought of home pressed upon MacFarlane, but he was required to stay at the base for a formal debriefing. It was not until mid-morning that he was in his van and on his way home. He didn't see the sun shining over the mountains and the snow glistening on their peaks; he was oblivious to the smells of the countryside, the cars on the highway, people in the malls of the little towns he passed. Instead, he saw a family enjoying a picnic and fishing from a riverbank on a summer's day. He imagined the father, his wife, her friend, and their four children enjoying a day of fitful sunshine and cool breezes that blew off the river. They must have looked forward to this quiet Sunday in early summer, with the wild honeysuckle and irises in full bloom, a perfect day for a picnic and a little fishing. It would be a wild taste of freedom in a new land, the husband and his wife having recently made it to Canada from Vietnam.

"I found out afterwards that they were immigrants," MacFarlane says. "I guess their number came up, and now here they were, free after—how long—maybe months, years even? They'd been stuck in detention centres in Vietnam while they waited to immigrate. It must have seemed pretty cool to them to go fishing and have a picnic on a riverbank after those camps. That's where they met each other, the husband and wife—in those detention centres, waiting to come to Canada. Later, they got married."

The families had fished and relaxed. The children played until a cold wind blew up off the river, so they decided to move to the car for shelter. The man continued fishing.

Their car had been parked near the top of a ramp facing the river so the children could watch the water while they ate. The man didn't mind the cool breeze and he knew the children would be warm inside the car, which was roomy enough—a white Volkswagon Jetta, standard gearshift. Then the nightmare began.

He was hunched over his line floating out in the water when suddenly he heard, close by, the crunching of tires on gravel, too close to be on the road. Then came a shout, and screams. He swung around and watched in horror as his car began a slow roll down the ramp with the women and children inside. This couldn't be happening! For a split second he stood and stared, heard banging on the windows, saw frightened faces pressed up against the glass. Oh, my God! He flung down his line and raced after the car, slipping and falling in the loose gravel, screaming instructions as he raced. "The brake, jam on the brake! Get the doors open, get out, get out!" But the car picked up speed as it approached the river. As the front tires smacked into the water, a rear door flung open and one mother, with a child in her arms, half jumped, half fell into the shallows. He grabbed her and the child and pulled them onto the bank. He raced back after the car, yelling at the top of his lungs, but it was in the water now, drifting slowly like a barge downstream, floating with the currents. Horrified faces stared out its windows; silent screams filled the doomed vehicle.

At first, the car seemed to float, but then the front end began its slow descent into the muddy water, the terrified faces of the children now pressed against the rear window. The car slowly submerged. The man, who had flung himself into the water, stopped when it reached his shoulders. He could not swim. He turned and raced along the riverbank, shouting, screaming, flailing his arms.

There was an empty spot at the top of the ramp where the car had been. There were no children laughing on the riverbank, just an eerie silence. Beside him on the riverbank, a prostrate mother and her child stared helplessly, unbelievingly, into the ruffled waters of the river where another mother and her children had disappeared.

MacFarlane swung his van into the driveway of his home about 11:30 in the morning, having reached the town of Abbotsford, about one hour's drive southeast of Vancouver.

"The street was pretty quiet, parents were at work and the kids were at school," he says. "My wife Robyn was upstairs with our baby daughter, bathing her. She was splashing about, naked in the bathtub and screaming, the way babies do, you know. I kind of freaked out. I couldn't bear to hear the sounds of the splashing of the baby. I'd just had dead babies in my arms, brought them dripping out of the river. I stood in the doorway staring at them, and I guess I had a funny look on my face because Robyn looked alarmed and asked, 'what's wrong?' I think I nearly went mad. I told myself I had to get a grip. This was my job and I had better learn how to deal with the stress. Get rid of the adrenaline from my body, that's what I had to do.

"Nothing, I'm okay," he told her. He smiled at his baby and went to the local pool to do some laps.

MacFarlane arrived at the pool ready for some strenuous exercise, even though he felt numb and exhausted. But there it was again: the pool was filled with two kindergarten groups. They shrieked and splashed about in the water. MacFarlane stood and stared at the chaotic scene, but instead of excited children splashing about in a swimming pool, he saw the lifeless babies he had held in his arms, babies who would never laugh again. Dead babies. Terror frozen on their faces, tiny limbs hanging limp. MacFarlane choked; he couldn't breathe. The world seemed to close in tightly about him. He thought he was having a panic attack right there at the edge of the pool; he had to get out of there. He moved slowly, like a person in a dream, along the edge of the pool, through an archway, and down a grassy path. But all he could see were small faces pressed up against a window. All he could hear were their gasps for air.

"I saw them in my mind for long afterwards and kept hearing their screams," he says. "It was such needless death, such a waste. Now they can't fulfil the purpose for which they were born, fulfill their destiny. We all have a purpose for being here, you know. I wonder about their lives, who that mother and her children would have been, what they would have become, had they lived. I risked my life just to find death, needless death."

Tim MacFarlane is still a rescue specialist and dive master for the Coast Guard at the Sea Island hovercraft base in Richmond. In addition to his full time job, he owns a company called The Canadian Amphibious Search Team (CAST), dedicated to the search and recovery of those for whom an official search has been abandoned. It also provides specialized training in courses such as capsized vessel rescue, swift-water diving, K9 handling (specialist handling of cadavers), and assistance to justice departments and government agencies worldwide. CAST's motto is, "When all else fails"; its symbol is the omega—the last letter of the Greek alphabet, symbolizing closure. CAST comprises over fifty professional men and women from various emergency service backgrounds, including forensic investigators, coroners, and underwater investigators.

MacFarlane understands the anguish of a family who cannot achieve closure at the death of a loved one because the body has not been found. One day, while watching television, he heard the impassioned statements of a father whose daughter had gone skiing on Whistler Mountain and not returned. No body was found after a weeklong search and the RCMP had given up.

"I can't believe there is no one I can hire to help me find my daughter," the grieving father said.

"That's what decided for me," MacFarlane said. "People need closure. They need to know where their loved one is. I can help them with that." So he created a company to accomplish his goal. He has since founded the Omega Foundation for those who cannot afford to pay for such services.

"Nothing is impossible if you have the drive and the resources," he says. "There's no limit to the amount of good you can do if you don't care who gets the credit. I feel I'm on a spiritual quest because rescue work is all about the living and the dead. When I look into the face of a person I've recovered, I wonder about that life, about all life. Doing this work puts things in perspective."

Brian Wootten is still commanding officer of the hovercraft at the Sea Island base in Richmond, and relieves as officer in charge of the station from time to time. He speaks of those who take risks to go to the aid of others.

"It's in the blood. It forms a primal connection, one to another, as well as to the group who shares experiences of a profound nature: life struggles, near death, and tragic death," he explains. "It's a bonding that's never lost. Even ten years after a dangerous and tragic rescue mission it's there; you can feel it. You never lose it."

Wootten tells how he goes out there as hard and as long as he can. "You have to be like a bloodhound, always in pursuit of this thing you can do to help someone. You do it even if you believe the situation is beyond all hope. You keep going, driving yourself, because you don't know that this might be the one time out of ten that your energy is not misspent. This might be the time you save a life, make a difference."

"And, the Canadian Coast Guard is an organization that is a repository for such qualities," he says. "That's why most of us are here."

A Hidden World

Divers in the Coast Guard

66 T he world's water is a beautiful other universe, and for those who dive beneath it, perhaps a last frontier," Angus Armstrong muses. He speaks of oceans, rivers, lakes, waterways, and the human wish to engage with them. He speaks also about the trauma associated with rescue diving from his perspective as a member of Toronto's Metropolitan Police and its marine unit.

"It's a hidden and secret world, available only to those who have the courage to brave its depths," he says. "But it's also an element of the earth that randomly takes people, devouring them like a monstrous, evil thing. Sometimes I think perhaps we shouldn't be there on the sea; it's not a natural place for us to be. Like flying—we're not meant to do this. But we have created devices for ourselves to travel over the water, and things can go wrong."

Armstrong grew up in Toronto near an area known as "The Beaches." Always, even as a small boy, he had an intense interest in water, paddling for the Balmy Beach Canoe Club from the age of eleven years, and becoming a lifeguard at seventeen. As head lifeguard for the Toronto Islands, he achieved local hero status through the dramatic rescue of a drowning man; Armstrong dove into the water and dragged him up from the lake bottom. His subsequent resuscitation efforts revived the victim.

As a young man, Armstrong joined the Toronto Harbour Police, a special unit where the officers carry no weapons. Eventually it was renamed the Marine Specialists, and Armstrong became a member of the dive team. He has remained with this team as the scene at the waterfront changed from industry to commerce to entertainment. Armstrong tells about his role in the marine unit of the police force, and about the trauma of diving deep into this netherworld to recover the bodies of the drowned.

"It's freaky," he says. "It can really shake you up. Drowning casts a strange light, a mermaid quality, on the person below the water's surface. Drowned people look eerily alive because they're

Among the most dangerous kinds of rescue work, diving is emotionally rigorous as well.

moved about by the sea or riverbed currents.

"When I dive and find myself swimming about in murky water where visibility is poor, I feel disoriented when I suddenly come face-to-face with a woman who appears to be alive because she's moving, rocked about by the currents. She seems to be looking at me, talking to me. Hair and clothes stream out behind her, limbs moving; her body is light in colour, almost transparent, all very life-like but with a sort of doll-like quality. The little sailboat that sank with her is bumping along the lake bottom, sails flapping, coming toward me."

Until recently, the Canadian Coast Guard had an underwater dive team at the Richmond Sea Island hovercraft base, near the south terminal of Vancouver's international airport, the only one of its kind in Canada. In the late 1980s, underwater rescue work was abandoned because it was considered too costly and not necessary due to the availability of commercial divers and the dive unit of the RCMP, who can be contracted as needed. Diving is an aspect of rescue work that is inherently risky to the dive team members.

The west coast unit pressured the Coast Guard headquarters in Ottawa to allow the dive team to continue as a pilot project, and the team of dive rescue specialists continued on this status until late winter, 2001. The dive team saved one life and has pulled several others alive from the sea, though these people died some time afterward. Eventually, the project was suspended, as the team is considered too expensive and risky to maintain.

All search and rescue workers agree about the trauma of finding drowned bodies, particularly those of children. Divers talk about the stress of entering a sunken car or plane on the bottom of the ocean, lake, or riverbed. It's a shock to all the senses, they say. What one knows as normal is turned topsy-turvy. Mattresses, pillows, and kitchenware swish about the ceiling; the commonplace utensils, blankets, phones—all the paraphernalia found in a plane—float past you, above and below.

"It's a search in a surreal world for equally surreal human beings one desperately hopes to find alive, but it's usually a forlorn hope. When you find the person you've been searching for," says Armstrong, "you're flooded with emotions. But the fact that you're required to be analytical helps, as if you're conducting a criminal investigation or a quick underwater autopsy. You concentrate on cold hard details; for example, abrasion to the upper right arm, scratch on the left foot, no marks on the face, torn blue jean jacket. You're locked into a set of procedures, and that's helpful." Armstrong describes how he holds the body of the dead person tight against him as he takes it to the surface, but at such an angle that the face is turned away.

"You feel comforted when you see that a person had died on impact, sorrow for those who have not," they say. This shock of discovering drowned victims is experienced differently by those who find them. In some parts of Canada—including Salt Spring Island, Newfoundland, and Nova Scotia—there is sometimes a particular fear among the crew, as the drowned person is likely to be a friend, a cousin, brother, uncle, someone the rescue workers know. The dread is heightened among SAR workers who were fishermen once themselves. They know, sometimes intimately, the people for whom they are searching, the people they sometimes have to drag dead out of the water.

"To know that the drowned man that you pulled out of the water is a buddy of yours, the one you had a drink with last week, went fishing with yesterday, is an especially difficult thing," says one SAR worker. "You can't brush it off lightly; you carry the horror and tragedy of it around with you for a long time, and it leaves its mark."

Tim MacFarlane of British Columbia ponders the life of the dead person. "You will never know what that person's life could have been, or the purpose for it," he says. "But whatever it was, now it will never be." Bob Teather, 'godfather' and guru of search and rescue for the RCMP, and a recently-retired diving leader, echoes many of these sentiments.

"You go when the phone rings, even when you are off duty," he says. "You have to, for yourself. You're always on a slope, gearing up or down. You're at a Saturday night dinner with friends. You don't drink because the phone may ring. The weekend comes, but not for you. There's a lot of stress because you never know, when you go out the door, what you might encounter. When you have to deal with the gruesome aspects of the job, you cry or get irritable; you can't sleep sometimes. You show empathy to the grieving families, make yourself available to them afterwards. But there's an emotional toll to showing compassion. In the end, though, it connects you; you feel truly alive."

How can people engage themselves in life and death situations and remain emotionally whole? MacFarlane shunts the horror and pain of it into one corner of his mind and closes a door on it, shoves it into the past. He explains that one can become desensitized, to an extent, but that this is usually a defense mechanism. When he's engaged in a rescue operation, he goes on automatic pilot, and afterwards he doesn't really remember what he has done. He has locked his pain behind 'black doors' in his mind, he says, but it refuses to go away, remaining there to exact its toll. MacFarlane describes how he began having terrible nightmares. When he eventually suffered up to three such nightmares each night, he avoided going to sleep; in the end, he could scarcely work or function, and he sought professional assistance.

"There is also vicarious trauma, a form of post-traumatic stress disorder," he says. "The cook at a makeshift kitchen at a disaster scene might not be directly involved in a huge and horrible recovery such as the Swissair disaster but is aware of the massive death all around him or her. It brings back memories of some past painful event and there is a reliving of the distress of it. Such a person needs someone to whom they can talk about it; they now need to deal with that event, need debriefing in order to recall what has happened and what he or she has done."

The Coast Guard has a program in place to help mitigate the emotional trauma experienced by search and rescue workers: the compulsory operational program known as debriefing, and a personal program known as 'diffusing.'

Diffusing is personal and takes place immediately after a mission is completed. Debriefing is operational, taking place in the following few days. Operational debriefing involves going over the mission in all its detail, while diffusing involves a discussion of how the rescue worker felt about what just took place, and how the person feels now, getting him or her to talk about it.

"Deep down inside, if I can't help someone today, I can't let myself get down about it. I think, I can help someone tomorrow," says Darryl Taylor of the Burin lifeboat station on the southwest coast of Newfoundland. "I can't tell myself I let this person die."

Strange Death on the Water

Richmond, British Columbia

J ulie de Grandpré looks forward to going to work because she loves everything about it. The place, her colleagues, the work (when it comes), and always the surprise element in it: the knowledge that she never knows what she is about to face during each shift—ten hour days or fourteen-hour nights—at the Coast Guard base. As is her custom, she comes on duty early for her 6:00 evening shift, allowing for a half hour crew changeover and a chance to get organized and oriented. She needs half an hour to slide into her stint as rescue specialist at the Coast Guard's hovercraft base in Richmond, British Columbia.

It is a beautiful late afternoon: the sun casts a warm, golden sheen across the slopes of the mountains. Light and shadow move across peaks dotted with remnants of winter snow. Today, the brown waters of the Fraser River are calm, with barely the suggestion of a ripple as they flow swiftly past the base.

Julie learns, when she arrives, that the second rescue specialist on this shift has called in sick, so she alone will be responding to

CCGC *Osprey* and others in training.

any medical or first-aid emergencies. This does not bother her; she has been more than a year into this work and feels well-qualified and experienced. Two specialists on one shift is ideal, but the work can certainly be managed with one.

The switch from one crew to the other begins but is not completed. Within fifteen minutes, an alarm rings through the two-storey building, an urgent call to go to the aid of people believed to be on board a sinking boat two miles from the mouth of the Fraser River—the only information the Joint Rescue Coordination Centre in Victoria has at the moment.

The crew races outside, the captain firing up the engines of the hovercraft that sits on the tarmac outside the base, just a short distance above the river. Julie prepares her first-aid and jump bag. The rest of the crew organize themselves and the craft for a speedy slide into the river.

"Let's go!" The crew is fast and efficient. "Let's hop on board; let's *go!*" Julie, like her counterparts, has done this many times— rushed out in response to a distress call about a sinking boat, dived off the hovercraft, rescued people off sinking boats—it's no big deal, almost routine.

Their destination is Sandheads, toward Easton, about two miles down river from the base. As the craft flies across the water, the crew learn few additional details, only that a man in obvious distress has called for help and all he can say is "Mayday, Mayday, sinking boat, sinking boat." Eventually he gives his position.

"I'm looking through the binoculars, scanning the water," Julie later describes. "Craig Rackhas is setting up the pump while Brian Wootton, commanding officer, concentrates on getting to the small boat that we can now see. A fishing boat is going back and forth between the small boat and the navy ship."

What is this all about? The crew is puzzled. "We find out that the fishing boat has gone to the navy ship in search of help for the small boat, but seems not to have received any," says Julie. She has prepared the first-aid equipment. Brian Wootton noses the hovercraft close alongside the small vessel; Craig prepares the pump while Julie pops the hatch and jumps aboard. She scrambles across the fore deck, scanning the boat for leaks, for open hatchways, and for people. She sees nothing untoward until she reaches the aft deck. She comes across him suddenly: a man lying flat on the deck, awash in his own blood, and the deck flooded by it.

The forty-two-foot cruising boat is not sinking, but the Vietnamese man in the fishing boat who had called in the Mayday had not known how to communicate anything else. He had seen his friend lying in a pool of blood and called frantically for help using the only English he could command.

Julie stares at the outstretched man in shock and dismay. She looks quickly around but there is no one else on board, and nothing to indicate what might have happened except for the presence of a broken shovel on the fore deck. The boat's motor is not running; blood pools around the unfortunate man, having poured from his head, his mouth—from everywhere, it seems to her.

She leaps back on board the hovercraft, grabs the jump kit and first-aid equipment, yells to Wootton something about what she has found, and jumps back onto the fishing boat. "White as a ghost is how she looked when she popped her head up," Wootton says afterwards.

Julie drops to her knees in the pools of congealing blood to take a pulse: nothing. She pops her head up from the deck to yell over to the crew on the hovercraft. "Get me the automated external defibrillator and the spine board!" This is all happening in seconds; Craig, handling the pump, still believes this is a sinking vessel; he stops and gets her the equipment she needs.

Julie bends over the immobile man. She can't get a pulse and so begins cardio-pulmonary resuscitation. Still no pulse. The Vietnamese man has now come aboard, slipping in the blood; Julie has it all over her, on her clothes, in her boots: "It's gagging up everywhere," she says. She continues her exertions, performing CPR on the man who is bleeding to death on the deck of his boat. "Within eight minutes, we got him on board the hovercraft as I continued CPR and first-aid," says Julie.

The trip from the base to the boat to this moment has taken just twelve minutes.

The defibrillator machine's computer now reads 'Shock advised.' Julie is the one who is shocked; she sweats all over, confused that the machine's computer initially instructed her not to perform defibrillation, and now is instructing her to do so. The man is cool, slimy from all the blood. Julie has an airway in place and has continued to perform CPR to try to get him breathing.

Using the defibrillator, she shocks him again and again. The computer does not read pulses, but Julie feels a very weak pulse. But the man has been bleeding for three hours from an apparent injury to his head, and does not have enough blood left to keep

An exhausted Julie de Grandpré beside the boat where the tragic death occurred.

him alive. Julie, on her knees in the bloody mess beside the dying man, knows it is hopeless.

They reach Steveston where an ambulance waits with advanced life support and paramedics. The attendants work on the unconscious man for forty-five minutes until a doctor arrives and pronounces him dead. Julie is told she did an excellent job; this man was a tough call, and she had given him his best chance. As many search and rescue workers do, she conducts her own post-mortem afterwards: What could she have done differently? Could she have done it better? Is there something she didn't do that would have saved this man's life?

Julie de Grandpré, at twenty-eight years old, is into her second year with the Canadian Coast Guard as a search and rescue worker and rescue specialist. The hovercraft base in Richmond is the place where she wants to work for the rest of her life. Eventually she wants to move to first officer and to captain's position.

Like so many of her Coast Guard counterparts, Julie seemed born to an outdoor, risk-taking life with a love of water and all things to do with the sea. She comes from a long line of ancestors who lived by and on the sea; her grandfather was a fisherman, and her father makes his living as a fisherman to this day.

After nine years in Quebec, she moved with her father and brother to Sechelt, north of Vancouver, following her parents' separation. They lived on a boat anchored on the shore of this small town in British Columbia. The thirty-two-foot sailing vessel was home for the remaining years of Julie's childhood and for part of her high school years. Living on the boat, Julie spent her spare time fishing with her father, swimming and working on boats—on their structure as well as their engines. She sailed. She loved the outdoor life and anything that involved physical challenge, anything that used her body and her hands.

It was a life of considerable poverty; when the fish were not jumping, the family did not eat, and hunger was an occasional companion. But there was plenty of love in that tiny sea-born home on the northern shores of the Pacific Coast, and Julie's father provided for his children as best as he could, sharing his experience and knowledge.

Still, poverty and life aboard a boat rather than in a home had a price. Julie felt different, set apart. While her father, and her life with him, had to be defended publicly, she sometimes cried over it privately.

After high school, Julie obtained ad hoc work aboard local boats as deckhand, and took any jobs related to the fishing industry; it was not difficult, for this is what she knew.

As a single mother in her late teens, she decided that she should make career plans. Three months at a career-counselling centre told her what she already knew: she was suited, physically and emotionally, for a life that involved physical challenge and outdoor activity, and work that somehow involved doing something for other people.

One evening she stood on the abandoned shore of Sechelt as dusk was falling, staring out over the sea. An extraordinary vessel roared into view just beyond the harbour—the Vancouver Coast Guard's hovercraft speeding its way to a rescue mission. Julie stared after it, mesmerized. What a remarkable sea vessel! She knew about boats and ships of all kinds; she had grown up in one, and had knowledge and experience that normally takes years to accumulate. She could work on boat engines, repair almost anything, tie knots. She understood the changing weather patterns and different types of seas; she could navigate and read maps. She knew suddenly what it was she wanted: a job on board a vessel like the hovercraft, which meant applying for a job with the Coast Guard. She stared after it this evening, listening to the roar of its huge engines, and watching the smoke belching from its smoke stacks.

The very next day, Julie phoned the Coast Guard's hovercraft unit in Richmond to ask if she could apply for a job. She looked at herself in the mirror, borrowed some clothes, and set off to the south terminal of Vancouver's international airport, where the hovercraft unit was located. There, she was welcomed by the staff, and John McGrath, the director of the unit, invited her on board the hovercraft and gave her tasks to perform. She found there was nothing she could not do—easily, quickly, and with no fuss.

"We'd like to have you on board," she was told at the end of the day. "We want to have you work for the Coast Guard, but we've recently taken in a few people, and there's no position available at the moment." While she waited for a position, Julie was told she might consider gaining a few additional qualifying certificates.

She did so, and applied for an office job with the organization so she would not lose touch for this was where she wanted to work for the rest of her life. She dreamed of it, thought about it, and waited. It took four very long years of being chained to a desk before a position became available, but, in 1998, Julie de Grandpré became a member of the Canadian Coast Guard's hovercraft unit.

"Chicks" to the Rescue

66 **I**t was a night memorable mostly for the fiasco it turned out to be. Well, not exactly a fiasco, because we did manage to rescue three guys and their boat." Julie de Grandpré described the night that she and another woman rescued a boat—with no thanks and some abuse for their efforts.

"Kim and I were on duty as the search and rescue crew," she said. "Brian Wootton was the commanding officer of the hovercraft. The whole thing began on the day shift. It was early spring, and the hovercraft was on search and rescue patrol in mid-afternoon on the Fraser River. Suddenly, a shape loomed up out of the haze that hung over the river— an eighteen- or twenty-foot boat with a small canopy in front and an inboard motor, called a "car topper." It had its propeller stuck fast on a shoal. Three men sat aboard among their empty beer bottles, stranded.

"Boat owners mostly know not to go up the middle arm of the river," Julie said. "It's the shallow arm—everything but a canoe will get stuck at low tide because, in many parts of it, the water is scarcely two feet deep. Even when the tide's in, there are shoals and sandbanks that can ground a big boat. That's why our hovercraft base is here on this part. We can get to anyone stranded, and we have to get them out because this arm of the river is used by seaplanes for landing. Boats should not be in it."

"A new boat, lots of booze, lots of show-off stuff, and three guys end up stuck in a part of the river where they shouldn't be," said Kim Meadows. "They didn't even know where they were. They looked pretty mad. Pissed and mad."

The Coast Guard search and rescue patrol learned later that one of the men had just bought the boat and had taken his buddies for a spin on the river. They had intended to travel up the north arm from Richmond to Surrey, to be met by a fourth friend who would bring a trailer to the shore to tow the boat home afterwards. They knew nothing about boats, nothing about navigation, and had little idea where they were. At this moment, they just knew they were stuck. They had actually

For search and rescue workers like Julie de Grandpré, gratitude is a welcome bonus after a successful rescue.

sailed past two breakwaters to get where they were now.

The day shift at the Coast Guard base made the decision to get the men off their boat and return them to it once the tide had returned. If there had been no danger to the men, they could have been left to await the tide, but their presence posed some hazard to seaplane navigation using that arm of the river.

Once ashore, the three men left the Coast Guard base and went off to a nearby pub to await the tides and the return trip to their boat, scheduled for 11:00 PM. As night fell, two men, like shadowy stick figures, lurched out of the gloom and along the ramp toward the hovercraft as the time drew near for the trip out to their boat. The third man had gone home. The night shift Coast Guard crew fired up the hovercraft and took the two men out to their boat, but it remained stuck.

"Look, we need to wait until the tide is full in, and we'll take you out again. Come back at 2:00 AM," said Kim Meadows, the rescue specialist on duty. The men slouched off once again.

The night crept on, and at 2:00 AM, one man returned and said the other had passed out in the pub. This one remaining man, the owner of the boat, phoned his friend with the trailer and arranged to meet him at the Coast Guard base. He himself was in an angry mood.

"We took this guy out there, and he got aboard his boat," said Kim. "We towed him down river toward the base, then let him go. We hung about while he started his engines. We watched for a few minutes, thinking we were clear of him at last. But no, his engines died."

The hovercraft's search and rescue crew re-attached the tow-line and struggled in the shallow water near the Coast Guard dock to bring the boat alongside and onto the trailer. Both women knew that this drunk and angry man knew nothing about boats. His friend with the trailer, hauled out of bed in the early hours of the morning, was not impressed. Neither had a clue what to do to maneuver the boat onto the trailer.

Julie prepared to jump on board the small boat to help get it aligned to the dock. "Look, I'm right here beside you," said Captain Wootton. As commanding officer, he had fulfilled his duty and was free to leave the scene. But after sizing up the two men, he'd chosen to hang around to make sure the rescue workers were all right.

Kim got in the water up to her knees to hook up a line underneath the boat, but the line jammed. The boat owner tried to pull the boat in with the winch line, which was too short.

"He tried to throw another line at me and pull himself in. I yelled at him that it wouldn't work. He yelled at me, at both of us, and tried to tell us what to do, but he didn't have a clue. I yelled to him that his way wouldn't work and we would do it our way. I put an extension onto the short winch line, passed the line to him, and told him to hook it up around the cleat. He didn't know what a cleat was. He got very frustrated and yelled at me. We were all yelling. Julie and I attached the winch line to the cleat, put clamps on the engine to keep it up, and he's just everywhere getting in the way and arguing. In the end, we did it. We got the damned boat out and onto the trailer."

"By now it was 3:00 AM," said Julie. "Both guys were pretty mad. But they turned to us, I thought to say thank you, but the owner of the boat tried to give us twenty dollars. Of course we said no, this is our job, we can't take any money. He argued. Then he looked at us and said, 'I can't believe we've just been rescued by two chicks.'

"We said nothing except, 'Just make sure you get home safely.'"

"I always thought I had to pretend I wasn't a girl to do these jobs," says Kim Meadows. "When I was younger, I did all the things boys usually do; I was just a big grubby girl who smelled like seaweed...I never thought of myself as pretty or not pretty, I just didn't care. I did what I wanted to do.

"But one day, I suddenly saw myself as so much like a guy that I felt not very feminine at all. At the same time, I figured that I didn't have to be a guy, that I just had to be—well, genderless." She stands in her greasy overalls amid old paint cans, reaching overhead to a wooden shelf to replace an assortment of tools: hammers, pliers, a saw, a high-powered drill. She wipes a dirty hand across her forehead and grins.

"When I got into the Coast Guard, I thought that to be taken seriously I had to be, not a guy, but like one; like the ones I had known growing up. I couldn't look pretty, wear make-up, nail polish, so I pulled my hair off my face and tied it up. I always wore jeans, shirts, or a lumber jacket, construction boots and baseball caps. I could do anything a guy could do, but I didn't go out to prove anything. All my life I just liked to do outdoorsy things, to build things and climb and swim and test myself physically all the time.

"When I was growing up, my Dad built the houses we lived in, and my sister and I helped him. We handed him tools and held the ladder. We cleaned up. We always lived in the country, way out beyond the suburbs, because of my mom. She's a very private sort of person and liked being away from other people, so our houses were always on the edge of a wooded area or bush. We—my sister and I—helped to clean up the grounds around the house, cleaned the yards...we worked on our Dad's boats; he worked with me on the car I had once. I guess these were the typical kinds of things that boys did. I found that a lot of what guys do is more interesting than what girls do, more exciting and challenging.

"When I went out on my first date at age fifteen, my boyfriend took me to a store that sold fishing tackle and scuba diving gear. He really showed off, like watch me, this is a guy thing, you don't know anything about this stuff. He picked up various bits of equipment, examined them, asked questions and made comments in a loud voice. Finally he bought some fins, and we left.

"'Tell me about diving, what it's like,' I asked him, suddenly intrigued with the idea of scuba diving. 'Oh, girls don't do that stuff,' he said and walked off in front of me. Well, here was a challenge. I always looked for them—challenges—you know? Things came up, like this, and there it was; being told I couldn't do something immediately made me want to do it. Besides, I liked that store and all the things in it, and I'd got this idea that I wanted to learn to dive. I sneaked back one afternoon after school on my own and asked how I could learn to dive, and how much the lessons would cost. Then I worked like mad at jobs after school and on weekends to save up for the lessons and the gear."

In Captain Cook's Wake

Bamfield Station, Vancouver Island

T he wild and rugged coasts of western Canada are the old seaways of captains Vancouver and Quadra. Both were navigational students of Captain James Cook, inheritors of the royal and ancient tradition of exploring unknown territories of the New World. Each charted the rocky and indented shorelines of Canada's far-flung western territory and its myriad, offshore islands.

In the nineteenth century, commerce in this awesomely beautiful place was sustained through rail and sea transportation from San Francisco, while steamer and sailing vessels travelled to and from Europe. Despite the dependence of early colonists on on the oceans, as late as 1871 there were few navigational aids for pilots. Those existing were adequate only for making sailors aware of the landfalls and of the Pacific Ocean's fogs and currents; lights existed only at Race and Fisgard Rocks in 1861, with one handrail at the base at Esquimalt.

Necessity drives the continuing evolution of the Coast Guard across Canada. Pictured here: *Assistance*, the first motorized lifeboat at Bamfield (1907).

In 1907, after a series of disastrous shipwrecks in the early years of the new century, a lifeboat station was built in Bamfield near Barkley Sound, a remote area of Vancouver Island. It was the first station in North America to be operated year-round, and to be supplied with a motorized rescue cutter dedicated to search and rescue: a thirty-six-foot mahogany diagonal. The station was

originally staffed with twelve men, but reduced to eight after World War One. A boathouse was built, along with a cookhouse, dining room, crew accommodations, coxswain house, tool and woodsheds.

Here, dense, pristine rainforests rise above a cruel shoreline—rocky, wind-driven, sea-sprayed, with drifting logs and kelp blown in by the near-constant onshore winds. The sea that washes these coasts has the unenviable reputation of being known as the graveyard of the Pacific.

Even the station lost its cutter. In 1909, anchored offshore instead of being taken up to the boathouse, the cutter broke loose from its moorings in a heavy gale and was wrecked on Robber's Island—one more shipwreck that led to a West Coast Trail and improved communication. Many a shipwrecked captain, along with his crew and passengers, had managed to reach the shore, only to perish among rocks and trees; those who made it to shore often froze or came close to starving because they were not able to communicate their plight.

In 1912, close to the point where the Coast Guard cutter *Valencia* went ashore, a road wide enough for a horse and buggy was built, and bridges extended across the many rivers and creeks on the fifty-mile-long West Coast Trail. A communications line was built; cabins stocked with a supply of food, medicine, and blankets. These became lifesaving materials and equipment for people stranded ashore and in need of food, shelter, and a means of communication with the outside world. By 1914, a new house had been built for the coxswain and his family; a house for the engineer came in 1922, and a new boathouse in the late 1940s.

The second *Assistance*, anchored in front of the Bamfield cable station (1910).

Today, the surroundings remain remote and rugged but a modern house sits among the trees, with a new seawall and a float ramp at its base. Beyond the station's windows, pines, spruce, and cedars still clump to the edge of the sea, but the once-lonely ribbon of road among the trees is busier: Bamfield is home to the Coast Guard's Pacific Region rigid-hull inflatable operations training school (RHIOT). In winter, four vessels train over 120 students from the Coast Guard and its auxiliary, the RCMP, the Department of National Defence, the United States Coast Guard, and other agencies. Bamfield is also the site of the Canadian Overseas Telecom Corporation—the longest running cable in the Pacific—and its staff of forty or more.

The Bamfield lifeboat station has a crew of four who rotate with another crew, each including an officer-in-charge, a motor lifeboat engineer, and two rescue specialists. Work schedules are two weeks on, two weeks off. A regular workday is followed by standby during evenings and nights. As at other Coast Guard bases throughout Canada, the station has a forty-seven-foot, self-righting cutter with a top cruising speed of twenty-five knots, designed to operate in seas up to thirty feet and in winds of fifty knots—the cutter here is *Cape Calvert*. Their fast rescue craft is a Zodiac Hurricane, with a cruising speed of forty-five knots.

"Our station is located right in the middle of the Pacific Rim National Park," says Clayton Evans, officer in charge of one of the crews. "We get from eighty to one hundred calls a year, busy because this is a playground for thousands of kayakers, sports fishermen, eco-tourists, and yachtsmen. Then there are hikers who come looking for the Broken Group Islands and the famous West Coast Trail. We also do lots of medevacs from the park and from the community, because there is no ambulance service, no paramedics—we're it!"

Technological advancements, like the self-righting surf motor launch at right, are welcomed by the Coast Guard.

Clay, as he is known, describes missions where the crew rescued overturned kayaks, vessels flipped over in the surf, and downed aircraft; he describes tourists washed into the sea by rogue waves, and missions to help First Nations women who give birth in dugout canoes. The Coast Guard crews at Bamfield also supply local lighthouses, repair navigation aids, assist the RCMP, respond to environmental emergencies, and take part in fisheries management patrols. Not least among all these duties is education; there is an almost constant flow of school groups from across western Canada, and the lifeboat station seems to be one of the principal attractions.

Dave Hegstrom is proud of his native place—the far northwestern reach of Vancouver Island where he spent most of his working life. This stark and beautiful spot juts out into the Pacific Ocean, which surges upon the rocky shores ceaselessly, restlessly. Great stands of pine and spruce are silent witnesses to the wreckage that floats about the seas of this desolate point. Dave was three years old when he first visited this area at Pachena Bay Beach, returning when he was six, to the Pachena lighthouse. It was here, in this same place, that Dave Hegstrom began his lifelong career with the Canadian Coast Guard as a search and rescue worker.

Almost half a century ago, the tall, blond, and energetic fifteen-year-old Dave worked at the cable station at Bamfield doing outdoor maintenance as a summer job. One day, one of the Coast Guard crewmembers approached to ask would he be interested in temporary work at the lifeboat station.

"One of our search and rescue (SAR) workers is off sick, and we need someone to fill in."

"Yes," said Dave, without hesitation or thought. He worked by day at the cable station, and ran, when he'd finished, to Bamfield where he worked from five in the evening until midnight as a relief rescue worker.

"The sick crew member died," he said, "and I got asked if I'd like to take on the position permanently. They made it so I was on evening shifts so I could stay at school." Dave remained at school until he entered grade nine, when he decided to quit in order to become a permanent Coast Guard seaman. The year was 1956.

In later years, Dave regretted that he didn't get his sea time on larger vessels, which would have allowed him to study to obtain his mates and masters certificates. With such qualifications he might have achieved positions of mate or skipper on the buoy-tending and supply ships that plied the coasts of British Columbia. But the shore-based work at the lifeboat station was helpful when his young family was growing up.

"And this lifesaving station work was more of a challenge for me than working on a bigger ship," he says. "I loved piloting the boats, and acting as acting officer in charge. Loved the adrenaline-filled rush that accompanied the rescue of boats and people in trouble. In 1972, I became acting officer in charge at the base when I won the competition for the job, and [was put in charge] of the forty-four-foot self-righting lifeboat, one of only three in Canada at that time."

Dave became officer-in-charge of a crew in a year that saw huge gales blowing off the coasts. The Coast Guard crew knew that they would be out in those storms, and not for a short period of time. "I remember that I grabbed a loaf of bread, some dried fruit, reached for some soda pop, and out we went," says Dave, telling how he and his crew struggled in their self-righting vessel, out to the fishing vessels caught in the storm. Each was towed in, one by one, by a Coast Guard crew for whom this was a marathon ordeal.

"Some were in trouble because of mechanical failure, no fuel, faulty plugs or water pump," Dave says. "Or breakdown of the impellor on the circulating pumps that cool the engines. Then there were the other vessels where the main drive shafts pulled free, the bolts got lost from the coupling, and these guys had no spares on board. Some got pounded by the weather, but others had dirty fuel tanks and had no spare filters. We got called out often for these kind of things, until a new Coast Guard policy told us we were not just to run out for people who have mechanical failure anymore. We used to go out for just anything; it didn't matter what the condition was, like a guy who ran out of gas. But now we had to leave them out there, sometimes for long periods, but only if we know they are not in danger themselves or to anyone else. Sometimes they got themselves started again, and, believe it or not, it's saved the taxpayers lots of money." Dave pauses. "We're here for life-and-death situations, not to look after boaters who should be taking better care of themselves."

In the 1950s, new rubber boats were supplied to the five-man crew at the lifeboat station, replacing the old fifteen-foot wooden dory and the sixteen-foot rowing boat with outboard motor attached, boats that were used to take supplies of groceries and mail to the lighthouse at Pachena.

"That was a great day when we got those rubber boats," says Dave. "Now we didn't have to fear being smashed up against the rocks; if we were, the rubber boat would just bounce off."

In those early years at the station, a crew of four remained on duty: the coxswain, engineer, and two seamen. There was an evening shift, and a graveyard shift. If extra crew were needed, others would be brought in on overtime; all maintenance was performed by the crew, who listened to the radio station at the Pachena lighthouse to hear about distress calls.

"The lighthouse keeper would ring us on a land line; the people would phone us at the station; the call would go from one line to another, and eventually they'd be switched over to someone else," says Dave. "There were eight lines at one time around Bamfield—a great way to listen in on other people's conversations!"

Changes crept in over the years, and, in the 1970s, the types of distress calls reflected the increasing numbers of pleasure craft out on the seas, and the sports-fishing boats that got into trouble because of mechanical failure. There were also more callers requesting evacuation of people suffering emergency medical problems.

The crew at the station worked closely with the 442 Rescue Squadron for the Canadian Airforce in Comox. The fixed wing Albatross aircraft, able to land on ground or on water, came into occasional use, as did a helicopter. The lifeboat crew ferried a sick or injured person from a vessel or an outlying island into the harbour, where the aircraft would land to transport the victim to the nearest medical facility. For more urgent medevacs, a helicopter technician would retrieve the person directly from the Coast Guard cutter.

Today, pleasure boaters and sports-fishing craft are out in large numbers on the ocean, along with commercial shipping vessels—large freighters, but particularly barges carrying fuel and logs. Coast Guard rescue workers still go out on calm seas and in violent storms, but now mainly to rescue people lost overboard, or to transport those with illness or injury, or to save those whose boats are consumed by fire.

Dave Hegstrom knows about fire at sea. Long gone are the days of steamships using fat in the boilers, or carrying logs full of inflammable sap for heating; but fire at sea is a hazard still. Dave is on duty when a call comes for the rescue of a tugboat on fire just off the Pachena lighthouse. The night is black with a heavy sea running. The old lifeboat with its crew speeds up the coast to try to help the stricken tug, learning as they go that it is an old wooden tug, the *LaForest*, and that it is towing a large barge. The tug's engineer had been filling up at a day tank used for the galley stove—a simple, everyday action—when it overflows, and pours down the two hatches on either side of the engine room, hitting the engine's two supercharges. The engine catches fire.

The tug's captain slows down and stops the engine, but the towline attached to the barge becomes tangled and sticks on the ocean bottom. On fire, and without power, the tug drifts perilously close to the barge and is in imminent danger of smashing against it.

When the fire breaks out, the engineer is at the back of the vessel putting oil in the lubricating system of the shaft. The skipper, assured that everyone is safely out of the engine room, releases the carbon dioxide fire extinguishers, all seven large tanks, and puts out the fire. All oxygen is effectively removed from the air.

The Coast Guard cutter draws up alongside the tug and hooks a line onto it, drawing it away from the barge. Dave, the only crewmember with first-aid training at the time, jumps aboard the burning tug to search for the crew. He finds the cook lying stretched out on the floor of the galley. Dave looks at him, and knows that the poor man has drawn his last breath. Flames had burst out of the engine room with a ferocity that prevented the cook from getting out. Flames had also burst through the floor of the pilothouse to burn a hole in the lifeboat.

Dave searches for the engineer and finds him at the bottom of the shaft. He holds a hammer in his hand, a tool he had used to bang on the canvas covering the hatch, hoping to alert someone that he was trapped. Dave immediately begins mouth-to-mouth resuscitation, periodically spelled off by another crewmember. During this time, a navy vessel has turned from its intended destination at Esquimalt and steams toward them, requested to do so by the Joint Rescue Coordination Centre in Victoria; the navy ship has a doctor on board. The Coast Guard cutter picks up the doctor and takes him to the blackened tug, but no doctor, and no medicine, can restore the cook or the engineer; both have died in the smoke and flames.

Moral Dilemmas

Salt Spring Island, British Columbia

S alt Spring is one of the Gulf Islands in the Strait of Georgia. The island has a small, year-round population scattered among the hills and trees of an undulating expanse of rock. Its hub is the village of Ganges on the southern shores, named for the *HMS Ganges*, the last sailing ship used as a man-of-war in the Royal Navy. The village has a hospital, police station, post office, fire department, and a high school for the Gulf Island children. A sheer rock face rises from the docks to meet the main street as it winds its way past Hastings House and Moby's Pub; the town itself is just two blocks away.

Ken Perry lives a short distance from the Ganges docks. A mobile marine mechanic and commercial diver, Ken has done countless dives, enjoys it, and makes a good living from it. But the phone call to his house in May of 1997—urgently summoning him to a rescue dive for a man drowning at the Ganges dock—is the beginning of a dive he would rather not remember.

Perry learns that the drowning man is Dave Raymond, his good friend and colleague. The two have dived together many times, working side by side in harrowing rescue missions, which makes this rescue effort particularly tough. Ken drops the phone, grabs the bag with his dive gear, and runs full-tilt down the road to the docks.

On the wharf, people panic—"A man is down there!"—they point to the water beyond the end of the dock. Perry looks. The dock is smashed, jagged pieces of it floating in water that is black with silt, diesel fuel, and oil. Shards from a barge swirl about. A local man is drowning among all this debris at the foot of the village, in full view of its inhabitants.

"Dave Raymond, a local guy, he was pile-driving," his co-workers tell Ken in rapid speech. "He was in the crane and it toppled off the barge—thought he jumped clear—he hasn't come up—must be stuck by something." The voices trail off. Ken has already removed himself from the confusion on the docks, climbed into his dive gear, and slipped into the water. The sea is black; he can see nothing. He swims among the debris, flinging out his arms and legs in a fireman's crawl, frantically searching. It is the longest forty-five minutes of his life, and he has to return to the surface. He goes back down again, but he cannot find the drowning man. He knows, then, that he is not going to get his friend out alive.

The next diver to arrive at the wharf is Simon Morris, who lives aboard his sailboat nearby, followed by Jeff Townsend from the island dive shop. Without a word, each throws himself into the inky water. They swim around as though blindfolded, flinging out arms and legs, hoping to bump into something. Coming up, they dive straight down again. A man is drowning, and they cannot find him. After forty-five minutes of frantic searching, they too resurface.

———

On this same sunny afternoon, Ian Kyle, coxswain at the Canadian Coast Guard base at Ganges, is off duty and enjoying his other life: farming the twenty acres of grazing land and old orchards where his horses wander. He is in the barn with his young son, the fourth generation of his family to grow up on this land, just a short mile from the lifeboat station. The sun is beginning its long slant across the sky when Ian's wife comes running into the barn, cell phone in hand.

"It's Andy Howell at the base," she says hurriedly. "It sounds urgent."

Andy is new to the Coast Guard base at Ganges, acting in the position of coxswain. "I heard a Mayday call go out," he says in hurried tones on the phone. "It's down at the wharf. I've got the cutter, the *Skua*, geared up to steam her to where the accident happened. But I need the dive lantern and can't find it. The water's been chopped up and there's no visibility down there, we can't see a thing."

Kyle jumps in his car and races down to the base. "I get there. It's almost four in the afternoon and Perry and Morris are already under the water looking for Dave," he says. "They come up twenty-five minutes later, without him. Visibility is zero, they say. By now, people are starting to crowd the wharf and gather on the banks above. Andy Howell, relieving for the off-duty coxswain, is made the on-scene commander by the Coast Guard Joint Rescue Coordination Centre [JRCC] in Victoria."

The JRCC has swung all its resources into action: divers from the Coast Guard hovercraft base in Richmond are sent to the scene, navy clearance divers are tasked to the area, and a helicopter is sent with military divers from Squadron 442.

Hope is high that Dave Raymond is alive and trapped inside an air pocket in the cabin of the crane. The crowds continue to gather and navy divers arrive. The fire department tries to maintain some crowd control and clears the school playing field for the helicopter to land. The Coast Guard's hovercraft arrives twenty-five minutes later, still well in time to save the life of a drowning man. John Merrett and Sue Pickerell jump from the hovercraft; they are the two on-duty rescue specialists and divers at the Coast Guard's Richmond base.

"We get the Mayday call and we're here in about twenty-five minutes," says Merrett. "There's still the window of opportunity to save Dave. People are everywhere. A sailing instructor is underwater trying to rescue him, guys from our Coast Guard base on Ganges, wharfies, Simon Morris and Ken Perry, commercial divers, and other local divers—like Dave himself. There's a mess in the water, oil and other fluids and cables, hoses and pipes hanging, very poor visibility. Perry, then Morris and Townsend, are the first to go down to try to get him out, but they can't find him."

It becomes a nightmarish experience for both Coast Guard divers. Pickerell is relatively inexperienced; Merrett, while having accomplished a hundred or more dives, has not been involved in many underwater search and rescue missions with the Coast Guard. "For a rescue, management is willing to take an extra risk with divers who are not very experienced, and so Merrett and Pickerell are allowed to go down," Jim Carson explains later. "But when it becomes a recovery, we try to get the seasoned divers to do the job."

"We have a frantic sense of time passing," Merrett says. "There's a lot of pressure. The awful part is thinking about the relatives on the shore when there is still the possibility of a rescue..."

The two divers feel a burden upon them: precious seconds ticking by, and tremendous pressure to dive and find this man. They know the window of opportunity to rescue someone is approximately ninety minutes. What if, by some miracle, the man is still alive? En route to the island, they have discussed who will do what, and are now about to dive. Firefighters, police, and a coroner all crowd on the dock. People on shore scream and yell. Pickerell and Merrett perform their final body checks.

Sue Pickerell dives down. Merrett stays on the surface, attached to her communication line, prepared to back her up. This is established protocol; if she gets into any difficulty, he will be there to assist.

Pickerell splashes into waters slimy with diesel and hydraulic fluid leaked from the toppled crane. Pieces of steel and chunks of wood thump up against her. She continues to search, until she comes close to using up her oxygen tank.

"She came up, and I jumped in then," Merrett says. "I'm down there looking for a man who might still be alive, but can't find him."

Eventually Merrett resurfaces to find the navy's search and rescue technicians from 442 Squadron arriving, and not long after, a helicopter drones overhead and lands in the school playing field, carrying navy clearance divers. They jump into the water to help search for the drowning man, while Pickerell and Merrett also dive down once again to do a wide area search. The Coast Guard divers remove their communication lines in order to extend the search area, remaining no more than ten to fifteen feet apart from each other, for safety. They fling aside the debris that crowds them, swimming under the wharf and all about the docks—down, up again, down—as the hope for finding the man and rescuing him slowly fades.

Then, close up against the wharf, near its end, they see a man's leg, and there they find Dave, the crane operator, pinned only by the sole of his foot, half dangling, half lying, on the sea bed, wedged between the crane which fell on his foot, and the float, a large wooden structure. It is clear immediately that he has already drowned. It is at this same moment that the navy and military divers also come upon him.

—

Tim MacFarlane whistles as he swings his van along the highway, watching the sun on the mountains, remnants of snow glistening white on their peaks, the roadsides a profusion of clover. Wild flowers bloom on the banks of the highway, and the slanting sun throws long shadows across fields. MacFarlane, at this moment, has no inkling of the accident at the Ganges docks.

His parents stand in the doorway of their home as he jumps out of his van and bounds up the steps of the front porch. The greetings are not yet over when the family is interrupted by the ringing of the phone through the open doorway. MacFarlane's ear is always attuned to its summons; he runs down the passageway to answer it, to hear the voice of his boss at the base.

"John McGrath here," says the voice. "We need an experienced diver on *Ganges*. If you can get to the base, Carson will take you over to Salt Spring. A man has drowned but no one has been able to recover the body. Seems the whole village, and a class of school children as well, are hanging around the shore. Bad scene, and closure is needed."

MacFarlane swings out the driveway and onto the highway, towards Richmond, where the Coast Guard's hovercraft sits on the tarmac above the Fraser River. Mike Carson, MacFarlane's dive supervisor and the commanding officer on duty, has already loaded the vessel with the extra diving equipment that might be required. James Garrett, MacFarlane's dive partner, it already there. MacFarlane jumps out of his van and onto the hovercraft, dive gear bag slung over his shoulder.

The sun slants low in the sky as the hovercraft speeds at twenty knots toward Salt Spring Island, racing across the smooth surface of the gulf waters and nosing its way into Ganges. The waters glisten pearly grey-green, mirror-smooth. In the velvety shades of a falling dusk, MacFarlane can see outlines of a pretty little cove with cruisers and yachts moored to either side of its jetty. Carson pulls back on the throttle and angles the hovercraft alongside the shore end of the dock.

The scene at the docks is still chaotic. One of the Coast Guard's two hovercraft is tied up at a dock, but the military are about to leave. The officers explain that there is nothing else they can do, and that they have time constraints—they are allowed a specified number of hours under the water, after which they must return and be replaced by a relief team. Carson looks around. It seems to him that the island's entire population is crowded on the jetty and the shoreline.

He does not like such emotionally-charged scenes with their intense pressure to do something, anything. This sense of urgency tempts rescuers to do heroic things without calculated planning and thought. Too many people involved, too many voices, the inevitable dissension, the crowding...Carson frowns again.

He is a young man who grew up on Egg Island in much solitude, with few outside influences, the son of a lighthouse keeper. During high school, he lived with his grandmother in Vancouver, but on school holidays he became the boy who built boats, who knew every rock on Egg Island and had a passion for all marine life. As a young man, he'd decided on a career as a doctor or lawyer—until his first summer job for the Coast Guard. He was hooked at once and forever to a life that would become his reason for living. Carson is, by nature, calm and reasoned, preferring to analyze a situation before rushing in, especially when the situation is a recovery and not a rescue.

"Tragic thing, freak accident." He briefs MacFarlane, explaining how Dave Raymond, a local man, had been hired by a small commercial outfit to do some pile-driving at Ganges. Driving jetty pilings, which are like telephone poles, deeper into the seabed makes for increased stability in the wharf. The owners of the marina had hired a barge, a big-lift crane, and an operator. The crane had been positioned on the barge, with a big steel sleeve or jacket that would fit over the piling. The operator lifts a large weight then releases it on top of the piling, which would then be driven deeper into the seabed. But on this day, the crane had somehow come loose from the barge—they'd said it wasn't chained—and toppled off. As the crane fell, Dave leapt out of the cabin; in his attempt to jump free, he had caught his foot between the dock and the steel tread of the crane. He now lay below the surface of the water, trapped.

Dave Raymond! MacFarlane, horrified, is scarcely listening. He did not know him personally, but by reputation. Dave was a great guy—people knew him all over the gulf, including the Coast Guard. He would do anything for anyone, drop what he was doing…and how many times had he come to the aid of the Coast Guard? At times he seemed almost part of it, always appearing at critical moments to help with a rescue. Here he was, drowning within a stone's throw of the Coast Guard base, and they couldn't help him; the Coast Guard and the military and the navy divers could not help him. MacFarlane's brain burns.

He hears more details in fragments as he jumps onto the dock, among the Coast Guard's day-shift rescue workers, and the commercial and military divers. "Crane not chained to the deck of the barge…he was reaching out to the boom of the crane—way out, farthest distance possible…pushed a weight farther out, like a big lever that makes the end of the barge where the crane was sitting settle into the water. The crane began on a downward slope...rolled off the barge and landed on a float where the gas pumps are. The float is not designed to take this kind of weight, and the guy knew he had to get out. He jumped out of the crane to a safe position, but the beams underneath the float broke and the crane and float went down to the bottom, Dave with it."

MacFarlane listens to all this as he and Garrett prepare to dive. Sue Pickerell and John Merrett, the Coast Guard's day-shift divers, brief them on the situation. The body has been found, and the military divers, directed to the scene by the JRCC in Victoria, attempt to free him. They make heroic efforts, asking for the jaws-of-life and for crowbars to remove parts of the wharf to try to get at him and release the trapped foot. In spite of their efforts, nothing budges; the dead man remains submerged thirty feet below the waves, stuck fast. The evening wears on inexorably and dusk settles over the water. The military and navy divers are anxious to leave and have been asked by the JRCC to wrap up their work because pilots are allowed only a certain number of hours on duty. They have concluded that only another crane can free the body, so there is nothing further they can do.

It is the mandate of the Canadian Coast Guard to provide search and rescue services, but once the rescue becomes a recovery, the responsibility passes to the Royal Canadian Mounted Police. When the RCMP learn that divers from squadron 442 are getting ready to leave, they approach the Coast Guard to ask if they will remain and help out. The Coast Guard crews readily agree that they will do all they can to retrieve Dave Raymond's body. Rescue workers on the *Skua* are advised to keep the Coast Guard cutter at the scene until the body is recovered and the incident is stood down. The crew contacts Captain John McGrath at the hovercraft base in Richmond to ask if he can send any of the Coast Guard's more experienced divers to the scene.

"Normally we would turn this type of situation over to the police," explains coxswain Ian Kyle. "Sometimes we stay to assist them, but often we have to return to the station to get rested and fed and ready to respond to another search and rescue call. It seemed very important to keep the Coast Guard here this time."

MacFarlane, his dive partner, Jim Garrett, and Mike Carson arrive at the wharf. If the family of the dead man are among the crowd, they remain unknown to the Coast Guard workers. An oil pollution boat arrives with gear for clean-up. On the dock, the atmosphere is tense and emotions high. In muted undertones, words are bandied about: 'can't leave him here for two days...have to get him up...saw off his leg...tie his leg with rope to the hovercraft and drive the vessel in reverse to pull off the leg...at least it will free the body.'

Garrett and MacFarlane prepare to dive into the water to do their own assessment of the situation by going down the line left by the military divers. Carson, refusing to feel pressured, puts himself into the frame of mind that he's not going to do anything that he doesn't think should be done. He has assumed the position as on-scene commander, and the responsibility to make decisions under difficult conditions weighs on him. He considers the family and the risk to the divers, and tries to ignore the emotions of the crowd and the demands of the press. He makes sure that plans are in place before indicating that it's safe to go ahead.

"Yes, there was a lot of pressure to chop off the guy's leg," he says. "If you arrive in a rescue mode, it's different. There's time urgency. You do a quick assessment, make a decision. You're likely to be influenced by people and crowds and the family; you feel you need to be seen to be doing things, but always you have to think about the rescue, and the risk to the divers."

Media representatives are in full force are up on the banks, prevented by the firemen from getting close to the scene. Because they are denied access to information about the tragedy, they resort to scanning the cell phones, and begin setting up hyperbolic microphones and cameras.

"It made things worse, created more tension for the rescuers," says Kyle. "Now we've gone to digital phones."

Garrett and MacFarlane have thrown themselves into the water beside the dock. Going down into a riverbed or ocean is difficult; there are pockets like caves, closed-up spaces that divers have to find their way out of. Like their counterparts in the Coast Guard and the divers in the military, Garrett and MacFarlane fight their way among flying wood and steel shards and other debris until they suddenly come upon the body.

"I stare into Dave's half-closed eyes, a few inches from my own," McFarlane says. "Here was a man in the middle of his life, working hard to support his family, and by some freak thing he's lying on the ocean bed, drowned, his life cut off, just like that. He looked like he was still alive, like people often do who have just drowned. I look at him, his face; he has a peaceful expression. His hair blows about his head with the currents and his limbs are flung out almost as though he was arrested in the middle of a swan dive. Here was a man, no longer a man, his life cut off by some freak chance."

"Garrett and I jump to the bottom of the seabed and our feet crunch the crabs that are crawling close to the body," says MacFarlane. "We go back down several times. First with a sledgehammer and chisel to pry away the planks. We spend about three hours in total and almost bleed our oxygen tanks dry. We can't move a damn thing. Then I say, 'give me some hydraulic equipment, give me the wrecking bars.' I try. God knows how I try to bust apart the steel and wooden planks. The float keeps swinging at me, and all the broken bits of dock. My feet crunch the crabs that crawl under me, but I can't move a damned thing. In the end, Garrett and I go back up to the surface."

There is turmoil on the dock. The dive team, led by Mike Carson, wants no part of sawing off a dead man's leg, even if it means that by doing so he will be freed from his watery grave. In his mind's eye, MacFarlane, can only see the body of the man being devoured by sea creatures. The Coast Guard crew, the firemen, and the police sit together in the hut at the end of the wharf to discuss all possible options: to dive once more and try to bust away the steel and wooden planks that pin the operator's foot or to wait for the second crane to arrive and remove the first crane—wait for who knows how long, a day, two days? Or the final option: one member of the crew can take a saw and cut off the crane operator's leg above the part where it is pinned.

"No one there is willing to do that," MacFarlane says. "But I would do it. To me, it's saw off his leg or leave him to the crabs. But others are against this."

"It's not our job to do that kind of thing," someone says. "This has become a recovery operation, not rescue, and what kind of image does it give the Coast Guard? We jeopardize all of our programs if we start doing things like this. If we do it, what else will we be expected to do? It made more sense to exhaust all other possible options before doing something so drastic."

Carson explains about the strong feelings he has about being pressured into making hasty or popular decisions, whether by a crowd scene, the family or the media. Especially when the operation has become a recovery, rather than a rescue. He will not have divers put in possible danger to recover a body. A rescue is different; one is willing to take extra risks.

The discussions on the wharf that night among all the parties are emotional. The police and the firemen say yes, to do it—saw off his leg. The discussions go back and forth; it is a difficult situation, a dilemma that assumes even greater proportions as the exhausted group works into the small hours of the morning on achieving a solution. The idea that a man's body will be left to lie underwater for a day or two in full view of the village is repugnant to all of them. None of them is sure what it is that the family wants. And what will it mean to all Dave Raymond's friends on the island? What about the community? You can't leave a man to be attacked by the sea creatures, and you can't pull a local hero to pieces.

"Some feel it to be absolutely wrong to cut off his leg, but I feel as strongly the other way," MacFarlane says. "I know about crabs and the dead beneath the water. We all ache for the family, knowing what agony they must be in not to know about him, terrible for them; something has to be done."

Closure is needed, everyone agrees. Get the job done and over with for the sake of the family and the community. After an interminable discussion that goes back and forth, it is agreed that everything possible should be done to protect the body from the sea creatures while awaiting another crane; the family did not want Dave's leg sawn off.

MacFarlane asks for Sunlight soap which repels crabs, body bags, and some rope—lots of it. Garrett and MacFarlane dive down once more to the dead man while the sea creatures hover about them and crabs crawl beneath their feet. They work to smear his body with the soap. They wrap him in body bags, inject the liquid soap into it, and then bind it all securely with rope. There the body will remain, its flesh protected until the second crane arrives to free it.

"I felt sick about it," MacFarlane says. "About everything: the diesel fuel that leaked out of the crane, my body aching from everything. I was exhausted."

The night dragged on. "MacFarlane and Carson finished wrapping Dave's body at three in the morning while we were on the dock among all the mess." says Merrett. "Sue Pickerell and I had been on shift for nearly twenty-four hours. The people had gone home. I didn't know where the man's family was, or what happened to them. The night got cold and we huddled on the dock and in the cabin of the hovercraft until it was light enough to fire up its engines and go back to the base. Then we had to hang around for the debriefing before we could go home."

"I've been working for the Coast Guard for thirty-five years," says David Howell, search and rescue worker at the Ganges lifeboat station. "These kinds of jobs are few and far between. The rest of the time, well, there are lots of good things: saving a life, and the day-to-day things like running the Coast Guard boat in a place like Clayquot Sound—it's a beautiful place, magical on a lovely day. You see the ocean, the killer whales sunning themselves at the end of the dock, twenty feet from the boat. I can take the million-dollar Coast Guard vessel—the best thing you ever saw—and run it in heavy weather, on water, or up on shore; I can use it to get to people and help them. It's a good working environment at the Coast Guard. Your work can make a difference in a positive way; even in a tragedy, you can bring closure to the family."

Howell speaks of the particular moral difficulty for the Coast Guard in the recovery of Dave Raymond's body. "The Coast Guard has a particular strength in that it allows room for people to hold their own convictions," he says. Indeed, it seemed that the rescue workers and divers from the different Coast Guard bases, as well their counterparts among the police and firefighters, held strong convictions about what should be done for the body of a respected local man. For everyone, in the end, it was all about passionate caring: for the people of the community, for the family of Dave Raymond, and for the dignity of the drowned man himself, even in death.

"In the Coast Guard, you are free to hold your own beliefs about a situation, and you are not judged for it," Howell says. "You can say, 'I'm going to do it,' or 'I'm not going to do it,' and it's okay."

The attempted rescue and eventual recovery of the man who drowned at Ganges had been a team effort. The community pulled together to get the local divers to the wharf; the Department of National Defence, which has overall jurisdiction for all national search and rescue work, coordinated the response, with the Coast Guard working alongside them to advise on marine search and rescue. Once the Mayday call had gone out, the JRCC in Victoria looked at the local resources and immediately dispatched what they had at their disposal. They fanned out to other agencies and called in their expert, off-duty divers. Other off-duty rescue workers rushed to the scene. The Coast Guard personnel, some of whom had been on duty for nearly twenty-four hours, remained on the dock in lonely vigil until dawn broke and another crane was on its way to free Dave Raymond's body.

Today, Mike Carson no longer works for the Coast Guard, but as a coastal pilot along the rugged British Columbian Coast. His ability to manage a scene such as the attempted rescue of the crane operator is well-known; his philosophy he attained at a young age and developed in the years he worked for the Coast Guard. His pursuit of a life of maritime search and rescue work is what he has deliberately chosen.

"People think it's changing too fast," says Carson of today's Coast Guard, "especially those close to the decision-making. But the actual work has not changed: saving people, fixing aids to navigation, breaking ice.

"When I first started in the Coast Guard, there were few dedicated SAR vessels; every Coast Guard ship had a job and did SAR as well, acting as a vessel of opportunity. If you were in the area, you did the search and rescue. If you were not, there were always other mariners about.

"The Coast Guard grew as an empire in the nineteen eighties," he continues. "It got really big. But training was really improved, and additional, specialized rescue work introduced." Carson is disappointed about the organization's more recent specialization. "You might be doing search and rescue work, or buoy tending, deckhand's work," he says. "You might wish to cross over, to transfer back and forth; this is supposed to happen, but it's actually something very difficult to do—to make the switch. Specialization is detrimental, because crossover is important."

"Things change; the organization gets bigger and then pares itself down, but overall, it's a good organization, and a very good job," he says. "In the end, I would choose it again. In the end, a seaman is a seaman, and marine accidents have been happening since the beginning of time. It is part of a seaman's duty to train to deal with them."